The
Calling

Books by Kim O'Neill

How to Talk With Your Angels
HarperCollins, 1995

Como Hablar Con Sus Angeles
HarperCollins, 2006

Bond With Your Baby Before Birth
Health Communications, Inc., 2009

CD's

Communicating With Your Angels

Finding Your Romantic Soul Mate

Communicating With Departed Loved Ones

The
Calling

My Journey With the Angels

Kim O'Neill

4th Dimension Press • Virginia Beach • Virginia

Cover design by Christine Fulcher

Dedication

This book is dedicated to all of the angels—
in spirit and in human form—who have
never given up on me.

The truth isn't always beauty,
but the hunger for it is.

Nadine Gordimer (1923–)
Nobel Prize Winner

Contents

PART THREE:
Slowly Building a New Life

PART FOUR:
Miracles Start Happening

Acknowledgments

I have been a professional psychic for over twenty-five years. One of the questions that I'm asked most often is, "How did you become a psychic? You seem so normal!"

I wish I could tell you that I have always approached my life's journey with seamless grace and dignity; that I've maintained emotional balance and unwavering optimism; that I have navigated my path buoyed by the utmost confidence in my ability to reach and exceed pivotal goals; that I felt entitled to receive the reward of unlimited abundance; that I chose to enjoy every moment of the journey fueled by my faith in self; and, that I remained humbly grateful for all of the teachers along the way who spurred my progress.

But that wouldn't even be close to the truth. In fact, you'll discover in these pages how clueless I was about where I was headed. I had no goals. I felt only anger and frustration toward my best teachers, like my father and my ex-husband, who had come into my life—completely unbeknown to me—to help with my forward movement. I had little self-worth or confidence, and had fallen into the routine of battering myself with harsh criticism in regard to my failings. I was consumed with self-doubt and was afraid to take even the smallest risk. I wondered why some people seemed to achieve great success, while I continually worried about whether I would get a paycheck after working around the clock in a business I had come to hate. Unaware that many of the people in my life were spiritual teachers for me, I fought them every step of the way, refusing to accept personal accountability for the terrible quality of my life. I blamed everybody else for what had become a self-sabotaging downward spiral that repeated itself day after day.

Many years ago, as I began to conduct private channeling sessions, I was stunned to discover that large numbers of people felt the same confusion and hopelessness that I had. Many of us resist our important lessons, feel disdain toward our best teachers, and have no clue about where we should be going. We can also be unaware of our life's purpose and how to achieve it, and live in a state of negativity and powerlessness. And, after all of these years, on some days, I still do! I've come to believe that no matter what your level of enlightenment, wisdom, or maturity, it takes remarkable courage to face your issues and take responsibility for what you were meant to accomplish while in your earthly life. There are certain days, even now, that I would much prefer to hide under my bed. We are all an ongoing spiritual work in progress.

While navigating my path, I've learned how to forgive and appreciate what my best teachers were trying to help me with . . . if only I had been open enough to realize it at the time. I want to extend a heartfelt "thank you" to two of them. My dad, with whom I so badly wanted a close father–daughter relationship, has now—in spirit—become a very good friend and guide. Not until I stopped lamenting over how hurtful his behavior had been while he was on the earthly plane did our friendship blossom into what it is today. My ex–husband was also a key teacher for me. I honor his presence in my life, and thank him for his resolute determination to carry his end of the spiritual apple cart. I wish, now, that I had possessed the maturity to have realized his contributions as they were being made.

The memoir you hold in your hands is a radical departure from my previous books. While working on this project, I had family members, like my brother, tell me, "Just don't talk about me!" Some people wondered aloud, "But you're not a celebrity . . . who would be interested in reading about *your* life?" Others told me, "You're crazy to share such personal details . . . I never would!"

I had to make difficult choices about which parts of my life I was going to share to prevent the book from evolving into 4,000 pages! In addition, following much deliberation, I have chosen to change the names of some of the people I talk about in these pages to protect their privacy. I've shared conversations that took place long ago to the best of my recollections. With the help of my angels, I have shared this narrative of my life as it has evolved to this point, in a way that I trusted would be insightful and encouraging to others who are struggling with similar issues. I hope you enjoy my story.

I'm sharing my personal story to demonstrate that you aren't alone, that others are struggling just like you are, and to convey, by relaying vignettes of my life, how making even the smallest—but *different*—choices, can yield big rewards. You can find happiness and peace in your life, no matter how flawed you feel you are . . . and I'm living proof of that! I discovered that the whole process isn't about becoming a perfect person as reflected in other people's estimation; but instead, by being true to yourself—releasing the need for other people's approval or endorsement for the choices you make—and being true to the particular, unique path that you feel is your destiny.

Introduction

On a sweltering midsummer night in 1966, when I was ten years old, seven young women were brutally raped and murdered in their dormitory by a lone assailant. The savagery of the crime inspired the biggest manhunt in the history of Chicago. Although the perpetrator was captured three days later, people never again felt as safe in their own homes.

When my frightened parents told me that we were, suddenly, going to start locking our front door at night, adding, "You're not old enough to know why," they didn't realize, and couldn't know, that I had already seen—firsthand—what the reason was. Because I had been a witness to the crime . . . in a psychic dream.

Unbeknown to them, my parents had triggered the onset of the terrifying psychic dreams that I was to endure throughout my childhood. The dreams always involved real-life events that took me to the scene of violent crimes, forcing me to become an unwilling spectator to events so unspeakable that they still haunt me.

My guardian angels were a vivid part of my childhood, too, providing tangible support and encouragement. But even they could not help erase the violent images that tormented me while I slept. In my mid-teens I began to wish, with all my heart, that my psychic ability would shut down and disappear so that I could be left in peace.

Miraculously, the psychic images came to an abrupt halt. Suddenly, I began to enjoy untroubled sleep. The terrible psychic images slowly began to fade—as did the tangible presence of my angels. I no longer had spiritual friends conversing with me. I did not miss the terrible nightmares, and I did not miss the presence of my angels. Quite frankly, I simply felt relieved.

By the time I was in my early thirties, I had created a life so dysfunctional that I didn't know where to turn. I had just gone through a very painful, demoralizing divorce. I was in a business with my ex-husband that was going bankrupt. I had no money and a mountain of debt. I had no friends. I believed that I had nowhere to turn. In a moment of sheer desperation, I called out to God for help. I was shocked when help quickly arrived . . . in the form of John Reid, one of my childhood guardian angels.

Although I had begged for assistance, I responded to the angel's presence with disbelief and resistance. But he refused to give up on me. Through his patient guidance, I discovered how I could develop my psychic ability and use it to help others, how to take a leap of faith, how to fully trust, how to face my issues, how to create abundance, and how to navigate the winding road that was to ultimately lead to my soul mate and my children. I was about to discover my true destiny.

Part One

Psychic Childhood

Chapter 1

The Calm Before the Storm

1966 was a different time. In the Chicago suburbs, people left their front doors open at night. Summertime brought everyone outdoors to celebrate the warm temperatures after a long, snowy winter. Children of all ages played outside and safely roamed the streets on brightly colored bicycles. Neighbors waved to one another and exchanged heartfelt pleasantries. Laundry hung to dry, caressed by a summer breeze sweetened with the captivating scent of sunshine, new-mown grass, and blooming flowers. Under an endless blue sky, kids in bathing suits frolicked through sprinklers that automatically fanned back and forth on lush green lawns.

We drank milk, Tab, Coke, and Tang. Water was considered a beverage with which to take an aspirin, make Jell-O, or stir into powdered Kool-Aid. If you wanted a cup of coffee, you made it in your own kitchen—for pennies—from a large can of ground Folgers. If you happened to see someone jogging, they were trying to catch a bus. Grownups exclaimed over the latest technological advancement—the color TV—and all of our friends hoped they would be the first to own one.

That summer, our apple tree produced fruit so tart that it was inedible but I nibbled anyway because it was *our* tree. Sporting brand new Keds, my brother and I dug up huge, squirming earthworms, captured monarch butterflies, climbed trees, played kick the can, read comic books, consumed endless boxes of root beer popsicles, and watched the fireflies work their on-and-off incandescent magic every night at dusk. In our suburb northwest of the city, the captivating smell of sizzling hamburgers and hotdogs regularly perfumed the neighborhood from backyard barbeque grills, even on weeknights.

Lyndon Johnson was president. Gas was 32 cents a gallon. Everybody smoked, including our doctor, who kept a metal ashtray on his desk. Radios were tuned to the Beach Boys, the Monkees, or the Cubs if they were playing a home game. While my brother teased me, I danced along to American Bandstand on TV, and developed a secret crush on Davey Jones. I nagged my mother to buy me the latest fashion direct from London. At ten years old, I argued, I was certainly grown up enough to wear the miniskirt!

Unbeknown to me, that innocent time was going to come to a fateful conclusion by two life-changing events that I would witness in the course of a single midsummer night. First, I saw my father try to strangle my mother. When I succumbed to an exhausted, terrified stupor that night, I found myself—in my sleep—at the scene of what Chicago *Tribune* reporters had dubbed The Crime of the Century. I watched in horror as a lone assailant brutally raped and then slaughtered seven young women. My psychic destiny had ignited, flared and caught fire. It was only the beginning of my journey.

Chapter 2

The Night My Father Tried to Strangle My Mother

Even as a kid, I knew that my childhood wasn't normal. Every Saturday night I worried about the abuse my mother would suffer—verbally and physically—at the hands of my alcoholic father. I never knew from one week to the next if we'd be spending Sunday morning watching cartoons and eating pancakes or waiting in the emergency room of the local hospital.

My father, the only child of Swedish immigrants who were themselves big drinkers, would have his first beer early Saturday afternoon. I would watch helplessly, like a practiced—but unarmed—soldier witnessing an all-powerful enemy mobilizing for the inevitable assault that was sure to come later the same day. Unlike my gentle Scandinavian grandparents, alcohol triggered a metamorphosis in my dad that would abruptly transform him from a sensitive, insecure, intelligent human being into a raging, abusive beast.

Despite the fact that my father drank beer all afternoon, he'd still be jovial at dinner. He would eagerly fire up his large Weber grill in the garage, and the flames would shoot alarmingly close to the raftered ceiling where our bikes hung along with the summer lawn chairs. Even in the frigid Midwestern winter, my father would patiently wait outside until the flames died down and the charcoal briquettes were properly red and glowing. While my mother made salad, sautéed mushrooms, and baked potatoes in the kitchen, he'd be in the garage grilling his thick–cut, specially marinated sirloin steaks. As they sizzled and crackled, the rapturous smell would perfume the neighborhood. Each tantalizing slab of Angus beef was painstakingly cooked to order for each member of the family. Unlike anyone else, I liked mine bloody rare. Somehow, he was always able to consistently present that to me. With anticipation, he would hover next to my chair as I inspected the heavily-charred piece of meat so tender that I could cut it with my fork. Inside, pale pink edges framed a red, raw center, and I'd squeal with excitement and tell him that it was perfection! My happy acknowledgment gave him a great deal of pleasure. My dad would comically roll his eyes, asking whether the semi–raw piece of meat needed more grill time, and I'd shake my head, already happily munching.

With the illogical denial of people in the eye of a hurricane whose full strength had not yet hit shore, we'd share a boisterous family dinner where we all laughed and talked over one another.

When we had polished off the last of my father's culinary masterpiece, my mother and I would clear the dinner dishes and prepare a hot apple pie or frozen chocolate whipped cream cake for dessert. Then we'd all retire—uncomfortably full—to the family room to watch TV. Besides my Dad's steaks, watching Jackie Gleason on our brand new color TV was also a Saturday night tradition. My parents loved watching the Honeymooners. My two younger brothers and I would sit with them, never quite grasping why grownups thought the fights between Ralph and Alice were so funny.

Following a Saturday afternoon of inhaling six packs, my dad would start on the heavy stuff right after dinner, announcing to no one in particular, "I've only had one beer!" He especially liked brandy and Greek Ouzo. He called it Firewater. When my father started getting really drunk, he began to imitate Ralph Kramden during the commercials. At the pivotal moment, he'd look at my mother and say, "Bang! Boom! One of these days, Alice! To the moon!" We knew then that the eye of the storm was going to surrender to the full force of the hurricane. My father's demons were about to be unleashed . . . full force!

In the flash of a second, my dad would snap and suddenly become unhinged. My two younger brothers and I had learned that when he exploded, we needed to become invisible. With the abruptness of a volcanic eruption, his mindless rage would spew and he'd lash out at my mother. She'd respond with tearful disbelief—as if it was the very first time—and try to escape by running upstairs to get away from him. He would charge after her, yelling, "Don't you dare run away from me!" They would cloister themselves in the master suite where the verbal tirade would escalate into a physical assault. With adrenalin pumping, we kids would retreat into our individual bedrooms where we'd hear him abusing her for hours.

"You're NOTHIN'!" he'd scream at the top of his lungs.

"No! *Stop!*" my mother would plead. There'd be the familiar sounds of muffled slaps. Because she was so terrified of him, I knew that she didn't dare fight back. That would have made him angrier.

"I'll see you and those kids in the GUTTER!" he'd threaten.

With my knees drawn up close, my whole body shaking, stomach heaving, I'd cower in my white provincial canopy bed, angry that the neighbors didn't come to our rescue. I was always certain that his demented, drunken raving could be heard echoing throughout our middle-class subdivision.

Why did he want us in the "gutter"? What did that mean? Why was he so mad at her?

Would Daddy come after us? Was he mad at us, too?

"No!" would come the muted voice of my mother. "Stig—no—*please!*"

"You're NUTHIN, you bitch! *Nothin!* DO YOU HEAR ME?"

My anger at the neighbors fueled a growing self-hatred. *Why wasn't I already a grown-up? I would fight him! I would save her!* I fantasized about grabbing him and throwing him to the floor, screaming at him to *leave her alone! Get out and never come back! We hate you!*

On Saturday nights, the unaffordable colonial house that my parents had acquired "just for you kids" became an inescapable prison. My brothers and I were literally trapped inside with no place to hide. From the time I was five years old—when I had first witnessed the abuse—I kept praying that my Dad would stop drinking, or that my Mom would somehow turn into a superhero and save all of us . . . or involve someone who could. But as the weeks slowly turned into months, and the months unfolded into years, it became apparent that no one was going to come to our rescue.

One particular Saturday night, after consuming a whole bottle of Greek Ouzo, my father went berserk. No more Ralph Kramden . . . he literally snapped. I had never seen such a look of hatred on anyone's face as he lunged at my mother. Bellowing and cursing at the top of his lungs, he tore after her as she tried to get away. Like a madman, he thundered up the curved staircase in close pursuit, and we heard them disappear into the inner sanctum of the master bedroom. As a terrible commotion ensued, we kids sought the little refuge open to us in our rooms. Unfortunately, mine was right next door to theirs.

As time dragged on, his explosive, throaty blustering went from aggressive to downright ferocious, and it struck an ominous chord inside of me. Although this kind of melodrama was typical for a Saturday night in our household, on this particular occasion I was truly worried for my Mom. I was too scared to just sit and listen, and I was too scared to act. *What should I do?* As if maneuvered by a force outside of myself, I acted upon my recurring I'm-going-to-save-my-Mommy fantasy.

Emboldened, I snuck out of bed and silently tiptoed into the hallway. Their door was ajar. I had to be extra careful; I didn't know what my father might do if he saw me spying on them. His voice was at fever pitch. I peaked inside, my heart pounding. The room was shrouded in semi-darkness; muted slivers of light from the outside streetlamp filtered through the closed blinds, casting a spooky glow. Light was reflected by the pale green ceramic handprint that I had made for them at school—now being used as an ashtray—that sat on the dresser close to the bed. Seeing it scorched and filled with cigarette butts made me feel hurt that they thought so little of my gift.

Then . . . as my eyes adjusted to the dim light, I was stunned by what I saw. I couldn't believe it! My father was straddling my mother in their bed . . . and he was *choking* her! He was trying to *strangle* her! Both of his large hands were tightly clutching her throat, and the muscles in his arms were taut with effort. He was so enraged that he was banging her head against the mattress like she was a rag doll.

"I'm going to KILL YOU, you bitch! You're NUTHIN! Do you HEAR me? NUTHIN!"

My mother was wildly scratching at his arms, hoarsely protesting, and kicking her legs in a futile attempt to knock him off of her. All the while, my father was screaming at her in a fury unlike anything I had ever seen. I stood, paralyzed, my mouth open in shock. Horrified, I quickly withdrew and jumped back into my bed.

I thought my heart was going to explode! What should I do? I wasn't strong enough to fight him! He was going to kill her! I loved her more than anything—I can't let him do that! She's my Mom! Who would take care of us? *Should I call someone? I didn't know the phone numbers of any other grownups in the family. Should I call the police? My Mom never called the authorities—or anyone else—about my Dad, so maybe it wasn't the right thing to do? If I did nothing . . . would her death be my fault?*

With tears streaming down my face, I sat quivering, ashamed, and very angry at my cowardice. I wanted to save her, but all I could do was shrink under my ruffled covers. I worried about my younger brothers and hoped they were okay. I was too frightened to be found in their bedrooms should my drunken father come looking for one of us. He could easily kill any of us kids if he tried.

"You're NUTHIN'!" continued the guttural shouting from down the hall. "You and those kids will always be NUTHIN!"

"No, Stig, *please—*"came my mother's raspy reply.

I stuck my head under my pink blanket and covered my ears. The drunken raving went on . . . and on . . . and *on.* I had never been so scared, and my head began to pound unmercifully. Almost as if I had been knocked out, I fell into an exhausted, trance-like sleep. The moment I dozed off, my first psychic dream began.

Chapter 3

Psychically Witnessing the Speck Murders

In my mind's eye, I saw a confusing kaleidoscope of indistinguishable sound and swirling color. Then, it rapidly crystallized into a clear and vivid picture, like a movie. However, unlike any film I had ever seen, I was actually a spectator *in* the movie as an unseen observer. I knew I was dreaming, but at the same time, I also had the ability to think and rationalize.

As the dream unfolded, I found myself standing in the living room of a large residence. A dark-haired, very petite girl who appeared to be in her early twenties was tidying the kitchen. She was surprised by several light knocks on the front door. Confused, she glanced at the wall clock. It read 11:06. Already dressed for bed, she had obviously not anticipated a visitor so late at night.

When the girl tentatively opened the door, she was confronted by a tall, young man with blond hair and badly pockmarked skin. Waving a gun at her, he pushed his way inside and quickly closed the door behind him. The girl's eyes popped open in surprise and she staggered a few steps back.

Oh, no! I thought. *This is a very bad man. I just know it!*

"Where's everybody else?" he asked quietly, in a slow drawl.

From the hallway, another girl cautiously peeked into the room, having heard the raps on the door. She was wearing cotton babydoll pajamas that were flowered and had puffed sleeves . . . just like mine! When she saw the man wielding a gun and threatening her roommate, her dark eyes widened in fear.

The intruder quickly slipped off his jacket and threw it across the back of a chair. There was a large, graphic tattoo on his left arm that read, BORN TO RAISE HELL. He immediately herded both girls down the hallway and into a back bedroom. I followed after them as if propelled by some unseen force. The big dormitory–style room held several sets of bunk beds. Three other girls were fast asleep in their beds.

"Ya'll do what I say," he said calmly. "I won't hurt you. I just need money." The man's voice woke the sleeping girls, who screeched in unison when they saw the armed intruder. A few of the girls ran to hide in the closet.

"I want everybody *here*," he told the girl in the babydoll pajamas, gesturing impatiently toward the floor with his gun. "Front and center. Ya'll gimme your money and I'll leave."

The girl hesitated for a moment, nodded nervously, and scurried to the closet. She knocked softly on the door and urged her roommates to come back out. They emerged with obvious misgivings. The man asked all five girls to sit on the floor facing him. Not wanting to prolong their ordeal or anger the intruder, they swiftly honored his wishes. They clung together, holding hands to bolster their courage. As if he was in no hurry to be on his way, the man sat on the floor across from them and comfortably extended his long legs.

"I'm goin' to New Orleans," he explained casually. "Where d'ya'll keep your money?"

The girls stared back at him.

"I promise I won't hurt nobody."

In rapid succession, each of the girls told him where he could find their purses. He got to his feet, slowly stretched, and left the room.

Get up! Don't just sit there! Run . . . while he's gone! Hurry!

Instead of attempting to escape, the girls remained rooted where they sat. Frightened glances passed between them. One of the girls

looked furtively at the windows that lined the wall behind them.
Can't you hear me? Run! Now!

The man returned holding what appeared to be a meager amount of cash. He was clearly disappointed. "This *all?*" he asked, his brow furrowed. The girls bobbed their heads. The outside door of the apartment opened and closed. Soft footfalls approached.

Another girl sauntered into the bedroom. "I'm home from my date!" she announced, her voice giddy as if she had been drinking. When she found five of her roommates huddled together on the floor, she frowned in bewilderment.

"Hello," said the intruder. Startled, the girl whirled, saw him, and yelped. The man gestured for her to join the others by waving his gun in their direction. She hastily complied.

Without speaking another word, he pulled a sheet off one of the beds, removed a large knife from his pocket and industriously began to cut it into a number of long strips. The girls huddled close to one another, their fear mounting as they watched him with wide-eyed confusion. When he had finished, he picked up two of the strips and approached the girl closest to him.

"Put your hands behind your back," he ordered quietly.

"But you've already got our money," argued another girl in a quivering voice. "You said you'd leave."

"And I *will,*" he answered. "I'm tyin' you up so I have more time to get away. I promise I won't hurt you. The faster ya'll do as I say, the quicker I'll be in New Orleans."

Clearly apprehensive, the shaking girl turned her back to him. The man proceeded to wind the strips of fabric around her small wrists in a special kind of knot.

"Now . . . I'm gonna tie your feet."

No! Listen to me! Don't believe him! He's lying! You'll be completely helpless!

Although her dark eyes were filled with distrust, she surrendered her outstretched legs, tightly clenched together.

He bound the girl's ankles with the same intricate knot. When he finished, he began to caress her inner thigh. Whimpering, she protectively drew her knees close to her body.

The man shrugged, and turned to the next girl. Crying, she shook her head, as if trying to rouse herself from a bad dream.

"C'mon, c'mon," he gestured impatiently.

Don't trust him! Run away! Why can't anyone hear me?

One by one, each of the six roommates reluctantly submitted, allowing him to bind their wrists and then their ankles. After they were all subdued, he stood and surveyed his captive prey. Unnerved and completely helpless, they anxiously stared up at him. The man smiled, clearly enjoying his position of power. Swiftly—without warning—the intruder reached for one of the terrified girls, lifted her into his arms, and carried her out of the room. Her shrieks echoed down the hallway.

All of the other girls gasped and looked at one another in alarm.

"Where is he taking Pamela?"

"He said he wouldn't hurt us!" cried another in a frantic whisper.

"God is watching," said the petite, dark haired girl who unknowingly admitted the intruder. She had an unusual accent. "Have faith."

The front door to the apartment suddenly opened again, and two more female voices could be heard chatting quietly as they made their way down the small hallway. The captive girls tried to call out and warn their friends, but it was too late—they had already stumbled upon the intruder. Two sets of footfalls flew down the hallway. The terrified girls escaped into the back bedroom but stopped in their tracks when they saw four of their roommates bound and held captive. The man was right behind them. He looked frenzied, eyes wild. He lurched at them, and they vigorously fought back. As they struck at him, he was able to grab a flailing arm of each girl in a vise-like grip. In desperation, they kicked, cried out, and fiercely resisted as he dragged them from the room. For the next few minutes, there was the sound of a tremendous struggle coming from an adjacent room. Suddenly, it became eerily silent. Then there was the sound of water running in the bathroom sink.

The girls in the back bedroom became panic stricken. They tugged against their restraints, and several tried to squeeze under the small bunk beds that lined the room. They couldn't fit.

Open the window and shout for help! No! He's coming! Look out!

The man strode back into the room. He eagerly reached for another girl. She was too frozen with fear to struggle. He untied her feet and marched her out of the room as she pleaded for him to release her. In a few moments, we could hear her loudly moan. This was followed by an ominous, palpable hush. Then . . . the sound of running water.

What is the man doing to the girls? He's hurting them! He broke his promise! And what is he washing?

Heavy footfalls strode down the hallway.

He's coming again!

The intruder returned, now covered in sweat, face flushed. Four petrified girls stared up at him with wide-eyed dread. "You're next," he informed the smallest girl, who had dark hair and eyes. She wasn't much bigger than I. With some kind of accent, she shrieked, "No! Please!" Like a ferocious, rabid animal, he snarled, barring yellow, uneven teeth. His helpless captives recoiled in alarm. He reached down, effortlessly picked up the tiny girl—who was still bound—and swept her out of the room. Endless moments passed.

The girl's voice echoed throughout the apartment.

"What did she *say?*" asked one of the girls.

"It '*hurts*,' in our language. Filipino," whispered the other slight, dark-haired girl. Her small body quivered as she began to sob. More time passed in silence. Water ran again. The heavy footfalls approached.

Oh, no! When will he finally go away? Why is he doing this?

The man reappeared, this time seeking out one girl in particular. He angrily confronted the pretty, big-boned girl. "Are you the one with the yellow dress?"

Eyes huge, she shook her head, but it was clear that she was lying. The girl cringed as he cut the restraints on her ankles and pulled her to her feet. In spite of her arms still tied behind her, she resisted athletically, but in vain, as he forced her from the room. From down the hall, there was the sound of grappling, then a powerful punch. *Thud!* "Ohhhh—stop!" the girl begged. "Please! Why are you—" *Thud! Thud!* "No! Noooo! . . . "* A body heavily fell to the floor. *Thud! Thud! Thud!* Then an awful silence that seemed to go on forever. Water splashing in a sink. Footfalls.

The intruder was back, his expression maniacal. Beads of sweat dripped from his face. Only two of the roommates remained, bound, on the floor where he had left them. It didn't take more than a second for him to decide who his next victim would be.

The man strode up to the girl who had fatefully returned from her date a short time earlier. He took out his knife, crouched down, and severed the binds on her ankles.

"No! Not *me!*" she implored, as he yanked her to her feet and shoved her onto a nearby bed. She fell back upon her arms, which were still bound behind her. Over her strident protests, the man used his knife to shred her blouse, her bra, her skirt, and her panties. Her naked body trembling, her eyes wild with fear, she pleaded, "No . . . please don't hurt me . . . " She clamped her legs together and tried to draw her knees close to her body.

In a deranged frenzy, he swiftly unbuckled his trousers, pulled them down, and brusquely spread her legs.

"No! *Please* don't! I'm *begging* you! *No—*"

The man roughly settled on top of her. "Put your legs around my back," he huskily demanded. Then he began to brutally push into her, grunting and moaning with each savage thrust. His movements were so forceful that the sturdy bed squeaked loudly.

What are you doing? Stop it! You're hurting her!

The dark-haired girl with the child-like frame now cowered on the floor nearby, all alone, tightly bound hand and foot. In a foreign language, she began to pray loudly in an attempt to drown out the other girl's tortured cries for mercy.

A spasm finally gripped the man's body. Then he became very still. After a few moments, he slowly stood and pulled off his pants and underwear. There was blood between the girl's legs. He dragged her to her feet, took the knife out of his back pocket, and cut the restraints that held her wrists. "I'm not finished with you," he said, poking one of her breasts with the sharp blade. "Not by a long shot."

"Oh, my god . . . no, *please* . . . " she whimpered, wiping tears and a runny nose with the back of her hand. He took her by the arm and forced her to limp behind him. Their footsteps traveled down the hall, and then they could be heard descending a flight of stairs. A few moments passed before the girl's loud cries rose from downstairs, followed by the intruder's bestial grunting that continued interminably.

In the back bedroom, there was only one girl left. Hours before, she had been the one who unknowingly opened the door to the intruder.

As she heard the man terrorize the last of her friends, her face became a mask of determination. It took several long minutes, but she was able to successfully wiggle under one of the bunk beds.

Abruptly, the first floor fell silent.

The dark-haired girl inexplicably scooted back out of her hiding place! From her position on the floor, she craned her neck to rapidly survey the room, her expression full of urgency—and the will to survive.

The sound of footfalls could be heard coming up the stairs.

No! What are you doing? He'll see you!

She propelled herself completely across the room in a series of jerky, panic-stricken movements. When she reached the other bunk beds, she kept maneuvering her small body until she forced herself completely underneath the low bed frame. Once again, she was totally out of sight. I trotted over and peeked underneath. She had scrunched up against the wall, and her breath was coming in huge, but silent, bursts. She closed her eyes and began to pray again.

You're hidden! You'll be safe under there! I sat on the floor by the bed, Indian style. I kept peering down at her to see if she was okay. I hoped she wasn't going to start sneezing from all the dust.

Right down the hall, water flooded into the sink. Then it stopped. Eager footfalls. Instinctively, I jumped to my feet and fled to the other side of the room. The dark-haired girl hiding under the bed stopped praying and was silent.

Here he comes! Don't make a sound!

The naked intruder strode back into the large dormitory bedroom, his lower body smeared with blood. He was a carnivorous animal ready to devour the last of his disabled prey, but he was visibly surprised to find the room empty. His cold blue eyes narrowed. He crouched to look under a bunk bed. No one there. Then he searched under an adjacent bed—the exact place where the girl had been hiding a short time before. No one there, either. Frowning, he stood back up. His eyes darted to the bed where the rape took place. Drying blood stained the crumpled sheets. There was an excruciating silence.

A shrill ambulance siren pierced the stillness, fading as it continued on its way. The intruder stealthily moved across the room toward the bunk bed that concealed the girl. I followed on tip-toes. Abruptly, he stopped. I paused. Like a predatory beast stalking with telepathic senses, he twisted his head slightly to listen. He turned around slowly, but deliberately . . . and looked right at—*me*! He had sensed my presence! I gasped and my hand flew to my mouth. *Can you see me? Please . . . .no!*

My heart began to pound out of my chest! Our eyes locked—and he leered . . . right at me! It made my skin crawl. "So you've watched everything, little girl?" he drawled, emphasizing every word. "Too bad I can't do you like all the others—but you'll never be able to forget me just the same."

I awoke from the dream with a start. I was so scared I couldn't catch my breath! I looked around my room. I grabbed a handful of my pink blanket to make certain I was really back home and no longer in that dormitory! I could hear my parents snoring loudly in unison. That meant my Mom was okay . . . until the next weekend.

Shaking, I turned on my bedside lamp. Outside my ruffled curtains, I could see pale strips of light just beginning to streak the dark sky. It was morning. That had been a long nightmare! And I didn't understand *anything* that I saw. It was the worst dream I ever had. I was so glad that it wasn't real . . . and that I was back home. Dorothy's voice from the Wizard of Oz ran through my mind: *There's no place like home.* Boy, was she right about that!

My cheeks were wet from tears, and I wiped them with the top of my flowered pajamas, pulled on my slippers, and trudged downstairs to the kitchen. I yanked on the door of the fridge, grabbed the orange juice, and drank from the carton. Standing inside the open door, I welcomed the peacefulness of being the first one up that Sunday morning. I placed the carton back on the shelf, closed the fridge, and walked outside through the unlocked front door to get the Sunday paper.

Although it was the middle of July, I was still shivering with goose bumps from what I had "seen" the night before. How would I possibly erase it from my mind? I bent to pick up the heavy rolled bundle from the front lawn and carried it inside. I dropped it on the kitchen table, untied the string that held it together, and sank into a chair to read the funnies.

As the *Chicago Tribune* unrolled, a picture of the man from my dream—

was staring up at me! I gasped and my eyes popped from my head. It was really *him!*

POLICE NAB KILLER SUSPECT
Picture Identified By Surviving Nurse

Richard Franklin Speck, 24, the ex-convict from Dallas, was seized by police last night . . .

Chapter 4

Tangible Proof

I looked up from the paper in total disbelief. What I had witnessed was *real*? It had actually *happened*? How could that *be*? I grabbed the front page and read further:

> . . . the killer left 32 fingerprints in the bloodstained townhouse where he methodically strangled or stabbed his eight victims after casually sitting on the floor and chatting as they lay trussed up on the floor. Speck was also was identified thru a photograph that was shown to Corazon Amurao, 23, the Filipino exchange nurse who escaped death only because she crawled under a bed and remained quiet and because the killer apparently lost count of the number of women.

I was stunned! I had dreamt about an actual *event*? I could feel Speck's cold blue eyes boring into me from the front page, and it made me shudder. As an all–powerful killer, couldn't he break out of jail? If he escaped, would he be able to find me? I was the only one—besides his victims—who had firsthand knowledge about the unspeakable events that had taken place. Shivering in fear, I stared down at his paper image. He had seen me—last night—in that apartment. He *talked* to me. I needed to share all of this with someone . . . and *right away!*

"You shouldn't be reading that," said my father, startling me. "It could give you nightmares. I'm going to start locking the front door. And I don't want you going outside anymore without adult supervision."

I was concentrating so hard on the newspaper story that I hadn't heard him come downstairs. I looked up at him. Because his behavior was so ugly, it made him ugly in every way to me. His hair was sticking up in every direction, he had a growth of beard, he wore his thick, nerdy glasses with pointed edges, his old bathrobe hung partially open, revealing his baggy boxers and skinny legs, and his brown slippers were faded and shabby. My dad looked ancient to me. He smelled bad, too, like bad breath, body odor, old booze, and stale cigarettes. I prickled my nose in distaste as he folded the front page section under his arm and searched through the rest of the Tribune. He pulled out the funnies and placed them in front of me. He patted me on the back.

"I'll make Swedish pancakes for breakfast," he called over his shoulder as he trotted double time to the toilet. "It looks like a beautiful day!"

The irony did not escape me. My *father* doesn't want me to have nightmares? Does he realize the trauma he creates every Saturday night? I hated him for what he put the whole family through. And he was acting like nothing had happened the night before. He tried to kill my Mom! At ten, I already recognized that I could never, *ever* go to my Dad with my spooky nightmare about the killings. From the first time I saw him abuse my mother—when I was five—I lost all of the trust and respect I had for him. What he had done the night before had chipped away at any remaining semblance of love or affection I once had. Emotionally, he was dead to me. I still needed a dad, but the kind of father I really yearned for just wasn't meant to be. I decided that I would have to father myself.

A few weeks before, I had made the mistake of asking my Mom if she was ever going to leave my Dad. Very surprised, she responded defensively, "Leave this *house* that we got just for you kids? Do you know how I have to *sacrifice* for us to live here? You want to live in the *inner city*—in a horrible *apartment*? That's all I could afford on my own, with my job! Is that what you want? You want to give all of this *up*? And move away from your *friends*? To go to a big, dangerous inner city school . . . where they bring *knives* to class? Is that what you want for your brothers? See—you're crying! This is why I could never consider it!"

Neither of my parents ever talked about what happened in our house on Saturday nights. My mom just always gave my dad the cold shoulder for days—erasing him from her emotional universe—like she did when she was mad at any of us kids.

Mom shuffled into the kitchen. "Good morning, honey," she wearily sighed, approaching to give me a light kiss on the cheek. Her face wore a dark expression. "Oh, God, I need a cup of *coffee*." I watched her go to the cabinets and grab the big tin of Folgers. As she measured the grounds, she turned to look at me. "Where's your father?" I gestured toward the powder room. She grimaced and turned away. She wore her robe over her nightgown, and I guessed that she must have been sporting a number of angry bruises from being slapped and choked. I knew then that I couldn't burden her with my creepy nightmare. She had her hands full with my father.

It was going to be a typical Sunday, with her giving my Dad the cold shoulder as punishment for his bad behavior. Of course, I could readily understand why she didn't want anything to do with him that day. It was a miracle that she was still *alive*! I thought that it was too bad that she didn't whip out the big wooden paddle she carried in her purse when one of us kids was naughty . . . and spank *him*. Even as a kid, it was apparent to me that she was hiding from what needed to be addressed—as if the relationship might magically get better on its own. Why did she allow herself to be his victim . . . over and over again? Perhaps, as a Catholic, she considered a disemboweled marriage her fault . . . like an unspeakable flaw? By disparity to some of my friends in school, no one in our family had ever been divorced. It was apparent that my Mom preferred to be in the marriage as it was . . . than to be on her own. *Any* relationship was better than none. Possibly, she felt that being a martyr every Sunday was the only way to really get my Dad's attention? Then again, maybe it had something to do with the fact that my Dad had a girlfriend. I overheard my Mom crying over the phone about it, and she was really upset. Evidently, he had taken his secretary bowling and then out to eat. I figured they must have bowled for an exceptionally long time, and that the restaurant must have had some pretty late hours, because he didn't come home until early morning.

My thoughts returned to the nightmare. My beloved, practical Swedish grandparents would *never* understand, and I predicted that my favorite Aunt Vera would be quick to tell my Mom, fearing that there was something terribly wrong with me. And who would blame her? Not even my closest friends would understand, either. I realized that I'd have to keep the dream carefully concealed—like an oppressive, traumatic secret that was mine alone to shoulder—just like my Mom kept the secret of my Dad's abuse from the rest of the family. My nine-year-old brother came downstairs.

"When's breakfast?" he groused.

"I'll start the bacon in a minute," answered Mom. "This is your summer vacation—you should enjoy it. You'll never have this carefree time back again."

My brother scampered into the family room. The TV sprang to life with noisy cartoons.

I glanced out the big kitchen window. The soft early morning sun caressed the budding roses in my father's garden, monarch butterflies danced among the petals, birds chirped busily, and just beyond the flowers, the sprinkler sat on the lush, green lawn holding the promise of another day's cavorting in our bathing suits.

The peacefulness of that Sunday morning utterly contradicted the brutal carnage I had witnessed the night before. In the course of a single night, my life had changed forever. I had learned that even a grown-up's life could be shattered at any moment by events that were completely out of one's control . . . because of a stranger! It wasn't only family members who could hurt you.

Both events struck a sudden, unexpected death knell to my childhood innocence. It was gone forever, almost as if it never existed in the first place. There was no way for me to retrace my steps and reclaim the mindset of the little girl I was—just the day before. And there was no one in my life with whom I could share this chilling new reality.

At that moment I was consumed by two burning questions. Why *hadn't* God saved those girls? And if I wasn't brave enough to save my mother from my own *father*, how would I save us from a merciless, diabolical killer like Richard Speck if he should escape from jail?

Over the course of the following months, I came to believe that what happened to those girls—and me—that summer night had been destiny. Later, on the TV evening news, I heard that the dark-haired girl, Speck's lone survivor, had returned to her native Philippines. I was glad she was safe. Still fearing for my own safety and that of my family, I snuck regular peeks at the Tribune to make certain that the killer was still behind bars.

When he was sentenced to death, I finally felt a small degree of relief from the corrosive effects of the unwavering fear and insecurity he had inspired. Once he was dead, he would never be able to come after me. I confess that I was never able to muster any pity or compassion for him as he faced the electric chair. Frankly, I didn't believe that it was going to be a fair punishment. Maybe, I reasoned, it might be more equitable if he burned in the electric chair *seven* times—one for each of the girls that he had tortured.

However, to my utter despair, that was not Speck's destiny. His death sentence was commuted to life in prison, where he expired benignly from a heart attack—overweight, addicted to drugs, and grotesquely parading around in a garter belt—even before he had served the first twenty years of his sentence.

Richard Speck had indeed marked me. But he was wrong about one thing. I *have* been able to forget him—except when the indelible memory of that long-ago midsummer night escapes from a vulnerable, hidden pocket of my soul to haunt my dreams.

Part Two

Coping with Adult Spiritual Amnesia

Chapter 5

Barely Surviving My Day Job

The old ship pitched and rolled on the heavy seas, just in sight of the British bombardment of Fort McHenry in Baltimore Harbor. A man could be seen on the deck of the American vessel; explosions of cannon fire illuminated his face against the dark, starless night sky.

Consumed with passion, he reached inside his uniform and pulled out a folded piece of paper and a writing instrument. The man unfolded the piece of paper on the ship's battered, wooden rail and began to write with deliberate intent. After a few moments, he looked once again toward the fort under siege, tears welling in his eyes. Inexplicably, the corners of his mouth began to curl and he burst into uncontrollable laughter.

"CUT!" yelled the director. "Goddamn, Jimmy—how many times we gonna shoot this scene? Get in character and stay there! You're supposed to be Thomas Jefferson, the father of our country, for chrissakes!"

"Francis Scott Key," I corrected the director with a heavy sigh. I was thirty-two years old, and I co-owned an advertising agency. My partner was my ex-husband, with whom I had started the business five years earlier when we were still married. At that precise moment, I was in the process of shooting a TV commercial for one of my clients who had planned a big sale over the Memorial Day weekend. I had created the poignant TV spot for the T-shirt company to ignite a spark of patriotism in the Houston community and, more importantly, to allow my client to unload his huge surplus of T-shirts emblazoned with the Texas state flag.

"Okay, Jimmy, you got your shit together now?" inquired the director.

The actor made a thumbs-up gesture, indicating that he was ready to begin shooting again.

"OKAY! QUIET ON THE SET!" the director barked. "ACTION!"

Once again, strobe lights began to flash on the actor's face to simulate "bombs bursting in air." His expression was so moving that I knew it would be a real tearjerker of a spot—just the tone and mood I wanted.

At the right moment, the actor reached inside the jacket of the rented military uniform for the paper and pen with which he would write the poem that was to become the Star Spangled Banner. He pulled out the piece of paper, but evidently, there was nothing else in there. Maintaining his expression and staying in character, he reached into the other side. Nothing in there, either. Suddenly, Francis Scott Key morphed back into Jimmy Willis, the fledgling actor from Driftwood, Texas.

"This time it wasn't my fault!" whined Jimmy. "Who took my pen?"

At that moment, one of the big strobe lights exploded with an ear-splitting BOOM!

"CUT!" bellowed the director. "BILL! Get that bulb replaced! I'm gonna be old and gray when this goddamned shoot is over!"

"What do you mean, *gonna* be?" I teased him.

"Yeah, you got *that* right," he responded dryly. "And my mamma said I'd never make it in show business." We both laughed. He then shouted, "Bill! Where are you?" When he got no response, he jumped up from his chair and strode off in search of his assistant.

We obviously weren't going to start shooting again for a few minutes, so I decided to call my office to check for messages. I held on the line while Shirley Stockwell, my receptionist and secretary, rifled through them one by one. First, the owner of the T-shirt company had called to say that his son, the advertising director of the family business, was on his way to the shoot. Second, the presentation I was supposed to give the following week to the big, new prospective client—a string of funeral homes—had been moved up to tomorrow, and I hadn't even *started* to work on what was supposed to be an extensive and complicated proposal. Four angry suppliers had called for money and were waiting for me to get back with them; and, a client in the computer industry who owed me $80,000 had called, stating his intention not to pay the bill. What's more, he informed Shirley that if I called him for the money, he'd consider it harassment. An unpaid debt like that could put our small firm out of business. Without it, we couldn't even make payroll the next day. The receptionist then told me that David, my business partner and ex–husband, had decided to take the day off to go on a long motorcycle ride around Lake Conroe.

I couldn't believe that David would take a vacation day when all hell was breaking loose! Shaking with anger and frustration, I told Shirley to tell the staff we had to work late that night to put the proposal together, and that I'd meet them back at the agency as soon as I finished the shoot. Suddenly, shouting erupted on the set, so I quickly ended the call and dashed back into the studio. The actor and director were in a heated argument.

"I simply will not do the scene again!" threatened Jimmy. "Everybody has their limits, and I'm creatively spent!"

"WHAT?" shouted the outraged director. "You'll do the scene as many times as I *tell* you to do it! Who do you think you *are*—Sir Laurence fucking *Olivier*?"

I saw that my ultraconservative client had arrived while I was on the phone in the other room. He had never been to a shoot before to see the creative process at work. He stood there unobserved in the corner, motionless, aghast, eyes popping.

"Hey, guys," I called to the actor and director. "Let's work out our little differences and finish the shoot." They completely ignored me. I waved to my client. He ignored me, too.

"And . . . I'm not going to wear this ridiculous wig," cried the actor, yanking it from his head. "I don't care if it *is* part of the costume—I look like a moron!"

"You look like a moron without the wig, you no–talent numskull!" replied the director.

"Look—the client is here!" I trilled, trying in vain to get their attention.

"Oh, *yeah?*" yelled Jimmy, his face beet red with anger. "Does a no-talent numbskull get to study acting under Bubba Jowarski in Texarkana?"

And with that, the actor tried to leap over the bow of the ship—presumably to attack the director. The big brass buttons on the uniform caught the sturdy wooden rail, and he fell flat on the floor, ripping out the entire back of the colorful jacket.

I winced when I heard the loud rending tear. Now I'd have to pay for the expensive rented costume. Jimmy unsteadily got to his feet, and I saw that he was bleeding from a small cut across his forehead. He touched his hand to the wound and looked at his fingertips.

"I'm bleeding!" he announced dramatically. "Somebody help me!"

A female assistant calmly approached the director with a small tube of antibiotic, which he passed to the actor.

"Look, kid," the director said in a fatherly tone. "I want you to understand that Kim has given you the opportunity to be the principle in a TV commercial that's going to be seen all over town. We have to finish shooting today, or we're over budget. Go and get cleaned up, and get your ass back on the set. Pronto."

The actor mumbled an apology and lumbered toward the bathroom. I made eye contact and nodded to my client, who was walking toward me with a thunderous expression. I quickly hissed to the director, "What are we gonna do, Fred? We can't use him with that cut in the middle of his forehead!"

The director waved away my concern. "Sure we can," he said. "Thomas Jefferson can look like he's seen action. It'll make it more authentic."

"Kim?" I turned around and saw my client. Although he was maintaining his control, he was fuming. The spectacle that he had witnessed was a clear sign that I was not capable of managing his family's impressive advertising budget.

"Hi, Arthur! I'm so glad you could make it to the shoot!" I lied, praying that he wouldn't stop the production, or worse—fire me.

"Kim, I don't think this is at *all* what we had in mind," he said ominously. "We need to talk."

"SO!" interrupted the director, with studied reverence. *"This* is the client you were telling me about?"

The owner of the T-shirt company looked at him coolly and said nothing.

"Yes!" I responded nervously. I couldn't afford to lose this client. "Arthur Freeman, I'd like you to meet Fred Peterson, our director—the man who is going to breathe life into the commercial that I wrote for you."

The director put out his hand and the client took it with obvious hesitation.

"Kim, could I have a moment?" the client asked, gesturing to a distant part of the sound stage. I gulped and nodded. I knew from his tone that I had lost the account.

"Hold on a second, Kim," asked the director in a theatrical tone. "Didn't you tell me that Art has acting talent?"

I regarded the director with astonishment. I had never said anything of the sort, and just the thought of my nervous, high-strung client performing was laughable.

"Actually, I did do a little acting in high school," replied Arthur.

"I thought so!" exclaimed the director. "I work with actors every day, and I can always spot talent."

I wondered if Fred had lost his marbles.

"You see, Art," said the director, putting his arm around the client's shoulders, "one of the principal actors didn't show up, and we were wondering what we were going to do. That's why we're all a little on edge. Kim is going to make this the best spot on TV. Did you know that *you* are her favorite client?"

"Well, I—"

"I just had an epiphany!" Fred cried dramatically, slapping his forehead with his palm. "The perfect answer to our problems! Art . . . might *you* consider filling in?"

Filling in, I thought? But the spot only calls for *one* actor—and we only have one costume! What the hell was he *doing?*

"Me? In a *commercial?"* responded the client, obviously flattered.

"Yes! You'd actually be saving the day."

"Arthur?" I interrupted. "Did you want to speak with me?"

Fred flashed me a look that said, *what are you . . . stupid? Shut up, already!*

"Uhhmmm, it can wait," my client replied.

"Come with me to our wardrobe department," said the director smoothly, leading Arthur to the tiny dressing room.

Jimmy Willis trotted back, ready to work. There was a noticeable gash on his forehead, but it had stopped bleeding. I asked if he was okay.

"Yeah, I guess so. I'm really sorry about the costume. And I'm sorry I was such an asshole. This role is important to my career."

"Then lose the attitude and do the best job you can. My client is here, and we all need to be on our best behavior. Got that?"

He nodded, head down.

A few minutes later, Fred arrived on the set with Arthur in tow, and I had to stifle a laugh when I saw him. Arthur was wearing pancake makeup that made him look positively orange. He had taken off his expensive suit jacket and stood in his shirt sleeves and trousers. Fred asked Jimmy to give him the jacket to the military costume. The actor obediently took it off and handed it to the director. The whole back of the costume was ripped out, but that wouldn't be seen on camera. Fred reverently held up the brightly colored military jacket to allow Arthur to slip into it. It was far too big for him. Fred called, "Wardrobe!" Bill, his stoic assistant, appeared with duct tape to temporarily alter the costume.

"Art, excuse me while I have a creative conference with Kim. She's the boss on this shoot." My client nodded happily, clearly in his element.

"What are you *doing*?" I asked out of earshot. "We can't use him in the spot!"

"If we don't, there won't *be* a goddamned spot."

"Shit! So how do we bring him in?"

"How about if he hands Thomas Jefferson his pen and paper? That kills two birds with one stone—then we don't have to worry about Jimmy fumbling with the props."

"You think it'll work?"

"It *has* to," he shrugged casually, accustomed to the unexpected. We walked back to the set.

"Okay, everybody—let's get this in the can," said the director, rubbing his hands in happy anticipation of finally finishing the shoot.

The two actors had already taken their place on the ship's deck. Jimmy had humbly donned the long wig once more and was dressed in a white ruffled period shirt. Arthur proudly wore the military jacket that had seen better days, and the tricorne hat that had come with the costume. Since we had only one wig, it worked perfectly to cover his modern hairstyle. Standing side by side, they were quite an odd pair: Jimmy was over 6'2", and Arthur wasn't quite 5'9".

"Alright! Now—Jimmy, you're Thomas Jefferson, witnessing a terrible battle from the bow of this great ship."

"Francis Scott Key," I corrected him.

"Which one *am* I?" cried the fledgling actor in frustration. "I have to *know*—so I can get into character."

"I stand corrected," replied the director. "You're Francis Scott Key."

"And who am *I*?" Arthur asked eagerly, now full of excitement.

"You're . . . you're . . . Sir Thomas Wellington! The ship's distinguished physician."

"My mother always *wanted* me to become a doctor. But I went into the family business because Dad—"

"—yes!" interrupted Fred. "And if it wasn't for that fortuitous decision, we all wouldn't be here right now, having the privilege of shooting this important television commercial. Some things are just destiny."

"That's *true!*" Arthur replied.

"So, you, Dr. Wellington, will walk up to Mr. Key and hand him his pen and paper. And then you will take several steps away from him. This is a very important responsibility."

"I am up to the challenge."

"Okay! Dim the overhead lights. Bill, start the strobes. Begin rolling. ACTION!"

Frances Scott Key, newly injured in battle, stood at the ship's rail, the lights from the cannon fire clearly illuminating his grave, but courageous, expression. Dr. Wellington approached, his face a combination of strength and determination. He gracefully presented a pen and a piece of parchment paper to Mr. Key. It was accepted with a distinguished nod, and Key placed the paper on the battered wooden rail of the ship and began to write. Dr. Wellington, the trusted physician, remained supportively by his side. Key wrote purposefully for a few moments. He then put down the pen and looked at the ship's doctor. In unison, both men, standing steadfast at the bow of the great ship, gazed across the water toward the fort under siege, war–weary tears in their eyes.

"CUT!" shouted the director. "WE GOT IT!" He leaped from his chair and strode toward the actors. "Unbelievable! We couldn't have planned that. Art, I'm glad you stayed put—it made the spot even stronger."

I approached my client and shook his hand. "Good work, Arthur. I think you're going to be pleased with what we've got."

"Wait until Dad sees this!" he answered, triumph in his voice.

"Go back and tell him that you had to kick some ass to get what you wanted," offered Fred jovially.

Arthur's face lit up. He was having a *very* good time. By the seat of my pants, it appeared I was going to keep the account.

Chapter 6

Hitting Rock Bottom

The moment I reached my car after the shoot was completed, I called the client who refused to pay the $80,000 he owed the agency. I fully believed there was some terrible mistake—that Shirley had gotten the message all wrong and misunderstood what he had told her.

"Hardcover Computers," answered their receptionist. "May I help you?"

"Hi, Barb, this is Kim O'Neill," I said, attempting to sound upbeat and positive. "Is Chuck there?"

"Oh . . . hi, Kim. He told me that if you called he wasn't going to speak to you."

"*What?*"

"I'm sorry," she whispered into the phone, right before hanging up.

I was incredulous. Suddenly, a little voice inside of me warned that Chuck Dugan and his wife, Dawn, who co-owned Hardcover Computers, were in the process of shutting it down. They didn't intend to honor any of their outstanding bills. I just somehow *knew* it.

My heart was beating so hard that I thought it would explode in my chest. Up to this point, my partner and I had weathered all the storms:

sporadically going without paychecks; working fourteen-hour days; pitching new business alongside much bigger agencies; trying to attract and keep good employees; and juggling bill paying, which included taxes. Hardcover Computers could force us into bankruptcy. We'd have to fire everybody and close the agency. All of our hard work would go down the drain. I had nowhere to turn for help. I began to cry. *How had it come to this?*

I thought about how everything had started. In the early 1980's, my husband and I had grown weary of the long, frigid winters in our home-town of Chicago, so we left to move to the warmer, subtropical climate of Houston, Texas. We quickly discovered that millions of other Mid-westerners had recently done the same thing. By the time we reached what the locals call "The Bayou City," even the renowned southern hos-pitality had apparently reached its limit. Every day we Midwestern ex-patriots were greeted with a growing number of bumper stickers that ominously proclaimed *Yankee Go Home!* and *We Don't Care How You Did It Up North!* and *Real Men Don't Eat Quiche—Real Men Eat Road Kill!*

My husband had worked in marketing in Chicago, so we decided to open an advertising agency. Our long hours and hard work quickly paid off, and soon the business was growing and appeared to have very positive prospects for the future. Unfortunately, our personal relation-ship was spiraling out of control, and after seven years together, we divorced, claiming irreconcilable differences.

At that time, the advertising agency was still a small enterprise, and all of our money was tied up in the business. Just after the divorce, the agency's financial situation started to nosedive, following the path of our personal relationship. It became almost impossible to handle our small payroll, and soon we found ourselves hurtling toward a frighten-ing crossroads.

Each new day became a mad, frantic scramble as I tried to handle the copywriting, pitch new business, collect the money owed to us, and negotiate with the angry suppliers hounding us for money, as well as handle the myriad of other tedious administrative responsibilities. Most days I ate lunch at my desk while creatively brainstorming with em-ployees, tackling an avalanche of routine paperwork, or returning nec-essary phone calls. I was so mentally, emotionally, and physically drained by the end of each work day that I couldn't see straight. There were many times when we had to work all night to complete an important project. I felt numbed, burned out, and trapped—not having the faintest clue of what else I could do professionally. I believed that I had nowhere to turn and there was no one to help me out of this dilemma. And now, after all of that turmoil and hard work, it looked as though we were in the awful position of having to shut our doors because *one client* refused to pay his bill.

Suddenly, the little voice inside of me suggested that I call the client's *wife* for the money. The idea hit me with such force that I stopped crying. Although Dawn Dugan was a silent partner in the business, I truly had nothing to lose. In better days, Chuck Dugan had given me their home telephone number and told me that I could contact him there if I needed to. My hands were shaking as I dialed their number.

"Hello," breezily answered Dawn, his wife.

"Dawn! It's Kim O'Neill."

"Oh . . . hi, Kim." She didn't sound pleased to hear from me.

I decided to skip the pleasantries and get right down to pleading. "Dawn, I *really* need the money Hardcover owes us."

"Well . . . I don't know what to tell you because—"

"Please, Dawn, I'm *begging* you," and I began to cry again.

"But I really don't make any of the decisions—"

"*Please, don't do this!*" I wailed uncontrollably. "Make out a check and I'll come pick it up before he gets home from work. *I'm begging you!*"

In the long pregnant pause that followed, I aged at least ten years. She finally responded, "I'd better give you cash. That way, he can't stop payment on the check."

I couldn't believe my ears. "You'll give it to me in *cash?*"

"How soon can you get here?" she asked worriedly.

"*Now!*" I answered, drying my tears. "I'll be right over!"

"Okay . . . but *hurry.* He usually gets home about three."

I looked at my watch. It was just after two, and they were on the other side of town. "I'll be there right away! Dawn, I'll never be able to thank—"

"Just *hurry up!* If he comes home early, I won't be able to give it to you."

Racing to their house, I could have broken Indianapolis 500 speed records. I worried about what Chuck Dugan would do if he found me on his doorstep. I got there at 2:45 p.m. I jumped out of my car and ran up the stone steps that flanked the entrance of their palatial home. I tripped, fell, ripped the sleeve of my white silk blouse, and bloodied my knee, but I had so much adrenalin pumping through my veins that I didn't even feel it. I frantically rang the bell. *Ding . . . ding . . . ding . . . ding . . . ding.*

The door quickly swung open and there was Dawn, holding a large Neiman Marcus shopping bag. She was obviously surprised by my tear-stained, disheveled appearance. Worriedly looking up and down the street, she shoved the bag at me, obviously concerned about her husband finding out about what she had done.

I grabbed the heavy multi–colored bag by the handles, looked inside, and gasped. I had never seen so much money before. Rubber bands held stacks of one–hundred–dollar bills that appeared to have been hurriedly assembled and stacked.

"I counted it twice," she assured me. "It's all there. I'll just tell him that I ran out of shopping money."

I looked at her in astonishment, my eyes wide, mouth open. *Shopping money?*

"Well," she said, reading my mind, "I have to have *something* to look forward to in this fucking marriage. Now GO!" She quickly shut the front door.

Limping, I scurried back down the stairs, opened the car door, threw the bag inside, and was on my way. When I got to the four-way stop at the entrance of the affluent subdivision, I saw Chuck Dugan driving past me.

I rushed to the bank. I wondered about the impression my appearance would make—a woman with red, teary eyes; a bruised and bloodied leg; and a soiled, torn blouse—holding a Neiman Marcus shopping bag loaded with $80,000 in *cash.* I had never made such a substantial deposit, and I was surprised that the teller didn't bat an eye—until she presented me with the deposit ticket, and I held it to my heart and began to cry. I felt like someone who had just survived a natural disaster.

Rush hour slowed my progress, so it was after 4:30 p.m. when I finally reached my office in the congested Galleria area. I didn't want to take the time to go home and change my clothes because the staff was waiting for me. I called Shirley from the car to let her know that I was minutes away.

The glass and steel mid-rise office building was a welcome sight as I swung my car into the multi-tiered parking garage. I pulled into my space, turned off the car and stepped out. My leg was now throbbing; I realized that blood had glued the pantyhose to my knee, which by this time also sported a swollen purple bruise. I grabbed my purse and briefcase, hobbled into the building, and got on the elevator. A man who owned an insurance company down the hall joined me just before the doors closed. He regarded my appearance with a startled expression.

"Typical Monday," I said.

The bell finally sounded, the elevator opened, and I limped down the hall toward the office. An ornate gold plaque inscribed *Advertising & Design, Inc.* hung outside the double glass and mahogany doors. I walked into the agency's large reception area and found Shirley hard at work behind the circular desk that served as her base of operations. The reception area was appointed with buttery-soft leather furniture and chrome and glass tables. The walls were lined with numerous framed ad campaigns that we had created, and we also showcased all of the design, advertising, and public relations awards that had been presented to us by our peers in the industry. Special lighting produced a soft glow that made the cavernous space appear like a warm, soothing, enveloping cocoon. Instead of feeling pride with what we had accomplished, I felt nothing but knee-buckling, gut-wrenching, mind-numbing stress each time I walked in the front door.

The moment she saw me, Shirley jumped out of her chair as though she had been shot out of a cannon. In her sixties, she was nurturing, stoic, capable, and able to thrive on stress. She had been with us since we opened our doors.

"Thank God you're back!" she exclaimed. "What *happened* to you?"

"I'm fine. Where is everybody?"

"They're all waiting in the conference room. You have a slew of messages," she announced, holding up a handful of pink *While You Were Out* slips with my name on them. "Want them now or later?"

"Later—we have to get going on the pitch."

She bent to examine my knee. "Ouch! I'll get the Bactine—I have some in my desk." Shirley was always ready for anything. "You're gonna need some aspirin, too."

"Thanks, Shirley."

"Kim, before you go back there, I need to share something. David has someone—"

"Did he *finally* come back? Good of him to join us. Call Star Pizza—"

"Done," she quickly replied. "Should be here any minute."

"Great! Bring the pizzas back when they're delivered. And would you make some good strong coffee?"

"Just finished brewing," she assured me. "I'll get you a cup. And the aspirin. You're going to need it." She then hurried through the reception area and across the threshold that led to the labyrinth of offices, the conference room, the file room, and the full-service kitchen. I limped behind her to my office, tossing my purse and briefcase on my desk. I grabbed the thick file I needed to create the proposal and hobbled down the long hall to the conference room where the staff had already assembled.

The door to the conference room was open, and I could see the seven staff members all sitting around the large oval table. They were unusually subdued. David, my business partner and ex-husband was standing just inside. I couldn't wait to share what had happened at the shoot and how I had collected the $80,000 from Dawn Dugan.

"I'm finally here!" I announced as I entered the room. It wasn't often that I felt a sense of buoyant pride. "I have big news!" I exclaimed. There was dead silence. Confused, I looked at the staff members, and I saw all seven pairs of eyes shift to another part of the room. I turned to see what they were gazing at.

There stood a beautiful blond who appeared to be around my age, looking at me with apparent shock. I wasn't exactly ready for the cover of a magazine, but there was nothing I could do about it. So, without apologizing for my appearance, I looked at her and nodded a hello.

"I have some big news, too!" shared David, with his most charming smile. "This is Monica. During our ride around the lake, we decided to get married. We haven't set the date, but when we do, you're all invited." David and Monica looked at one another as if no one else was in the room.

His news hit me like a ton of bricks. I found it utterly demoralizing that at the same time he was romancing his new sweetie, I was still emotionally reeling from the divorce. It had been a monstrously painful time, and my self-worth had never been lower. Like reliving a bad dream, those years of marriage flooded over me in a sudden, nightmarish flashback.

Not long after the honeymoon, David had begun to express hurtful criticism about my looks. He would routinely point out a young, pretty girl and suggest, "Why don't you wear your hair like hers?" or "Why don't you wear tight jeans and a tank top? Wow! Look at her!" It certainly wasn't long before I began to believe that David looked at other women because I just wasn't *enough*. As time went by, I found myself lacking in every way. After all, my husband—ten years older than I—was handsome, charming, funny, creative, and undeniably charismatic. I tolerated years of that abuse because I loved him; and, if the truth be known, I really didn't want to be alone. I was also terrified that a separation would lead to the demise of the business.

David started spending most of his time away from home, either with friends or staying late at the office. When I tried to get him to talk with me about his feelings, or our relationship, his reaction was always a stony silence. There came a time when, apart from pitching new business, we didn't see one another. I had become controlling because of my insecurity, desperately needy, and lonely. I routinely confronted him, pleading to know why I was so physically and emotionally lacking, and he would turn his back and walk out of the house without a word. Finally, one day, I decided that I simply couldn't endure any more hurt, anger, rejection, or emotional melodrama. I reasoned that no matter what happened in the future, it would somehow be better than the lonely, living hell I had been experiencing. I realized that I couldn't change the past, or make David the husband I wanted him to be. Nor could I waste any more time beating myself up over having stayed in the relationship so long.

And now, without a word of warning, my ex-husband was going to remarry so quickly—while I remained hopelessly single. I wanted to be reasonable. I certainly didn't begrudge David moving on with his life. I had realized, of course, when I filed for divorce that he would very likely remarry. I truly didn't care. His engagement had just taken me by surprise because it had occurred so soon after our breakup. I guessed that he had been seeing Monica while we were still married. He was going to enjoy a brand new future with gorgeous, skinny, adoring Monica—and I would spend the rest of my life alone, eating Chinese carry-out in front of the TV in a dismal apartment with my cat, Winston, as my only companion.

Shirley tapped me on the arm, holding out two aspirin and a small cup of water. I blinked several times, trying to neutralize the kaleidoscope of events and feelings that were threatening to make me cry. That was the *last* thing I wanted to do in front of Monica and all the staff members.

"Congratulations," I told the happy couple, trying valiantly to muster a smile.

"So, Kim . . . what's *your* big news?" asked one of the art directors, trying to diffuse the tension.

"Oh . . . the shoot ended up with Arthur in the spot," I answered in a small voice, shrugging my shoulders. My news now seemed dull, anal, and unimportant. That's *me*, I thought: dull, anal, and unimportant. "And . . . I was able to collect all the money that Hardcase owed us."

"That's nice," casually declared David, without taking his eyes off Monica.

The agency staff, on the other hand, was delighted. They knew they were going to get their paychecks the next day—and have continued employment. They clapped for me in unison. Biting my lip to keep from crying, I silently nodded my thanks.

"Well, I guess we're off to celebrate," said David to Monica.

"W-W-What?" I stuttered. "You can't leave! We have to create the proposal for the big pitch tomorrow—we haven't even started it! We're all going to stay late."

"You can handle it," he replied, nuzzling his new fiancé. "This is a big day, and I can't disappoint my Baby Girl." And with that, he led her from the conference room.

I felt all eyes on me. No one spoke a word. I was so incredulous at his behavior that it took me a few moments to get my brain around everything that was transpiring. Anger started to bubble up inside of me, and I was on the verge of exploding like a bottle rocket. I silently wished David a bout of a long, lingering, hideous disease that would cause painful hemorrhaging from every orifice of his body; and then, when all of his internal organs began to liquefy and he'd scream for mercy, I'd just watch and laugh at his misery . . .

"STAR PIZZA!" a young male voice shouted from the reception area.

"I'll go," said Shirley, and she scurried down the hall.

I gave a deep sigh and shook my head. I looked at the staff, and I could see the fear and uncertainty in their eyes. My knee started to throb again. I felt dizzy and lightheaded. I yearned to go home, pick up my cat, and feel him purring against me. Then I would eat at least three pounds of chocolate.

"Okay, guys," I heard myself say, thankful that they were so loyal. "Let's make this the best frigging proposal we've ever done. If we pull this off, I promise you all a big, fat bonus."

"What will you give us if we don't pull it off?" teased one of the designers.

"An evening with Chuck Dugan," quipped Shirley, who had returned with the four large fragrant boxes and numerous cans of soda. The starving staff began to inhale the pizza. Then we settled in for a long night's work.

The proposal was finished at 3:30 a.m. I sent the staff home and stumbled back to my apartment. I fed Winston and then took a long, hot shower to help ease the pantyhose off the wound on my knee. I threw myself on top of the bed, too exhausted to sleep. I couldn't stop thinking about how David had walked out—not just on me—but on the whole staff.

I was suddenly so desperate to get away from David and the relentless stress of the agency that I decided to put a resume together and look for a job. I'd be starting all over again at ground zero. I fantasized about having a Mr. Wonderful, children, my own business, and the ability to earn an income—completely on my own—without someone always working against me and belittling what I was trying to accomplish.

But that fantasy seemed a million miles away and completely unreachable. The thought of that made me feel so overwhelmed with fatigue, frustration and despair that I began to sob. Through my tears I pleaded aloud, "I need help! Why does everything have to be so difficult? What am I going to do with my life? I have no husband, no good friends, no children, no professional security, no savings, and I'm in debt up to my eyeballs! I'm thirty-two years old, and I have absolutely nothing to look forward to. I'm a complete failure. I can't stand this anymore!"

I began to wish I could die right there in my bed and be done with it. I had made a disaster of my life, and I had never felt so defeated and demoralized. I finally cried myself to sleep, feeling nothing but self-pity and hopelessness.

Chapter 7

Angel John Reid to the Rescue

The next day, the advertising agency was a typical whirlwind of activity. I was so upset with David that I couldn't even stand to be in his presence, and I decided not to mention Monica or what had happened the night before. I didn't have the time or energy to invest in a quarrel, and I knew that nothing I could say would make any difference. We had to make the big presentation together that morning, and I wanted David to concentrate on the business at hand. We were pitching a big, conservative, male-dominated funeral company, and they had given us a two-hour audience in which we had to demonstrate how Advertising & Design, Inc. was the best agency in town to handle their advertising and public relations. David and I instinctively recognized that they were going to respond more favorably if he handled the major part of the presentation, with me playing a supportive, subservient role. That was fine by me, as long as we won the account.

As usual, David was running late, so we had to rush to be on time for the meeting. I drove so he could review the fifty-page, elaborate pitch that we had created the night before.

"Kim!" he shouted in alarm, after reviewing the first part of the proposal.

Startled, I jumped in my seat, almost swerving into another lane of traffic. *"What?"* I asked him.

"Goddamn, son–of–a–bitch—we've lost the fucking account!"

"How? We haven't even gotten there yet! What's the problem?"

"Who proofed this goddamned thing?" he yelled.

"We all did."

"You sent Shirley home early last night, didn't you?" he asked accusingly. Shirley was our best eagle–eyed proofreader. She always caught all the mistakes.

"Not until after midnight . . . she was exhausted! We were still working on it at 3:00 a.m."

"We're *doomed!"* he whined. "Why don't we just close our doors right *now?* Do I have to do *everything?* Can't *anything* be done right without me being there?"

I felt my blood pressure rising so high that I expected to have a stroke on the spot. I hated him so much at that moment I couldn't see straight. He had never acknowledged that we remained at the office more than half the night after he had left to have fun, and now he was calling us all *incompetent* as well? He didn't appreciate *anything!* We did all the hard work. All he had to do was review the proposal and waltz into the boardroom to do what he loved best—starring in the David Morgan Show—with me and all of the prospective clients serving as an admiring audience.

"I can't stand it when you get like this!" I shrieked. "What's the frigging *problem?"* I wanted to pull over and start beating him over the head with the proposal he was waving in front of my face as I drove.

"Your proposals are always so *predictable,"* he wailed, continuing to criticize. "Once again, you decided to promise a new client that Advertising & Design, Inc. is going to make them a recognized 'force' in their industry."

"Doesn't that make sense? Why else would they hire us?"

"Well, there's a little problem with a typo."

"Tell me!" I demanded, as I drove.

"Oh . . . it's just that you promise that Advertising & Design, Inc. is going to make them a recognized 'farce' in their industry."

"That's impossible!" Now I was wailing, too. "But spell–check didn't indicate—"

"That's because 'farce' is spelled *correctly*," he explained, as if to a simpleton. "Here . . . look!" he waved the proposal in front of my face. I rudely pushed it away from my field of vision, and it struck him squarely in the face.

"You just cut me!" he hollered, as if I had just plunged a butcher knife into his throat. I glanced at the left side of his cheek, and I saw a minute paper cut. A pinpoint of blood started to appear. He pulled down the visor and peered into the lighted mirror. "I can't spill blood on my new shirt. It'll never come out!"

"You idiot! Go in my purse and get a Kleenex," I replied. He rifled through my purse and pulled out a tissue.

"But it has lipstick on it," he whined.

"So? You've been exposed to my lipstick before. Just turn the tissue around and use a clean part." He looked at me with a beleaguered, helpless expression. I saw him try to stifle a smile. Evidently, he had finished his tirade.

Although his anger was now completely spent, I was furious. Since the recent divorce, I found it impossible to tolerate or ignore the mood swings that caused explosive outbursts one moment and funny, soft coziness the next. I was no longer drawn in by the extraordinary charm, humor, and charisma that compelled so many people to indulge the bouts of temper that erupted now with such increasing frequency. Everyone always enabled David to do just what he wanted to do without having to endure appropriate consequences. I narrowed my eyes, tightened my mouth, and returned my focus to the highway.

"Don't smile," he teased in a melodic voice, trying to coax me out of my seething frustration. Rather than apologize, it was his way of making nice. When we first met, he had shared the story of how, when he was a boy and had done something mischievous, he would approach his exasperated mother and try to diffuse her annoyance by being charming and making her laugh. It had always worked, he had told me. After we were married, he started to use the same tactic whenever I'd get upset.

"Shut up," I snapped, keeping my eyes on the road. "I'm *sick* of your temper. You're like a six-year-old."

"Don't do it . . . " he teased again.

I did everything I could to keep from breaking into a smile, but the edges of my mouth started to quiver. I just couldn't help it. It made me even angrier.

"Don't do it . . . " he repeated, tickling my side as he coaxed.

Despite all my efforts to resist, I started to chuckle. "David, I *hate* when you do that!"

"I know," he grinned. "That's why I do it." He picked up the proposal he had been waving and said, "We don't have time to correct the typo, so let's just hope they all have a good sense of humor."

And luckily for us, they did. When David reached that part of the presentation, he dramatically pointed out the typo; and, with a beguiling, self-deprecating smile and the most earnest of expressions, he promised that we'd never make them a "farce" in their industry. Although it was logically nonsensical, he created the impression that we had deliberately used the word "farce." David stole a glance at me, and we collectively held our breath. Then all the conservative male board members had a hearty laugh. It was then that they told us that we had won the account. Nobody had more magic than David when he wanted something.

It was mid afternoon before I finally had a moment to close my office door and begin to return some urgent phone calls. I suddenly felt shivers running up and down the length of my body as if I had been connected to a low voltage electrical current.

At that moment, I felt an invisible hand encircle my left wrist. By the size of the fingers, I knew it was a male hand. Although there was no one else in the office, I could tangibly feel the hand grasping my wrist in a very gentle, nonthreatening way. Then, in no more than a few seconds, the sensation stopped. I was spooked and utterly dumbfounded. Nothing like that had ever happened to me before!

I jumped up from my desk, scurried to the door, and looked down the hallway. Everything seemed completely normal. I was still spooked, so I walked down the hall to the reception area and found Shirley hard at work in front of her computer.

"Have you seen anything out of the ordinary this afternoon?" I asked her.

"In *this* office? You're kidding me, right? When *isn't* something weird going on?"

Her sarcastic, down-to-earth response made me smile, and it calmed me. Striding back to my office, I assumed that what I had experienced was stress-related. The agency was going through a severe financial downturn, and I was still in business with David, my temperamental ex-husband. Who *wouldn't* be going crazy?

Blessedly, the rest of the afternoon was uneventful. I was able to leave the office around six-thirty. I picked up some Chinese carryout and got caught in a typical gridlock of Galleria rush hour traffic. Once home, I changed into a nightshirt and crew socks, fed Winston, poured a glass of Chardonnay, put an old *Thin Man* movie in the VCR, and in an exhausted stupor sat down in front of the television to eat.

The moment I picked up my fork, the goose bumps electrical-current sensation started again. This time, it was much stronger. Then some movement caught my attention. My eyes widened with shock as a ghostly apparition began to take shape in my living room. In mere seconds, it assumed the discernible form of a man who appeared to be in his mid-thirties. He was wearing a dark suit that looked as if it could have been at the height of fashion in the late nineteenth century. He had piercing blue eyes, dark hair combed away from his face, a strong jaw punctuated with a cleft, and a rugged build. He just stood there and smiled at me.

My fork clanged to the plate. In a panic, I screamed and leapt to my feet. I had never been so frightened. A man had just broken into my apartment! But he wasn't a man . . . he was a . . . *ghost?* Can a *ghost* . . . *break in?* Was I clearly seeing an *apparition?* Was I becoming delusional? Did I need a padded cell? I quickly surmised that this was definitely *not* the result of money problems or working with David.

Nearly hysterical and flooded with adrenaline, I quickly realized that I had no escape route. The apparition, *or whatever it was*, could easily grab me if I tried to dart past him. In the small apartment I had nowhere to run. The apparition just stood there smiling.

My scream awakened Winston. With obvious irritation, he yawned and then caught sight of our uninvited guest. I was still poised to flee, as I watched Winston casually stretch and then eagerly trot along the back of the couch toward the apparition. The spirit held out his hand and gently stroked Winston under the chin. My cat began to purr loudly.

By all appearances, my Persian cat, who was disdainful toward all humans but me, was interacting with someone he apparently knew and liked. But then it occurred to me that this being wasn't . . . human.

The apparition made no move to approach me. He simply stood and smiled. Then, to my further amazement, he spoke to me with a resonant voice that had a British inflection.

"I'm sorry—I didn't mean to frighten you. My name is John Reid." His blue eyes were full of quiet amusement. He was not at all surprised by my reaction to him. I stood without speaking, mute with disbelief. Things like this simply did not happen to me. Nor did I want them to start happening now. When I didn't respond, he continued to explain his presence in my living room.

"I'm an angel. You asked for help. They sent me."

I could feel the same disquieting wave of energy running through me, just as I did that afternoon in my office. Shivering with goose bumps, I wondered silently if he had visited me earlier.

"Yes, I did," he answered, reading my thoughts. "It was my way of making an introduction." His voice took on a somber, earnest tone. "I want you to know you're not alone anymore. Now you have me."

My mind was racing but not comprehending. My first instinct had been to protect myself from a stranger who had broken into my apartment. As a woman who lived alone, I had become very protective about my safety. Now I was confronted by the scenario I feared most. What was he going to do to me, I wondered? Logic told me that if he wanted to hurt me, he could have easily already done so. But he didn't appear threatening in any way. He just stood there smiling peacefully; his manner seemed very warm and reassuring. Did I really just see him materialize out of *thin air*?

"Why would an angel want to visit *me*?" I blurted suspiciously.

"You asked for help," he replied.

"How do I know you're an angel? Do something to prove it."

"Like a party trick?"

"You *can't* be an angel. Angels don't talk to human beings."

"You're misinformed."

"But it's not natural!"

"It's the most natural thing in the world. You'd be feeling it if you weren't being so anal retentive."

"*Anal?* I'm not anal!"

"You think not?" His eyes twinkled with merriment. "You're the poster girl for what we guardian angels refer to as the Human AA Syndrome. I should have asked for hazardous duty compensation when I signed up to work with you again."

"Human AA Syndrome? What's *that?*" I asked fearfully.

"You're anal and you're angry."

"I'm NOT angry!" I shrieked. "And I'm NOT anal!"

John Reid started to chuckle.

"Are you making fun of me? Angels don't tease people!"

"You're misinformed. With all due respect, having a good sense of humor is de rigueur for an angel to work with human beings."

"It's *what?*"

He smiled with affection and indulgence, as one would with a small child who had just asked a quaint question.

"Leave me alone . . . or . . . I'll call the police!" It was an empty threat. The phone was in the kitchen, and there was no way I could scurry in there fast enough and make the 911 call before he grabbed me. "Get out of here!"

"It's not that simple."

"Why *not?* If you're really an angel, then you can do anything you want!"

"You're misinformed. We have commitments to attend to. It isn't happenstance that I arrived on your doorstep. You asked for help. I agreed to work with you again. I'm perfectly willing to overlook your initial rudeness and your lack of hospitality."

"What do you mean you 'agreed to work with me again'? I've never been visited by any angels!"

"I wasn't expecting this to be easy," he sighed to himself. "Have you forgotten your childhood? You used to refer to me as your best friend. Let me take you back . . . "

As if by magic—in my mind's eye—I returned to my childhood, and I was flooded with snippets of traumatic memories that hadn't surfaced in years. The horrific dreams about violent crimes, my father, drunk, ranting, beating my mother. The never-ending fights about money, gambling, other women . . .

I "saw" the night he tried to strangle her, and how she begged him to stop. Then I "saw" the apartment where Richard Speck had murdered the student nurses. And there was John Reid! He *had* been there. Revisiting the past helped me to recall the presence of an angel who stood by me through it all—offering comfort, support, encouragement, and protection. I never felt alone because he was there—the very same angel that stood before me now. How could I have *forgotten*? I had developed amnesia about my entire relationship with him.

Reading my thoughts, he responded, "Most human beings forget their childhood companions by the time they reach adolescence. They want to grow up and put away childish things; and, so often, the memory of we guardian angels is relegated to a dusty shelf like so many beloved toys, books, and games. And because you abandon us, you assume that we, in turn, abandon you."

"But we're misinformed?"

He smiled at me.

I was clearly hearing and seeing him, but my brain still couldn't comprehend. Was this a sign of some terrible mental illness? "This is impossible! Insane!" I wailed. "I'm becoming delusional . . . people just don't have conversations with guardian angels."

"You're disturbed but not in the way you think. Don't I *look* real? Don't I *sound* real? How *else* would I know about what happened to you? I was *there*."

I stood silent, still afraid to move—rooted to the spot, brow furrowed, eyes squinting with suspicion.

The angel continued to reminisce. "Remember when you sprained your ankle ice skating on that pond? Remember, when you were eight years old, the first pair of glasses? If memory serves, they were speckled pink, and came out in little points at the temple—"

"I *hated* those glasses! I was completely blind!"

"In many ways, you still are. You asked for guidance in regard to your direction in life. Because of the success of our past relationship, it was decided that I should come to help you get on track. It's time. You have important work to do. That's why I'm here. You have not only forgotten about your relationship with me when you were a child, but you have blocked all the dynamics of your destiny, as well. I've asked myself time and time again why you are so impatient and why you deliberately choose to do everything the hard way. You make everything so much more difficult than it has to be."

"I have a destiny?" I asked.

"Every living soul has a very unique destiny that will lead them to true happiness, if only they can discover what it is."

"I've made such a mess of my life," I lamented.

"That's precisely why I'm here. Your life has stalled. If you're willing to listen and do the necessary work, I can help you move forward."

"So what is it that I'm supposed to do with my life? I'm desperate to make changes right *now!*"

"All in good time," he answered. "A journey of a thousand miles begins with the first step. And believe me, I understand the necessary time frames. That awareness is part and parcel of an angel's responsibility. By the way, the voice you heard inside of you that suggested you contact Dawn Dugan was none other than mine. Do you see how well we already work together?"

"How long are you going to stay and help me?" I asked.

"As long as it takes," he replied.

Chapter 8

Hard Lessons in Faith

My journey of a thousand miles began that fateful night with guardian angel John Reid at my side acting as a navigator. I must admit it took some time before I could really feel confident that he wasn't just a figment of my imagination. For a little while I still worried that I was having some kind of breakdown, but I dismissed that notion as I recognized that my life was slowly and steadily improving just as he said it would.

Initially, I was hesitant to depend on him too much, out of fear that he would vanish as abruptly as he first appeared. But true to his word, he remained faithfully by my side. In fact, he accompanied me everywhere I went. John Reid progressively earned my trust and respect, and our relationship became very natural to me, as it had when I was a child. However, because I was the only one who could see him, I was often embarrassed at work or in public places when I'd forget myself and respond out loud to something that he'd said or done. I was quickly labeled an eccentric due to launching into animated conversations with thin air, or worse, suddenly laughing hilariously at nothing at all.

I'm naturally a very pragmatic, skeptical person, so I was always asking John for *proof* of the intuitive process. Still fearing I was far too anal retentive to leap headlong into the process, he slowly began to reveal intuitive information to me by sharing simple predictions about the weather, the outcome of the presidential election that was taking place at the time, and what was going to occur within the advertising agency on a day–to–day basis.

As I opened up to the process of angelic communication and began to develop faith in what I was hearing from John, he started to provide intuitive information about other people. That was fascinating! I became much more discriminating with the prospective clients I was pitching because he would warn me about folks who didn't pay their bills on time. He also saved me from several potential car accidents by saying "Wait!" to prevent me from driving into the path of a vehicle speeding through a red light. John even shared information about present and future health concerns for my family and me.

What's more, I began to receive intuitive messages about strangers standing next to me at the grocers, dry cleaners, and the neighborhood video store. This information included specifics about their health, physical safety, love life, career, finances, and past life experiences. Just as he had promised, a whole new world was opening up to me.

However, in spite of the fact that I was receiving consistent psychic information about other people, I had no real way of validating the accuracy of what I was picking up. So, once again, I found myself asking John for tangible proof.

John told me that he would be delighted to provide the proof I had been asking for. The next day while I was getting ready to leave for work, he disclosed that he had some intuitive information about a door–man who worked in the apartment building I lived in, and he requested that I pass along an important psychic message to him.

"What? *Me?* I can't do that!"

"Why not? When you present the information to him, he'll provide the proof that you've been asking for."

"I don't even know him! He'll think I'm crazy!"

"And your point is . . . ?"

"I don't want to make a fool of myself!"

"You'd better get used to that, Kim. I'm amazed that you care so much about what other people think. You have to let go of needing other peoples' approval. Your life will be so much easier when—"

"Of course I care about what other people think! Unlike you, I live on the earthly plane with them. I'm not going to do it, John. I *can't*."

"Okay," he shrugged. "I just wanted you to tell him that his sister is ill and needs to go to a doctor."

"Doesn't the sister know that already?"

"No, she doesn't. Some illnesses do not have classic, telltale symptoms."

"Like what kind of illness?"

"Cancer."

"Oh . . . " I answered in a small voice. My aunt had recently died of the disease, and her passing was horrific. At first, she complained of a chest cold and a cough that wouldn't go away, but she never connected those symptoms with cancer. She finally went to the doctor, who diagnosed bronchitis and sent her home with a prescription for an antibiotic. The disease quickly spread throughout her body like wildfire, finally reaching her brain. The woman who had been so vibrant and beautiful was left incapacitated and bedridden, and she spent the last weeks of her life muttering to herself incoherently. Aunt Patsy died in a world all her own, having lost the capacity to recognize any of the loved ones who hovered around her bedside.

"What would I have to do?" I asked in a resigned tone.

"Just pass along *exactly* what you hear from me."

"You make it sound so simple."

"It is."

"Okay, let's just get this over with before I come to my senses. Maybe the doorman won't be here today? Maybe I won't be able to find him? You know I have to get to work, so I can't wait around."

"He's here. Stop stalling." And with that, I stepped out of the elevator and literally bumped into the man we had been discussing. I got the goose bumps sensation again—and I suddenly had the distinct impression that the universe somehow *meant* the two of us to have contact that very morning. I didn't know if it was nerves or one of my characteristic blond moments, but I couldn't recall his name in spite of the fact that I frequently said hello to him.

"Hello . . . Pete?" I stammered.

"I'm *Sam*," he replied with a puzzled expression.

"Sam! Of course, Sam. I'm sorry."

"You stressed out today? Anything I can do for you?" he asked kindly.

"Oh, no . . . I'm just on my way to the office! You know . . . where I work. I . . . I . . . think I'm late. Well . . . good bye, Pete!" I hurried through the door.

Go Back. Now! John insisted. I stopped in my tracks. *You said you would do it. Aren't you a person of your word?*

Damn! Why, oh why, did I promise? I took a deep breath, turned around, and walked back to the unsuspecting doorman.

"Forget something?" Sam asked.

"Uhmmm, yes, actually . . . " I stood woodenly, eyes darting this way and that, not knowing how to proceed. My heart started to pound, and my breathing sounded labored.

"Are you okay?" he inquired, now looking worried.

I simply nodded.

John started to speak. *Just repeat after me . . .*

"Just repeat after me," I said to Sam, who furrowed his brow in confusion. John winced. I quickly surmised that I wasn't supposed to repeat *that*. Too late now!

Your sister needs surgery, John said. *Right away.*

"Your sister needs surgery. Right away." Sam looked extremely surprised. As virtual strangers, he had never discussed his personal life with me.

Not the one in New York—I'm referring to Karen, the sister in Florida.

As I repeated what John was saying telepathically, the doorman's eyes widened. He stood rooted to the spot, oblivious to the other people coming and going.

"There is a hazardous growth developing in her left breast. The lump is pre-cancerous and has to be removed . . . now."

With that, Sam took several steps away from me. He was clearly frightened.

"You must call her this afternoon," I continued. "She's depressed because of her marital problems, and she needs to hear from her big brother. You'll make her laugh, like you always do. Then you need to tell her about the cancer. You're going to save her life with that phone call."

I proceeded to tell him that the psychic information he was receiving was courtesy of my guardian angel, John Reid. Poor Sam looked like someone who had just undergone electric shock treatments.

"But I don't *understand*," he replied, looking frightened, shocked, and suspicious. "How did you know I *had* a sister? And how did you know she was in *Florida*?" Then, raising his voice, he sputtered indignantly, "Karen doesn't have *cancer*! And she doesn't have marital problems, either! What's *wrong* with you? Are you some kind of *nut case*?" And with that, the doorman turned and strode away from me.

I stood there staring dumbly, beet red with embarrassment, still clutching my purse and briefcase. I literally had no clue about what to do next. Should I chase after him and apologize? But that might scare him even more and make things worse—if that was possible. I would never deliberately hurt or scare anyone, and I felt miserable.

"Kim, good work! I'm proud of you," John exclaimed happily.

"Why did you make me *do* that? Did you see how upset he was?"

"I didn't make you do anything. It was your choice. And you did admirably—except for saying 'repeat after me.' That wasn't the most auspicious beginning," John chuckled with amusement.

"Don't you *dare* laugh at me! Because of you and your cockamamie psychic predictions, I just scared the hell out of that man."

"May I submit to you that if you had remained quiet and his sister had gotten malignant cancer, *that* would have scared the hell out of him."

"You always have a glib answer for everything," I hissed, tears flooding my eyes. I didn't know why, but besides feeling humiliated, I felt incredibly emotional. The tears started to stream down my face, and I clumsily dug through my purse for a tissue.

John tried to reassure me. "If I know Sam, and I think I do, he'll get over it pretty quickly. That's why I picked him as a test subject for you."

"So you look at human beings as nothing more than guinea pigs in the cosmic experiments you're conducting?"

"You're taking a rather melodramatic point of view. You asked for proof and now you have it. Remember what Oscar Wilde once said: 'Be careful what you wish for . . . because you may get it.' Did I ever tell you that Oscar was a friend of mine? A *platonic* friend, I might add. Very amusing fellow. We used to go to the theater in London . . . "

I was clearly overwrought, and he knew exactly why—and yet, he was casually launching into one of his old *stories*? If it wasn't for the relationship with him and all of the psychic information he shared, I wouldn't have traumatized another human being . . . and I wouldn't have been humiliated in the process. I had never felt so discombobulated, and I was keen to separate myself from the source of my anxiety.

I listened as he described a night at the theater in times gone by—as if nothing was wrong. His dismissive, casual manner about my feelings and everything that had just happened reminded me of David, which ignited a firestorm of anger inside of me.

I had gotten along just fine until John came into the picture. I had been leading an independent and empowered life—a little stressful, maybe—but I was taking care of myself just fine. *Who did he think he was?* Incensed, I interrupted his monologue.

"John, I want you to listen to me very carefully. *Leave me alone.* I want you to *go.* I don't want to *see* you any more—and I don't want to *talk* to you anymore. You're *not* going to tell me what to do *ever again!*"

"But I didn't—"

"*Don't speak to me!*"

"But—"

"NO! I want you to *disappear.* Just go back to the planet you came from." I continued to cry, and my voice became shrill. I had become unhinged, and I furiously gestured with all the force I could muster while still holding my purse and briefcase. "I want my normal, anal life back. *Leave me alone* before everybody starts to think I'm completely *crazy!*" John vanished immediately.

"*Good,*" I shouted. "And *don't ever come back!*"

Out of the corner of my eye, I saw a woman and a little boy of about five standing by the bank of elevators. It was obvious from their expressions that they had witnessed the whole exchange. I realized that I had just made a terrible scene in the lobby of my apartment building. I had never been a person who created scenes—*ever.* Now I was really embarrassed. The mother placed herself between me and her young son in a protective gesture that was not lost on me. She stood staring as if I were a space alien.

"MOM!" The little boy urgently tugged at his mother's sleeve.

His mother shushed him without taking her eyes off me.

"But . . . MOM!" More tugging.

She shushed him again with a stern expression. The little boy peered at me from behind his mother, his eyes huge with amazement and curiosity.

I was at a complete loss for words. Managing a constipated smile, I said, "Sorry. PMS."

A soft *ding* sounded, the elevator doors opened, and the woman shoved the little boy inside. He couldn't restrain his excitement any longer.

"MOM! Did you see that guy just *disappear* in *thin air*? That was AWE-SOME!"

The mother was aggressively pushing buttons inside the elevator. "Lower your voice, Michael! And stop making things up, or you're going to have another time–out."

"Mom . . . what's PMS?"

The elevator quickly closed. I stood looking at my tear–stained image in the mirrored doors, wondering what was becoming of me.

As the day unfolded, it went from bad to worse. Unfortunately, by the time I reached the office, my eyes were still red and swollen. It was apparent that I had been crying, and, because I wasn't my usual perky self, my coworkers could easily detect something was very wrong. Although they had the sensitivity not to ask what was going on, they did inquire, in soft, subdued tones, if I needed some coffee or a chocolate fix. I remained in my office with the door closed. I didn't want to be disturbed. I needed to think.

I kept seeing Sam's face full of fear and anger, and I was really worried about him. I fervently wished I could go back in time and retrace my steps. I promised myself that I'd never again share psychic messages with anyone; nor would I be interested in receiving channeled information about my own life from John or any other spirit.

I was certain that, by now, the doorman had shared the freaky experience with everyone who lived and worked in the building. My vivid imagination was conjuring up nightmarish images of Sam calling an emergency meeting to warn people about me for their own protection, and turning them into an angry mob who would be waiting for me when I got home. I pictured all my neighbors, including the woman and the little boy, in the lobby of the building listening with rapt attention to the shocking tale he had to tell.

"There's a weird woman who lives here in the building, and she's dangerous and delusional. She thinks she can talk with spirits. Her name is Kim O'Neill!

"Our *neighbor?* The one in advertising? But she's hardly ever home—and she always seems so quiet."

"Those are the ones you have to watch out for."

"What *happened?*"

"Just this morning, she told me that my sister has cancer—and that she is going to get a divorce."

"Why would she say such a thing?"

"She said an angel told her."

"An *angel?* Did you see the angel?"

"Of course not! She just made that up. Angels don't talk to people."

"How *awful!* Who would predict something so *negative?* So *hateful?* How did you escape?"

"I ran as fast as I could!"

I imagined an ugly mob forming. "She should be locked up. Let's call the police! Or a hospital for the criminally insane."

"We must avoid her at all costs—let's unite and force her to leave. Light the torches—we'll be ready to run her out of town if she has the audacity to show her face here again!"

I shuddered at what they all must be saying about me. I would be a laughingstock, at best. And I was convinced that everyone would believe that I was mentally disturbed. And was I?

My first foray into sharing psychic information had gone terribly wrong—in spite of the fact that I had faithfully repeated everything John had said. I couldn't understand why he would have deliberately put me in such a compromising position. After all, wasn't I doing everything he told me to do? Wasn't I really trying to work through my issues? Wasn't I a good person? Why would he encourage me to humiliate myself and purposely frighten another human being? I had asked him for proof—but did he really think that I would walk away from that experience confident and encouraged? Perhaps I *was* delusional. John could be nothing more than a figment of my imagination. Maybe I needed intensive therapy and I was just trying to avoid it by creating a spiritual pal who would assure me that I was mentally stable. But what kind of person seeks reassurance about mental and emotional health from a *spirit*? If John really *was* a guardian angel, then wouldn't the information have been perfectly correct? I decided to call an acquaintance and ask for the name of her therapist. There was no time to lose.

What's more, I'd have to find another place to live. I simply couldn't stay there under the circumstances. I hated the thought of returning to the apartment building. I wished I never had to go back. I considered spending the night in a hotel, but it occurred to me that I didn't have a change of clothes or my toiletries. Of course, common sense told me that I'd have to go back to my apartment. I was thankful that Sam worked the day shift so that I wouldn't have to face him that evening. But what about the following day? I wondered what time he arrived in the morning. Maybe I could leave extra early so I wouldn't have to face him. Had he really told everyone in the building about what happened? And how would all of my neighbors treat me now that they knew I spoke with spirits?

Trying to put off the inevitable, I remained at work until after eight. Feeling sick and edgy, I reluctantly drove home, parked my car, and walked quickly and quietly with my head down. I was hoping to avoid contact with anyone in the building. I reached the bank of elevators undetected and then was startled by someone who abruptly shouted my name.

"KIM! WAIT!" I jumped ten feet. I turned and saw Sam, the doorman, quickly approaching. I flinched, fully expecting an angry tirade. Instead, he threw his arms around me in a warm hug. I stood motionless.

"Finally! I've been waiting for you all day. I thought you'd never get home. Guess *what*?" He pulled away, breathless with excitement. He looked at me expectantly, waiting for a response. I had none to give, so

I just blankly stared at him. He waited for just a second before continuing, eager to share his big news.

"Remember this morning?"

I nodded mutely. Did he think I could have *forgotten*?

"At first, I thought you were *nuts*. A kook. You really scared the shit out of me. But then I got to thinking. I was already having this feeling that I needed to call Karen. I just didn't know why. So I thought *what the hell*—why not? What could it hurt?" He stopped to catch his breath. "It was really weird! Karen is always at work during the day and I don't have that number—so I called her at home and was going to leave a message—but she picked up the phone. She'd just come from the doctor's office. When she heard my voice, she started to cry. She said that the doctor wants to remove a lump from her breast, but she was too scared to let him do it. I told her I'd plan a visit whenever she decided to have it done. She promised to call the doctor and schedule the surgery."

I was mute with disbelief.

"And there's more. She told me that her husband just left her and ran off with the eighteen-year-old babysitter! Can you believe that sorry SOB? When I fly down there, me and my brother-in-law are gonna have a little talk. Karen said she never would have called me because she knows how busy I am—and she didn't want to bother me!"

I was in shock. All I could muster in response to what he was sharing was a wide-eyed, confused gaze.

"If it wasn't for you, I probably wouldn't have called her. And if she didn't have the operation, who knows what would have happened?" He grabbed me again, eyes filling with tears. "You might have saved her life. Thank you!"

"I'm so glad," I muttered.

"Listen," Sam said, leaning toward me and whispering confidentially. "No offense, but I thought you were bullshitting me. Did you really get the information from an *angel*?"

"Well, I . . . "

Without stopping to listen, he quickly looked around to make sure no one could hear him. Then he leaned in even closer. "Does the angel have any more stuff to say? I mean, the information was right on target.

If you ever hear anything else about me, or my family, would you tell me?"

"Okay," I answered hesitantly, clearly remembering that I had given the angel in question his walking papers.

Sam repeated his enthusiastic thanks, pushed the elevator button for me, and wished me a good evening. I stood there staring after him as he walked away. He turned the corner and began to whistle as if he didn't have a care in the world.

I had just received the proof I had been asking for—in spades. As the mirrored doors opened and I stepped inside, I suddenly had a mental flashback of the mother and her young son getting into the same elevator that morning.

"MOM! Did you see that guy *disappear* in *thin air?* That was AWESOME!"

The little boy had seen John! Why hadn't I picked up on that this morning? Even more proof. Maybe I'm not crazy after all!

At that moment, I was overcome with the now-familiar goose bumps sensation. I heard a masculine, disembodied voice say, "Oh, ye of little faith." John Reid materialized by my side in the elevator. "PMS is *right,*" he said with his usual handsome grin. "I keep telling them I need hazardous duty compensation."

"John! I got my proof! Just like you said!"

"Maybe next time you'll believe me before you jump to conclusions and make false assumptions."

"I'm sorry," I replied humbly. "I should have had more faith in you." Then I had a pivotal realization. "So, I guess—at times—psychic information is not going to resonate inside of us right away—but that's okay—because it doesn't mean that it's *wrong* . . . right?"

"I'm not quite certain about what you just said, but I think you're getting the picture," he replied. "You've had a big day today. What you're going through isn't easy, is it?"

"No, it isn't. And everything is happening so fast. But, John, I'm so relieved. Do you know what I realize now? I'm not a crazy person! There's nothing wrong with me. Even though I talk to you."

"I am impervious to flattery, I warn you," he responded dryly. I smiled at him and he smiled back at me.

"And I'm sorry that I interrupted your story. What were you saying earlier about Oscar Meyer?"

"Oscar *Wilde*," he corrected me, in a mock lecturing tone.

"Sorry!"

"As I was saying," he began with hesitation, in the same lecturing tone, as if convinced that the story might be wasted on me. "My friend Oscar and I used to frequent this small theater in London's West End. Did you know that a very handsome young lady who used to perform there inspired him to write *The Importance of Being Ernest?*"

"I loved that movie!" I chimed.

John hung his head and looked resigned.

"What's the matter?" I asked.

"Nothing," he replied. "Shall I continue?"

"Yes, please!"

"Well, originally, he was going to call it *End Over End*, but I convinced him otherwise; I didn't think such a title would appeal to the carriage trade. He was already in quite a bit of trouble over some unfortunate incidents that occurred at a little soiree he had given at his country home—"

"Really?" I asked eagerly. "Like *what?*"

"Your sensibilities are far too delicate to hear the details," John chuckled at some distant yet vivid memory. "I've never known anyone before or since who could throw a party like Oscar."

The elevator doors opened and we exited, John still holding court as we walked down the hall to my apartment. I was glad my spiritual companion was back.

Chapter 9

Slowly Building Trust

Under John's capable guidance, I continued to eagerly explore the process of channeling, and soon my ability to receive angelic information seemed to explode. At this point—without conscious intent—I was receiving intuitive sensations about everyone who came close to me, and this became extremely distracting—especially in business meetings.

In spite of the experience with the doorman, and the fact that I was consistently bombarded with psychic information, I remained insecure about the accuracy of what I was picking up. However, I discovered that if I maintained faith in John, and myself, and in the whole intuitive process as it unfolded, that proof would always be there for me.

One of the most telling psychic experiences I've ever experienced happened at that time, and it really helped build my confidence that I was, without question, accessing accurate information. This event reminded me that things are rarely what they seem on the surface.

I was visiting a client in the health care industry. It was a big closed-door meeting attended by more than a dozen people. One of the executives of the company sat on my left. As the meeting got underway, I was

shocked by the very unpleasant waves of dangerous sexual energy coming from him. I couldn't help glancing in his direction. But he appeared
as professional as ever. He certainly didn't have a flirtatious manner like
my ex-husband. To the contrary, he had such a dignified demeanor that
I was quite unprepared for the intuitive information I was receiving.

My newly found psychic ability was telling me that he was taking
sexual liberties with female patients—a huge, inappropriate no-no in
his position at the company. Of course, I immediately questioned the
information because it seemed so far off the mark based on my prior
experience with him and what logic was telling me. It seemed absolutely preposterous! I felt guilty and disloyal to a man who had awarded
our little agency with his big, prestigious account, paid his bills on time,
and who had shown nothing but respect and appreciation for all of our
hard work.

Very shortly thereafter, confirming my psychic information, I received
a call from a colleague of his. She told me that he had just been fired for
sexual misconduct involving several female patients. She began to
worriedly ask about how I was going to handle the potential media
scandal—but frankly, all I could think about at that moment was how
on-target my intuitiveness had been. It was my first experience in receiving information that appeared completely unbelievable and nonsensical on the surface but was, nonetheless, occurring behind the
scenes.

At this point, about six months had gone by. John believed I was
ready to learn about my life's work. Up to that time, in spite of the fact
that he knew I loathed advertising and was eager to move on, he had
consistently discouraged me from job hunting, indicating that it
wouldn't be necessary. I had absolutely no clue as to what my destiny
was, and I was bursting with curiosity. This was the moment I had been
waiting for!

Initially, when John revealed the news to me, I was crushed with
disappointment. My destiny was to be a *channel* and a *medium*? A *psychic*?
I suddenly pictured myself wearing a turban and lots of costume jewelry, working out of a small trailer with a big neon palm outside that
proclaimed, *I solve all problems of life! Magic potions prepared, voodoo hexes guaranteed, packets of animal by-products available for curse removal . . .*

John impatiently interrupted my train of thought by providing a job description of exactly what a medium does. He explained that a medium, or channel, is a conduit, much like a pipe that carries the flow of water. My "water" was going to be the messages from "the other side" that I was going to share with others. What's more, he told me, like a physician who specializes in a certain area of medicine, channels specialize, too. One of my areas of specialty was going to be accessing specific information from guardian angels and deceased human beings to help a living individual find out about his destiny.

Destiny, he explained, pertained to life's work, issues to be resolved, the nature of our relationships with other people, finding a soul mate, as well as building greater levels of emotional and financial abundance. The psychic information I was supposed to provide was going to help people become more aware of who they were and why they were here, to allow them to create a quality of life filled with purpose, direction, and meaning.

He went on to say that every channel, or medium, is a work in progress; and, as I continued to develop my ability, I would receive more detailed and specific information.

"You mean I'm going to be talking with *dead people?*"

"We don't refer to anyone as 'dead,' " John explained. "Every soul continues its existence, regardless of whether it possesses a physical body."

"That's absurd!"

"A short time ago you thought talking with angels was absurd."

"But I don't want dead people hanging around! I don't know the first thing about—"

"So you'll *learn.* Babe Ruth had to hit his first baseball, didn't he? Julia Child had to cook her first soufflé. You had to write your first radio commercial, didn't you?"

"But that's different."

"How?"

"Because that's *normal.*"

"Since when did you ever aspire to being *normal?*"

I frowned, suddenly at a loss for words. It was true—I had never aspired to settle . . . to lead a conventional life. He was right, damn him.

Double-damn him, I thought. Was he *always* right?

"Now, now," he teased. "Remember . . . I can hear what you're thinking."

I kept forgetting that.

"Oh, *no!*" he said loudly, comically slapping his hand against his forehead. "I suppose that means that *I'm* not normal, *either!*"

I smiled. "Maybe that's why we're such a good team. Did the universe match us up because we're both misfits?"

"Thank you for that great vote of confidence. I think I've just changed my mind about asking you to provide a testimonial for my guardian angel resume."

"Do you guys *really* have resumes?"

From the look on his face, I was glad that I hadn't yet developed the ability to read *his* mind. With a resigned expression, John went on to explain that it was my spiritual responsibility to spend my life providing intuitive information to others to help them move their lives forward, just as he was helping me with mine. In addition to that, I was supposed to teach others to channel for themselves so they could receive their own messages from the other side whenever they needed them.

I just stared at him. The left side of my brain had abruptly kicked into gear, and I began to tell him that the whole notion of me being an intuitive conduit was too ridiculous for consideration. After all, I was a serious businesswoman. It had taken me years to establish my credibility in the ultraconservative Houston business community. And I was to give all of that up? To start my own channeling practice? I'd be laughed right out of town!

He allowed me to rave on. His unruffled attitude indicated that he rather expected this negative reaction from me. A short time later, when all my negativity was spent and I could quiet my brain, I began to balance and center myself.

"May I remind you that everything happens for a reason?" said John.

It suddenly occurred to me why I had begun to receive so much intuitive information about other people. I did yearn to have my own business outside of advertising, and I was certainly enthusiastic about leaving the business partnership with my ex-husband. And oddly, I had been recently fantasizing about doing something meaningful that would allow me to make some small difference in other peoples' lives.

John suggested that I test the waters by actually providing channeled information to someone else—just as I had done with Sam, the doorman. Only then could I make a rational and informed decision.

The thought of channeling for someone else filled me with immediate apprehension. In a relatively short period of time, channeling for myself had begun to seem like the most natural process in the world. Channeling for another individual—that struck me as a completely different undertaking.

What if I got it *wrong* somehow? What if I couldn't do it again? John told me that all I had to do was *listen* and simply repeat what I was hearing. Spiritual beings would provide all the necessary information. What's more, he promised, he'd be right there by my side. We'd be a cohesive team.

In spite of my objections, he remained firmly convinced that I was ready. I listened to him with a growing sense of doubt. How would anyone *know* I could channel for them? John pointed out that it would be my responsibility to approach people and offer to pass along messages from their angels or deceased loved ones. It was part of my process, he explained.

But how would I accomplish *that*, I wondered? Ring somebody's doorbell like a Fuller Brush salesman and say, "Hello! You don't know me, but I have a message from Ignatz—your guardian angel." Or, perhaps I could approach an advertising client and say, "You know, besides producing your television and radio commercials, and writing your new ad campaign, I could make psychic predictions for you." Maybe when I went out on one of my very infrequent dates, I could suggest, "Why don't we go back to my place? I'll make coffee, turn on some romantic music, and then I'll conjure up your dead Uncle Buford so he can explain how you can finally get rid of that pesky athlete's foot fungus."

I was amusing myself with these various scenarios until John disclosed that this was going to be the very process that would allow me to eventually leave the agency and go off on my own. Suddenly, I wasn't laughing anymore. I had to approach others, he explained, because I would be showing intent to the universe that I was serious and committed to my life's work. After I started demonstrating my intent, then it was up to him to fulfill his end of the partnership by bringing clients to me.

As shy as I was, I wasn't crazy about the idea of approaching hapless, unsuspecting strangers and offering to channel for them. I asked John if he could just wave some kind of cosmic magic wand and get things going immediately. He made it clear that the universe didn't work that way.

He pointed out that each human being has to develop an awareness of his or her particular destiny, and then begin to demonstrate deliberate intent to follow through before a spiritual being has the permission to assist by pushing things forward. When the process is in full swing, he explained, my life would move forward faster than I had ever dreamed possible. All I needed was to do my part. I had to *earn* the opportunity to move to another chapter of my life. The ball was clearly in my court.

Chapter 10

Finally Setting Boundaries

When I awoke that Tuesday morning, I had no clue that it was going to be a day like no other. Little did I know that I was going to disclose—for the first time—my growing psychic ability with David, my business partner and ex-husband.

Just after lunch, a brainstorming session had begun in my office. Rebecca, a copywriter, and Phil, the art director, sat across from me in the two chairs that flanked my large pine desk. Craig, one of the designers, perched on the small couch that sat in front of the floor-to-ceiling windows to my left. Audrey, an account executive, stood across the room taking careful aim at the dartboard that hung on the back of my door.

"Our new client, Dr. Edison Lowe, is planning to meet with us next week," I shared with them. "He expects some brilliant creative ideas for his upcoming ad campaign. I've been thinking—why not recommend radio and TV appearances, too? I think he'd be a natural."

"Hey, that would be great," said Craig. "If his target audience could *see* him and *hear* him, it would really breathe life into his campaign. And I've got some ideas for a new ad—the one he's been running looks like crap. No wonder he hasn't been getting any response."

"I'm going to have lunch tomorrow with the producer of *Good Morning Houston*," said Rebecca. "I'll convince her that Dr. Lowe would make a great guest. He could answer questions from viewers."

"Why not try to sell him as a host of his own radio show?" asked Audrey. "I can contact the program director of KPRC."

"Fantastic!" I answered. "Dr. Lowe needs a new publicity picture, too."

"Jesus—does he ever!" said Phil. "Who took the last shot? He looks like Quasimodo."

"Well, he might not be pretty to look at," I observed, "but he's got the goods. His CV is as long as my arm."

"His *what?*" asked Phil.

"Curriculum vitae," I explained. "It's what physicians call their resume."

"CV sounds like an unmentionable disease," the art director quipped.

"Audrey, call your contact at the station," I said. "Let's get the doctor on a radio program while we're developing the new ad campaign, and I think he'll be one very happy boy."

"Will do," she answered, still throwing darts. "That's how I make the big bucks."

"From your mouth to God's ears," I responded, reviewing the doctor's CV. "Let's see here . . . Harvard Medical School; Johns Hopkins residency; currently on the staff of Baylor; has a private practice as an OB-GYN and is also researching fertility." I looked up from the papers I held. "Lowe told me he needs to increase his patient population because his malpractice insurance has just gone up to over a hundred thousand a year."

"No *kidding?*" cried Rebecca. "I wonder what he *earns?*"

"Hey, I wouldn't mind working in a business where women took their clothes off all day," mused Phil. "And they paid me to feel their tits."

"You idiot," said Audrey. "He's a *doctor*. He doesn't look at his patients from a sexual point of view."

"Bullshit," he answered. "Tits are like pizza—even when they're bad, they're good."

"We also need to come up with some kind of slogan or tag line for the good doctor," I told them. "Something that will position him as an authority in his field."

"Hey, I know," offered Craig. "Dr. Edison Lowe—At Your Cervix."

We all groaned at the pun.

"No, wait!" he argued. "Think of the hot logo design I could come up with for his business cards."

There was a sharp rap on the door before it opened. Shirley stuck her head around the corner. "Sorry to interrupt. The marketing director for Grand Oaks Mall is on the phone and she's hysterical."

"What happened?" I inquired.

"Remember the new guy she just hired to dress up like the Easter Bunny so all the kids could come and get their picture taken with him?"

"Yeah . . . " I answered cautiously.

"Well, he got drunk during his break, and when he returned to Bunnyland, he yanked off the hood to his costume—and, in front of all the kids in line—pulled a mommy on his lap and gave her a kiss that she'll never forget."

I pursed my lips and shook my head, while everyone else laughed heartily. I wondered how long it would take to handle all the damage control.

"There's more," warned Shirley, in her deadpan voice.

"Do I really want to hear it?"

"The mommy has already hired an attorney and has called all the TV stations in town. HPD is over there now investigating the assault charge. You wanna take this?"

"Kim, could I handle this?" begged Audrey, turning her attention away from the dartboard. "Please?"

I looked at her and made a quick decision. I swung around and grabbed the phone on my credenza. "Hi, Kate . . . it's Kim. Yes . . . I just heard. I'm *so* sorry that happened," I said, while motioning to everybody to quiet down. I didn't want the traumatized client to hear my staff laughing. "Listen, I'm going to send my best PR person to handle this. Her name is Audrey O'Connell. You'll be in wonderful hands. Okay— don't worry, she'll be right over."

I hung up the phone and turned toward my eager staff member. "Audrey, be sure to call your contacts at the TV stations from your car. If you need me, I'm right here. Get to Grand Oaks as fast as you can."

"I'm already gone!"

"Okay, everybody, so much for the brainstorming session," I said with a sigh. "Let's meet again tomorrow, same time." As the last staff member left my office, I shut my door for some privacy.

John abruptly appeared. "Today is the day you're going to come out of the closet at Advertising & Design, Inc.," he happily announced.

"What do you mean?" I asked with a little concern. He seemed to have an important agenda.

"You're going to spring all of your plans on your partner, David."

"I can't do that!" I gasped. "I'm not ready!"

"Yes, you are. Let's get it over with . . . right now."

"But I'm worried, John. What if he laughs at me?"

"So? Better men than he will laugh at you."

I shot him a worried look.

"Perhaps that was a poor choice of words," he noted.

"And what if he asks me to *leave* once I tell him?"

"Believe me; he will not do that. Remember who you are!"

"Who *am* I?"

"You're one of the founders of Advertising & Design, Inc. Don't you run the company?"

"Yes," I admitted. "But David doesn't realize that, does he?"

"He does . . . in his own way."

"I'm scared, John! I'm self-supporting, and this is the only income I have. I have no savings—"

"All right, dear one, let's not get anal."

I bit my lip and protectively crossed my arms.

"Approach the gathering storm with courage," said John. "With strength—with independence—with empowerment. Don't let him frighten or intimidate you. And beware of his manipulations. You need to see him more clearly for who and what he is."

"But I do!"

"Horsefeathers. There are still times when you see what you want to see. But all of that is about to change."

I pulled open a desk drawer and reached for the dark chocolate that I had stashed there for emergencies. I munched while regarding the angel with a worried expression.

"Where is your backbone?" he demanded. "You can do it. And I'll help."

"That's what I'm afraid of."

"Your opportunity is fast approaching."

My phone suddenly buzzed, startling me. John gave me a thumbs-up gesture. With my heart beating rapidly, I picked up the receiver. David was calling from his office at the opposite end of the hall. He was screaming so loudly that he didn't need the intercom.

"KIM! I NEED YOU! I CAN'T FIND THE GODDAMNED SON-OF-A-BITCH FILE FOR—" I hung up while he was in mid-sentence.

Whenever he lost something—which occurred with regularity—he would summon me to find it. I had learned from experience that if I didn't make an immediate appearance, he would continue with his tirade until I did, creating a huge distraction for everyone else at the agency.

"Fire in the hole," chuckled John. "It's show time!"

I grabbed a yellow tablet and a pen, as was my habit. I never knew when a good idea would strike, or when I'd need to make notes about something, and I always liked to be prepared. I opened my office door, and John and I quickly navigated the long corridor. When I reached his office, David was violently rifling through the file drawers in his credenza.

"WELL, FUCK ME . . . FUCK ME . . . FUCK ME . . . "

"David! Lower your voice!" I hissed at him.

"KIM! Where is the file on the ACM Chemical account? I KNOW I gave it to you! GODDAMN SON-OF-A-BITCH . . . "

John started to speak to me telepathically. *It's in the file room where he left it.*

"It's in the file room where you left it," I repeated.

David looked at me with genuine surprise and then strode out of his office. In no more than twenty seconds he was back carrying the file in question. His anger was completely gone, and he was smiling.

"How did you know it was there?" he asked casually, without thanking me.

John sat in one of the chairs opposite David's desk. I took the other chair, placing my yellow pad and pen on the small table next to me.

Now is the time to tell him, John nudged. *I've been looking forward to this!*

"David—uhhmm—there's something we need to discuss," my voice trailed off nervously.

"I think I know what you're going to say."

No he doesn't, said John, eyes full of merriment.

David looked down at his watch—which he always did when I was talking to him. It was a not-so-subtle reminder that he didn't have all day to invest in a conversation with me.

You'd better make it snappy, advised John. *His time is obviously very important.*

I nervously bit my lip and frowned as I tried to choose my words. Where would I begin? My life had changed so much in the past few weeks . . . and how would I share the news about John?

"Let me see if I can help," said David impatiently. "You started to become distracted right after I announced my engagement to Monica."

"Yes, that's right," I responded. "But—"

"You're upset that I'm getting married. It's only natural that you'd be depressed. So in essence, you'd like me to break up with her and come back to you."

I didn't think that I heard him correctly; I just sat there staring for a moment. Was he out of his *mind?* Had he always been this way? Was I just starting to really notice how ego-driven he was because, with John's help, I was starting to finally move forward and resolve some of my own dysfunction?

"David . . . " Shirley's voice crackled over the intercom. "Monica's on the line."

A big smile played upon his face. Forgetting all about me, he turned toward his credenza and picked up the phone. In a provocative voice, he purred, "How's my Baby Girl?" After listening for a moment, his smile faded into a scowl. He remained silent for some seconds before he responded, "But, Monica, I told you last night, I wasn't flirting with that girl. I didn't even know who she was. I'm an artist . . . I like to watch all people." Then more glowering silence. "You don't *believe* me?" he asked, feigning hurt. After a few moments of listening, he said, "Don't smile . . . "

My eyes popped open. Some things never change. I should have known—he used to call *me* Baby Girl when we first met. And it didn't take a mental giant to figure out that he probably said all the same things to the ex-wife before me. He didn't vary the script from woman to woman, and that brought home just how transitory and unimportant all of us were to him. Wouldn't it be interesting if we all got together and shared notes? I imagined that we'd all come to the same conclusion: that his Harley Davidson motorcycle was his only true love.

"Don't do it," he repeated. Then he listened for another moment, chuckled, and said, "Okay, Baby Girl, I'll see you tonight. And why don't you wear those sexy jeans and the high heels we just bought? I love you." And he blew kisses into the phone.

My nervousness was turning into resolute determination. Did I want to be shackled to this man for the rest of my life? Did I want my personal or professional reputation tied to his? Did I want to be summoned to his office every time he went into an immature tirade? Did I want to continue being the recipient of all the can't-you-keep-him-on-a-shorter-leash stares from employees, clients, and suppliers every time he acted like a nincompoop? Did I want to be in business with a partner who never—ever—acknowledged any of my contributions? Did I want to keep someone in my life who didn't treat me with respect? Was I going to keep settling for a business relationship with someone who did nothing but manipulate and disregard other people, especially women? I suddenly decided it was time to make my stand! I was more desperate than ever to get out of there and away from him.

David hung up and turned back toward me. "Now, what were we discussing?"

At that moment, Craig knocked on the doorframe. "Oh, sorry," said the designer, when he saw that we were in a meeting. "David, you asked me to tell you when I was finished with the ACM stuff."

"Yes," David answered, to my chagrin. He stood and announced, "I'll be right there."

To my partner's surprise, however, before he could rise from his leather chair, I said firmly, "He'll be out in a second." Craig quickly retreated as I got up and closed the door.

"I have something to tell you."

"I don't have the time right now!" he complained, in his usual effort to dismiss me. Now that he had found the missing file, I was yesterday's newspaper. "You don't realize how busy I am. I have the ACM Chemicals meeting tomorrow, and then the goddamn idiots at Porter Electronics expect me to—"

"David," I interrupted him in a quiet voice, but my teeth were clenched. "You're going to listen to me for one minute."

Oddly, he quieted immediately, and it was one of the rare occasions when I had his full attention.

"I'm going to move on with my life."

"Good," he answered. "Did you meet somebody?"

"Well . . . in a sense, yes."

"I wish you all the best. When do I get to meet the lucky guy?"

"*I'm* the lucky one. In fact, he's an angel. Would you like to meet him right now?"

David looked puzzled. "Is he waiting outside?"

"No—as a matter of fact, he's sitting right there. His name is John Reid." I made a sweeping gesture to indicate the chair next to me.

David looked at the chair, obviously finding it empty. Then he looked back at me with a curt expression. "I don't have time to play games. Do you have something to discuss or not?"

"Yes, I do! And I'm not playing games. I don't do that to other people— I treat them with respect. You don't understand me and you never did. You just don't have the time to think of anyone but yourself. That's just one of the reasons I'm leaving the agency."

"Leaving the *agency*? When? Is it because of Monica?"

"*No!* I just can't stay here with you—I can't stand it any longer."

"But you can't leave!" he whined. "What about the pitch next week— and all the copy for ACM—and all the taxes have to be filed—and—"

"Well, unfortunately I'm not leaving right *now*," I explained. "But I am planning to go, so I wanted to be ethical and give you plenty of notice. You'll need time to find a replacement for me so it's not a Chinese fire drill when I leave. In fact, if you want, I'll interview people myself . . . and even spend a couple of weeks showing the ropes to my replacement. I've put everything I have into this business, and I wouldn't hurt it for the world."

I was suddenly the mouse that roared. He sat staring in amazement.

"Did you find a job?" he asked quietly.

"No . . . I'm starting another business. As we speak, I'm working to get it off the ground."

"What are you going to be *doing*?"

"Working as a professional channel."

"A *what?*"

"A psychic."

He searched my eyes for several long moments, and then he burst out laughing. "Okay! Who put you up to this? You really had me going." He put both sets of fingertips on either side of his head in mock concentration. "I see all . . . and I hear all. Chuck Dugan, can I tell your fortune? Just hold out your palm, you rotten son-of-a-bitch, and I'll tell you about the future! You're going to fuck everyone you come in contact with." He took his hands down and laughed uproariously. Then he started to hum the theme song to the Twilight Zone. "Too bad you weren't psychic before we picked up that tick-infested account! Hey . . . Kim, just think of the award-winning logo Craig could design for your business cards! How about a big palm on the front and a crystal ball on the back? We could include your picture—you could wear a turban. No more bad hair days!" He put his hands back to his head and began to mimic a sideshow phony. "I'm using my own amazing psychic ability to figure out how you came into your powers . . . I know! Those thick glasses of yours allowed you to tune in to the other world. They will also help you connect with aliens . . . but the way you *look* in those glasses is so scary that it will make them think twice about an abduction—"

For the first time, instead of feeling stung by his caustic remarks, they just made me feel sorry for him. His own insecurities made him hypercritical of others. I had the sense that he would never choose to change. I narrowed my eyes and spoke very softly and very deliberately. "Are you ready to listen to me or should I leave? My time is important, too."

"And didn't you used to call me the 'Vanishing Indian' when we were married?" Then he motioned to the chair next to me. "Who's *this*—the Invisible Man? I guess you haven't yet subjected him to the long, drawn-out lecture on needing a man with depth and substance? A man who'll always *be there* for you?" His laugh was full of sarcasm. David knew how to hit all my hot buttons—and I *despised* him for it. I felt close to exploding with the bottle rocket anger only he could inspire.

"You—you—" I sputtered, and John stopped me by reaching out his hand and placing it supportively on my arm.

Well, I think this conversation needs to come to a close, John said telepathically. *Why don't we show your business partner what the channeling process is all about?*

Although I was seething, I nodded in agreement.

Tell him he'd better not go to the Strip Club tomorrow night to meet the girl who dances there—Monica will find out.

I smiled. My anger and resentment were quickly washing away. I repeated what John said, and David's eyes almost popped from his head.

"How did you *know* that?" he asked suspiciously. "Are you having me followed?"

And last weekend he bought the expensive car that he promised he wouldn't. He's going to pick it up this afternoon. That's why he's in such a hurry to leave.

"You bought the *car?*" I shrieked at David accusingly. Now my eyes were popping. "After you promised you wouldn't! You know we have such money problems. How could you have *done* that?"

"Who *told* you? Did the dealership call? I told them *not* to!" David then put his hand to his mouth as if wishing he could retract his statement.

"Did you think I wouldn't *find out?*" I yelled. "I pay all the bills!"

"Well, that big account I've been pitching is right around the corner—"

Don't forget, Kim—you'll be leaving soon, reminded John. *You won't have to struggle with all of the agency expenses much longer.*

"That's right, John. I can't even imagine how wonderful that will be!"

"Who the hell are you talking to?" David demanded.

"My guardian angel, John Reid. John—meet David. David—meet John."

David didn't look at the empty chair. He began to regard me with a worried, concerned expression. "Listen, Kim, honey, how long have you been hearing voices? Maybe you need a good therapist—"

"Just because *you* can't see him doesn't mean that he isn't there."

"My God . . . I hope none of the clients ever find out about *this*—we'll be completely *fucked*," he wailed, placing his head in his hands. "How am I ever going to explain your mental problems?"

"I don't have any mental problems except for *you*," I responded, with a newfound assertiveness. "And things are going to change around here, effective immediately. You're going to stop your profane, screaming tirades. I'll be damned if you're going to embarrass me in front of all of my psychic clients."

"What do you mean . . . 'psychic clients'?"

"I'm going to start giving readings for people here until I have the money to get an office of my own."

"Like hell you are!"

"Like hell I'm not! Who do you think you're *talking* to?"

"Somebody with serious delusions! You'll never make it on your own! You wouldn't be here right now if it wasn't for me. You don't have the ability to run your own business. Once you hang up your shingle as Madame Lagonga, you'll be making a royal fool of yourself, and there will be no retracing your steps. No one really takes you seriously *now*, but if you go into *that* business, they'll be laughing at you all over town. And don't think you can come crawling back here, begging me to take you back. Once you walk out that door—you're *gone*."

The oddest thing happened as I listened to David threaten me. It had always been a great fear of mine that he would decide to leave me behind and abandon the agency as he had our personal relationship. But, as he ranted, he actually fueled my determination to leave him. *Why* had I ever married him? And *why* had I ever chosen to enter into the business partnership? Had I been that dependent? Had I been too scared to try and make it on my own? Had I needed someone who could act in a leadership capacity because I was too weak to do so myself? Had I felt that the only security I could have was tied up with another person? I knew I wasn't *lazy*, because I was willing to work around the clock. I suddenly realized that I had been paralyzed by the fear of being completely responsible for myself—and every day through-out all those years I had continued to tolerate David's abuse in order to have security. But the irony was that I had never felt so insecure! It had been a terrible trade-off. I hadn't gotten married—I'd been adopted. I had recreated my mother's patterns.

In those pivotal moments, I was bombarded with a new level of self-awareness and understanding. And I didn't like what I was discovering. I was ashamed and disheartened that I had made so many degrading, unfortunate choices. I wasn't just angry with David—I was angry with *me*. I was the one who allowed him to treat me the way he did. Al-though I had no control over his behavior, I certainly had control over mine and how I chose to react to him. I decided that I wanted to build independence and empowerment; and, at thirty-two, I was finally ready to demonstrate that I had backbone. I *could* and *would* make it on my own. I had never been so determined about anything in my life. David was still raving, but his words no longer affected me. He could no longer use them as weapons to hurt, demean, or frighten me. I looked across the desk at him, and suddenly, I knew that I was emotionally *free*. I felt validated, inspired, and invigorated by a newly budding self-confidence. It was a watershed moment.

" . . . you've *never* been that creative—and all the clients know that *I'm* the one who runs—"

I interrupted his tirade by standing up. I calmly looked at my watch. "David, I really don't have the time to continue this discussion. I will work as hard as ever doing agency business, but I'm also going to be conducting channeling session whenever I can. If that isn't agreeable, I'll pack my things right now."

He stopped talking, his mouth open. He clearly was not expecting that.

"Your choice," I said casually, shrugging my shoulders.

"You can't be serious—"

"Okay," I interrupted, gathering my notebook and pen. "Have a good life."

"No! Wait!" he replied. "Maybe we can work something out."

As with most bullies, once they are confronted, they back down.

"Good," I said. "You'll have to excuse me . . . I have a session to conduct."

David stood up, opened his mouth, but chose not to speak.

"C'mon, John," I said. The angel, still unseen by David, rose from his chair and followed me out of the office. I strode down the hall smiling, knowing that I had just survived a seven-year chapter of my life that had almost consumed me.

Chapter 11

Coming Out of the Spiritual Closet

David never mentioned his introduction to John. I guessed that he had decided to ignore the provocative angelic messages I had shared because he didn't embrace any beliefs that were religious, nor did he embrace anything even remotely spiritual or New Age. He also had the habit of dismissing things that he had no control over, or that weren't his idea in the first place.

Shortly after that meeting, however, David did approach me to ask that I refrain from sharing my departure plans with anyone—especially Advertising & Design, Inc. clients and colleagues—and, of course, I readily agreed. He was right. It would undermine everything I would try to accomplish at the agency before I left. I also knew that he was hoping I would change my mind.

Unfortunately, his bullying and manipulative tactics sharply increased in the days and weeks that followed as he grew increasingly agitated and angry at the prospect of me leaving. He continued to tell me in no uncertain terms that he didn't believe it was possible for me to be successful on my own, and that once I declared myself as a psychic, doors all over town would slam in my face, and everyone would ridicule me. I'd be ruined professionally, and I'd have burned all my bridges in the process. Of course, I didn't expect him to be supportive or encouraging in any way, but his cutting remarks frightened me because they mirrored my own concerns. He continued to make it clear that once I left the agency, he'd consider our business relationship severed and he wouldn't have me back under any circumstances. What he didn't realize was that his words only served to fuel my determination to move on and create a brand new existence.

At the same time, I couldn't help but worry about the agency's financial situation, and I was naturally concerned about departing without any type of compensation. I handled the company finances, so I knew firsthand that David didn't have the resources to buy me out, and I felt in my heart that the business would not, in the future, turn around and become viable or profitable. I would walk away with nothing but my last paycheck and a few pieces of office furniture. Although I was keen to leave Advertising & Design, Inc., common sense dictated that I'd have to be patient a while longer until I was earning enough as a channel to pay all my personal monthly expenses and foot the bill for new office space, as well.

As much as I tried to remain positive and optimistic, it became very clear that starting all over again in a very unique profession was going to be nothing less than a gigantic leap of faith; and I couldn't ignore the fact that the whole enterprise was based solely upon what my guardian angel John, a *spirit*, was communicating with me. All of the dynamics of the transition seemed overwhelming! However, for the first time in ages, I had something to work toward that had inspiring possibilities.

Once I had informed David about my future plans, John told me that the next step was to demonstrate intent to the universe by revealing to as many people as possible that I was a fledgling channel. I decided to take the plunge by approaching members of the women's executive networking group that I had been a member of for several years.

We met every Thursday at 6:30 a.m. for breakfast in a ballroom of the Ritz Carlton Hotel. Because I believed that I had already proven myself as a serious businesswoman within the group, I hoped that the other members would look upon my new venture as extraordinary and avant-garde rather than kooky or bizarre. I had several advertising clients who were also members of the group, so I had to be careful not to mention that I was ultimately planning to leave the agency to avoid breaking the promise I had made to my partner.

I was the last member of the group to speak that day, and I stood up in front of the seventy-five women with my heart pounding wildly. "Good morning! I'm Kim O'Neill, a partner in Advertising & Design, Inc. We offer full service advertising, marketing, and public relations services. In fact, we just received an award from the Art Directors Club of America for a logo and corporate identity we designed for Dr. Eve Blaine." I gestured toward the plastic surgeon who was sitting at one of the big round tables to my left. Everyone looked at her and clapped their approval. She smiled, pleased with the recognition.

"The power of networking!" cried one of the members in the back of the room.

"So," I continued, "if you'd like to update your current logo or corporate identity, please don't hesitate to contact me. And don't forget that Advertising & Design, Inc. also produces radio and television commercials, and we'd love to put our expertise to work for you." When I started to sit down, John began to strongly object.

Stand back up! You have to tell them! demanded John telepathically. His words stopped me, and I remained in a clumsy crouching position halfway to my seat.

I can't! I responded in my thoughts. *Maybe next week!*

Now!

But—

NOW! DO IT NOW!

I literally sprang back to an upright position. The members obviously thought I was finished with my usual spiel, and the room was once again abuzz with conversation, laughter, and the clinking of coffee cups. I had to recapture their attention.

"Uhmm . . . excuse me . . . " The noise quotient was so high that no one took notice that I was speaking again.

"Excuse me!" I shouted, and the room quieted again. Except for a few isolated conversations in the back of the ballroom, I had regained the floor. "Well . . . I . . . " and my voice trailed off. *What* had I planned to tell them? For a moment that seemed like an eternity, my mind had gone completely blank. Then it all flashed back. I giggled nervously.

"Do you know what the term *channeling* means?"

The women shook their heads in unison. I immediately guessed that they assumed it was some kind of advertising lingo.

"Well . . . it means communicating with spirits . . . like guardian angels and departed friends and family members."

Eyes began to widen. There was a pregnant pause as the breakfast came to a standstill—forks and coffee cups remained suspended in mid-air. Even the no-nonsense Ritz waiters stopped what they were doing, stood, and stared at me expectantly.

"Well . . . *I've* been channeling." I tried to appear upbeat and confident, like interacting with spirits was the most natural thing in the world. The bustling ballroom was suddenly so quiet that we all could have heard a pin drop in Poughkeepsie. "And . . . I'm trying to hone my skills. So . . . I'd like to offer you, as members of this group, a complimentary psychic reading."

The other women just stared back at me, brows furrowed and mouths open in apparent astonishment. The smile froze on my face. Instead of sitting down, I made the mistake of brightly adding, "Channeling has really changed my life. In fact, it was my guardian angel John Reid who suggested that I share this with you today."

The ballroom remained as still as a tomb. I just stood there for a few moments, staring back at all the women who were gaping at me. Finally, I had the presence of mind to mumble some awkward thanks, and I hurriedly sat back down. The silence in the room was deafening. It seemed to last forever. I wished that I could take my words back. I felt seventy-five pairs of eyes focused in my direction, and my face had gone crimson with embarrassment. Hives began to bloom in big, red welts across my forehead, cheeks, and chin.

To make matters worse, I began to psychically pick up on some of their thoughts: *Kim has lost her marbles! She is in advertising and you never know about those people, but this is too much. Now she thinks she can talk with angels? And dead people? She needs a good therapist and a serious prescription, fast!*

I wanted to bolt from the room, but I just sat rooted to my chair for the rest of the networking meeting. My stomach was so upset and I was shaking so badly with nerves that I couldn't drink my coffee or eat the small fruit plate that cost a whopping eighteen bucks a week. The power of networking, indeed! I decided to duck out early to avoid the more aggressive members who wouldn't hesitate to voice an outspoken opinion about my new passion. Just as my ex-husband had warned, I feared they would ridicule me.

By some miracle, as I drove back to the office, a small sense of pride began to wash over me. I had mustered the courage to declare myself in front of a big group of people. I had shown intent. As embarrassing as it was, it was also rather freeing. I was taking the initiative and moving forward with my life without any help or assistance from David. I was consumed by a wonderful heady rush that I hadn't felt in a long time, and I relished it.

As time went on, I didn't receive a single call from anyone in my networking group asking for a complementary channeling session, nor did anyone call to inquire as to how my life had taken this sudden new path. In spite of their negative reaction and continuing disinterest, John urged me to carry on with courage and conviction. So, every Thursday morning, in the ballroom of the Ritz Carlton Hotel, I stood up and reminded the members of the group that I could provide them with a complimentary psychic reading. With repetition, my announcement barely caused a stir. In fact, the women ignored it entirely.

I came to believe that they regarded the channeling as some kind of mysterious, esoteric hobby inspired by the stress of my recent divorce. In spite of the lack of interest, the weekly meetings provided continual opportunities to demonstrate intent; and, completely unbeknown to me at the time, they were helping to build the momentum that was fueling my forward movement.

Chapter 12

Psychic Nightmares Return

As the new chapter of my life unfolded, the chilly winter months came to a close. In Houston, the month of March heralds the true initiation of spring. The temperatures soften; the sky becomes a clear, radiant blue; lawns regain their bright, vivid green; trees bud; and a soft breeze carries with it the promise of longer days and the renewal of a milder season.

Delicate azaleas, the pride of so many gardeners along the Gulf of Mexico, start to bloom in a profusion of luxuriant soft pink, fuchsia, white, and peach. Roses of every variety grow full and lush in flowerbeds, gracefully winding their way across trellises and arbors. Daffodils, tulips, daisies, marigolds, begonias, and dogwoods come to life in a riot of splendid color that blankets the city in preparation for summer; when the southern crepe myrtles and mimosas blossom, the majestic Magnolias reveal their large pale flowers, and the wild blue-bells carpet the countryside.

Since I had moved to Texas, I had come to *dread* this time of year. I hated all of the pollen that hung in the air like a yellow fog, clinging to everything outside. Sometimes it was so thick that it fell from the sky looking like yellow snow.

It was a Friday evening in mid-March, and like many other hapless Houstonians, I was sick with allergies. I had gone to bed early in the hopes of catching up on my rest so that I could begin to feel better. As I fell asleep that night, I didn't realize that, like the advent of spring, I, too, was about to experience a revival of sorts. Not since early childhood had I suffered from violent, gruesome nightmares that foretold events that were to unfold in real life.

I was in a deep sleep when the dream first started as a swirling mix of color, smell, and sound that quickly crystallized into a clear, vivid picture—just like when I was a child. In the dream, I was standing in front of a busy strip center. A blonde teenage girl hurried out of one of the stores carrying a big box of doughnuts. As she approached her car, a man grabbed her from behind and thrust her into the open door of a van that was parked next to her. He pulled the door closed, ran around to the other side, jumped in and drove away. The girl didn't have time to mutter a sound.

The dream continued as I was transported to a densely wooded area that looked like a forest preserve. The van had been driven off the main road and was hidden from view by some high brush.

The girl, now naked, was tied to a tree. She appeared to be alone. She was fighting wildly to free her wrists from the thin plastic cord that bound her arms behind her, but it held firm. Her torn pink shirt, ripped blue jeans, sandals, panties, and bra lay scattered on the ground. The terrified girl was startled by the shrill *caw! caw!* of a bird flying overhead.

The door of the nearby van swung open again and the man climbed out. He approached the helpless teenager and began to unzip his jeans. Immobilized with fear, the girl stopped yanking at the ropes. Her breathing became fast and shallow. Tears rolled down her flushed cheeks. She begged him to let her go. She promised she wouldn't tell anybody what had happened. He took obvious pleasure in her tearful pleading.

"You and me are gonna have a real good time," he told her in a guttural voice. The girl started to scream and thrash her legs. Enjoying the desperation of his victim and his control over her, the man grinned as he carefully unrolled a condom onto his erect penis.

"NO!" she screamed. *"No! Please don't . . . don't . . .* NO—"

I awoke with a start. I was shaking . . . horrified by what I had seen. I switched on the bedside lamp. My clock read 4:20 a.m. Winston lay next to me, irritated that his sleep had been disturbed. He yawned and, with great resignation, sat up with his eyes half-closed. I padded to the bathroom, then got a drink of water from the kitchen and climbed back into bed in an exhausted stupor. I turned off the lamp, Winston snuggled close to me, and I quickly fell into another deep sleep. In a few moments, the same dream continued.

I was still in the forest preserve. The brutalized teenager remained bound to the tree, obviously in shock from the trauma she had endured. She was shivering uncontrollably. There were bruises around her mouth, her throat, and her inner thighs . . . and I could see bite marks on her small breasts. There was a small amount of blood smeared on her abdomen. The girl was moving her head from side to side, muttering incoherently. Bloody condoms and their hastily torn off wrappers littered the ground.

A loud noise jarred the girl back to reality. It sounded like her attacker was impatiently rummaging through a tool box in the van. Then there was the sound of muted footsteps. In a matter of seconds, the naked man was standing in front of her. He held a hunting knife with a jagged edge.

At the sight of him, the young girl began to sob. Her body trembled violently. In a tearful whimper, she begged to go home to her mother. Smiling, he moved even closer. The teenager cowered away from him. "How will you like to be gutted like a little doe?" he asked her. "I went through your wallet, Claire. You only had two bucks."

The young girl regarded him with wide-eyed fear.

"You'd better make your peace with God," he told her, waving the knife menacingly. "Do you want to say a last prayer?"

"What . . . what . . . do you mean?" she asked in a whisper. "I don't understand why you're hurting me . . . "

"This is my hobby," he told her. "Some guys hunt deer . . . or bear. But why hunt something you can't fuck—before you kill it?"

"Please let me call my mother," the girl begged, her voice hardly audible.

"Is she as pretty as you?" the assailant asked. "Maybe I'll go pay *her* a visit. I have the address from your license."

"NO! Leave her alone!" cried the girl.

"Shut up!" he growled, thrusting the knife directly in front of the young girl's battered face. Her breathing became terrified gasps. The pretty teen never had time to say her prayers. Mercifully, she fainted moments before her captor began to disembowel her.

I startled myself awake by screaming at the top of my lungs. I sat bolt upright in bed, gasping for air, my heart racing. I looked around my room to make certain I was safe. The terrible images had only been a *dream!* I smoothed the curly, tangled hair away from my face. It was wet with tears. The bedroom was still dark. I looked at the clock and was surprised to discover that it was only five-thirty, but I knew I'd never get back to sleep. I didn't *want* to go back to sleep, afraid that I might find myself transported back to the horrific images in the forest preserve. I sensed with all of my being that the dream was true—that it wasn't some weird, horrible figment of my imagination. I *knew* that I had dreamed about a real event; I just couldn't pinpoint the specific time frame or discern the exact place where it had occurred. The childhood nightmares that provided graphic, firsthand knowledge of kidnappings, rapes, murders, and arson had started again. That meant I would never know what to expect after I surrendered to sleep; what terrible horrors I would witness. It was like watching a movie about true life events, except for the fact that I became *part of the movie* as a silent, unseen spectator.

The dreams were always identical in the way they unfolded. At first, as the images began to crystallize, I'd be transported to the locale where a crime was going to take place. The victim and the perpetrator then arrived on the scene, and the crime immediately transpired with me as a witness. I would remain on the scene until the crime was completed and the perpetrator left the premises. It was only then that the nightmare would release me, and I would wake up emotionally traumatized and physically exhausted.

Unfortunately, these frightening events—like the Speck murders so many years before—continued to haunt me long after the intuitive nightmare ended. Each new dream indelibly imprinted my heart and soul with the memory of the fear and suffering the victims had endured.

The specifics remain to this day—the recall of what I had seen in those dreams is so intact that they can be easily triggered by a song, a type of weather, a particular kind of smell, or a location. And suddenly, in my mind's eye, I'm traveling back in time, reviewing a crime as it first took place just as I "saw" it in my dreams. Apparently, the nightmares had returned—with a vengeance. I wondered if more psychic images would follow. How would I cope? What would I do?

My thoughts returned to the forest preserve I had visited the night before and the horrific crime I had seen there. I wondered if kidnapping, rape, and murder had always been the teenager's tragic, unspeakable fate? Who was her assailant? How does someone *become* a rapist and a murderer? Claire couldn't have been over eighteen, and I shuddered to think of the agony she endured while being savagely raped. Why did the man choose *her* as a victim? I felt an overwhelming rush of compassion for the girl. Claire had taken her last breath at the hands of a maniacal killer who cruelly snuffed out her life as if it had no meaning. She would never go to the prom. She would never go to college. She would never accomplish her life's work. She would never get married or have children. The brutal killer had stolen all of that from her and her family.

I said a small prayer for the young girl, wishing her well in heaven. I assumed that Claire's family was frantically searching for her. They had probably contacted the police and were, perhaps, dispersing flyers in their community with her name and picture. Would they ever find her dead body—or would she always remain a missing person? Would her grieving family ever know what really happened to her?

I couldn't erase the image of her small, naked body tied to the tree. I angrily assumed that the man in the dream always chose victims who were weaker, helpless, and vulnerable. I wondered if the high school girl had been chosen at random, or if he had known her in some way before the kidnapping? Why did he pick *her*? Did she remind him of someone—like an abusive mother, or an ex-wife or girlfriend who rejected him? Did he target her because he hoped she would be a virgin? Or did she represent the caliber of woman he thought he could never have because she was so beautiful?

Although I had firsthand knowledge of what was occurring as the crime had unfolded, all I could do was stand there helplessly as an unseen spectator and witness what was taking place between the participants. In the worst way, I wanted to go back in time and smash the killer over the head or hold him at gunpoint—anything to *stop* him from hurting the girl. Better yet—prevent him from abducting her in the first place!

I fantasized about having superhero strength and being able to stop him from terrorizing the girl by forcefully knocking him to the ground while the teenager ran away to safety; and I could have held him there while we waited for the police to arrive and drag him away in handcuffs. Then he would be sentenced to life in prison where he could never hurt anyone again.

But in reality, as the nightmare unfolded, all I could do was helplessly *stand there*—just as when I was a child! I wanted to go back inside the dream and *save* the girl. I wanted to *do something* to change what had happened. *Why did I have that dream?* I would forever be haunted by the terrible images.

Chapter 13

Befriending a Teenage Murder Victim

In my nightshirt and white crew socks, I got up and stumbled to the kitchen to make some coffee and feed Winston. I was really scared. I needed to talk with John. I couldn't believe that the dreams had started again. And *why* had they started? I grabbed a fresh cup of decaf before the pot finished brewing, and saw that John was watching TV in the living room, relaxing on one of the chairs opposite the couch. He was entertaining himself by watching the *Three Stooges*.

"Good morning," he called to me. "Were you aware that Moe Howard and Larry Fine are now working as very respected guardian angels? However, they often receive a rather comical reaction from the human beings they work with when they disclose their identity. Seems *everyone* on the earthly plane has seen the *Stooges*."

"Never mind that!" I answered rudely. "I'm so glad you're here. You won't believe what happened!"

"You had one of your nightmares," he answered, turning off the TV by simply looking at it for a moment. "I've been waiting for you."

I quickly took a seat on the couch and gathered my legs up under me. "John—it was terrible! A high school girl was kidnapped in the parking lot of a strip center by this guy—a lunatic! And he brought her to what I think was a forest preserve, and—"

"Yes, that would be Claire," he noted somberly.

"Do you *know* her? Is the dream *real?*"

"Yes, on both counts."

"Oh, my God! That poor girl . . . " My tears were flowing again, and I ran to get some tissues. Clutching a handful of Kleenex, I dashed back to the living room and resumed my seat on the couch.

"Okay," I said, still sniffling, tissue to my nose. I was now all business. "What can I do? Who can I call? Should I contact the police? Claire's family? I know! Let's go after the killer. We can make him confess. I wonder how *he'd* like to be tortured—his balls *pinched*—and *twisted*—and then *ripped off?* John . . . you could do that part."

"What am I now—your *accomplice?*" he asked. "Guardian-angel-turned-partner in crime? I don't think torture or dismembering testicles is in my current job description. I've already signed up for one hazardous tour of duty—"

"We have to do *something!* I'm not a scared, helpless little girl anymore. Now I can help. I'll track him down and make him wish that he had never even *seen* Claire. He'll be sorry he ever approached that sweet girl. What if he grabs somebody *else?* We have to stop him!"

"The testosterone is really flowing this morning. I've never seen you like this."

"John, you're my best friend! You should know how I'm feeling. All of those years of cowering in my little bed, scared shitless of what I was seeing in my dreams . . . and then being haunted every day at school with all of those awful sights . . . and sounds . . . and smells."

"Yes . . . these days they refer to that as post-traumatic stress disorder. I was one of the guardian angels for a poor chap who returned to London in 1919 after serving in the Great War . . . and every time a car backfired, he hit the ground, whimpering."

"Come *on!*" I urged him, jumping to my feet. "Let's *do* something! We'd better *hurry.*"

"What would you have us do?" asked the angel.

"Let's call the police."

"Which department? Do you know where the crime took place?"

"No . . . I didn't get a clear picture of that. Okay, then . . . what about the girl's parents?"

"Who would you call if you don't know where the crime took place?"

"And I don't know *when* it took place, either," I admitted. "Do *you*?"

"Yes, as a matter of fact, I have all the particulars."

"So why are we just *standing here*? I'll go get dressed—"

"Wait! What is your plan of action?"

"First . . . we'll contact the police wherever the crime took place. We can help them nab that frigging lowlife—before he hurts anyone else."

"After they apprehend the 'frigging lowlife' . . . then what?"

"We could point them to where he buried Claire. So the police have evidence that a murder really took place. Then her body can be returned to her parents, and—"

"How do you know the remains were buried?"

"Well . . . I just figured that the killer would want to dispose of the evidence."

John remained silent.

"So?" I questioned. "What did he do with her?"

"Do you really want to know?"

"Yes! Tell me."

"After he pulled out her entrails, he cut up the rest of her body, and then—"

"STOP! Enough! I don't want to hear any more." I reached for another tissue. "It's unbelievable that there are people walking around like that."

"It's just as frightening to think of how he became the person that he is right now."

"No matter what happened to him, it couldn't be worse than what he did to Claire."

"That is debatable. His mother was a prostitute. From the time he was just a little chap—about the time when your dreams first started—he was a witness to the parade of men who visited their flat. He saw everything. The mother hated her life and felt victimized by the men she took money from. So she victimized her small son with a torrent of verbal, physical, and sexual abuse throughout his childhood. He was too weak and vulnerable to fight back. He used to cower in *his* little bed at night, too."

"What happened? Evidently, he didn't get therapy. Did he escape once he was old enough?"

"When he was twelve, he retaliated by killing her. He was sent to an institution for boys where he remained for six years. He was released at eighteen . . . and has been killing ever since. To date, there have been five murders."

"Why haven't they been able to catch him? What about his fingerprints or other DNA evidence?"

"His prints are not in the system. And because he kills strangers at random, there is no evidence to tie him to any of the crimes. Plus, he moves around, never staying in the same place from murder to murder. He won't be apprehended."

"*What?* How could that *be?*"

"A girl goes missing without a trace—and no body is ever found. So the authorities cannot determine foul play. With no body, they cannot establish the cause of death. The method by which he kills his victims would indicate a specific pattern, and that could help the authorities identify him as the perpetrator. But then there's another problem. At this time, police departments in America do not always share information amongst themselves about crimes that take place in their far-flung jurisdictions. Therefore, because this man moves around so much, even if the authorities found the remains of one of his victims, it wouldn't lead anywhere. It would appear to be a single killing by a man who was nothing more than a phantom. It is his destiny to remain free until he passes from the earthly plane."

"But then he never has to pay for his crimes? He just gets away with them? That's not fair to his victims and their families."

"Kim, there is nothing remotely 'fair' about life on the earthly plane. That is why it is considered the best spiritual boot camp in the universe."

"So . . . he doesn't have to face any consequences?"

"I didn't say that," quickly answered John. "Every living being has to atone for his transgressions against others . . . whether these transgressions are in thought . . . or in deed."

"Then he will be held accountable for what he has done? Once he gets to heaven?"

"As are all living beings."

"I just don't understand," I whined. "How can such a mentally disturbed person keep getting away with murder?"

"Make no mistake—he's very clever. He knows exactly what he's doing. What's more, he is perfectly aware that he will never be caught."

"But don't all criminals think that?"

"Yes, many do believe that they can continue a crime spree without apprehension. However, in this young man's case, he is correct. He is just as psychic as you are. However, he uses his ability to cause great harm to others."

I was quiet for a moment, pondering everything we had discussed.

"Murder happens all the time on the earthly plane," John observed. "It always has—and getting away with it is commonplace."

"It *is*?"

"Certainly," he answered. "There are people in every walk of life who have committed more heinous crimes than you can imagine. And they will never be caught for one reason or another. It depends on the destiny they have chosen for themselves."

"But if *everyone* has guardian angels, can't you *do* something to stop it?" I asked, incredulous. "Where were Claire's angels when all of this was going on?"

"If we guardian angels stepped in and prevented all of the injustice, malice, cruelty, and suffering we witness on earth, there would be no learning experiences. We would be eliminating the opportunity for an individual to evolve into greater wisdom, enlightenment and maturity—"

"But can't people learn an easier, simpler way?"

"Unfortunately, human beings often choose to grow only when facing great danger or adversity. That is the reason great numbers of individuals encounter so many trials and tribulations during their earthly lifetimes—to allow them to expand spiritually and emotionally."

"It's all so unbelievable!"

"Kim, I find something curious. When you were a child, you asked a good many questions about your clairvoyant dreams."

"Yes?"

"But you've never asked the most important question."

"What's that?"

"The *purpose* of the dreams. Why you have been, and will continue to be, privy to such information."

My eyes widened, and I was flooded with the goose bumps sensation. I shivered in my warm apartment. So there was a *reason* why I had been a witness to so many crimes over the years? I had never considered that the dreams were coming to me for a specific reason. I just always assumed that it was my weird cross to bear. Suddenly, I didn't know if I wanted to hear the answer.

"I have a surprise," John told me. Then he called out to someone I couldn't see. "I think that's your cue!"

In a moment, I could see a ball of silver light. It started to spin and grow and take shape. Seconds later, the teenager I had watched being raped and murdered the night before was standing in front of me. She was dressed in the same pink shirt, jeans, and sandals that I had seen crumpled on the ground in the forest preserve where she had been killed. I gasped, disbelieving.

"Hi," she said shyly, with a little self-conscious wave. "I'm Claire."

"I know," I said, my eyes popping with amazement. I couldn't believe that I could see her as clearly as I saw John. But I wasn't scared.

"Are you *okay?*" I stupidly inquired, never having been in this situation before. I honestly didn't know what to say to someone I had just seen hideously murdered, and who was standing before me in *spirit.* John wasn't kidding—this *was a surprise!*

"Claire, may I introduce Kim?" said John with a flourish.

We both nodded to one another and smiled. It appeared as if she felt as awkward as I did. We both looked expectantly at John.

"Kim, you and Claire share a spiritual contract."

"A what?" I asked, while still staring at the dead girl standing in my living room. *Should I ask her to sit down?*

"No, thanks—I'm fine," she said shyly, reading my thoughts.

"A spiritual contract is a promise, or a commitment, made between two parties in regard to what they're going to do for one another when one—or both—are in an earthly lifetime."

"Oh . . . " is all I could respond.

"You and Claire have been sisters in a number of past lifetimes."

"Really?" I said. "I've always wanted a sister."

"Me, too," quietly offered Claire.

"Well . . . now you have each other. Kim, you'll be able to see and hear Claire as clearly as you perceive me. Claire—you will be able to communicate with Kim much like you could if you were still on the earthly plane. Unfortunately, you're going to discover that most other human beings will *not* be able to see you or hear you. Even your family members may not be aware of your presence—no matter how hard you try to communicate with them."

"I know! I've already tried to talk to my Mom—but she can't hear me. I need to tell her that I'm alright."

"But you're *not* alright . . . you're . . . " my voice clumsily trailed off because I didn't know how to continue. John had taught me that "dead" was not a polite word to use. I seriously doubted that Claire's mother would consider her "okay" at this point.

"Yes, she would!" replied the girl, again reading my thoughts. "She already senses that I'm . . . gone. She just needs to know what happened to me. No one is ever going to find my body."

"This is so terrible! I *saw* what you went through!"

"Don't cry," she said gently, comforting me. "It's too late to change what happened. I just want my Mom to know where I am."

"And that's where you come in," John explained, gesturing to me.

"What can I do?" I asked, confused.

"A short time ago you were all fired up to do something about what you saw in your dream. Rather than search out the killer and rip off his privates, I submit that you put your ability to better use and consider channeling messages from Claire to her mother, to allow the poor woman to communicate with her daughter one last time."

"Are you *crazy?*" I said. "I can't do that!"

"Why not?"

"Well . . . what if I can't *do it?* What if I get it *wrong?* Wouldn't it be horribly upsetting for her to hear about what happened to her beautiful daughter?"

"It's more upsetting for her *not* to know," insisted Claire.

"I'm nervous about channeling the simplest of information, and you want me to call Claire's mother and—"

"Claire's mother is going to call *you*," said John emphatically.

"Why would she call *me*?"

"Because she is going to hear you on the radio," he told me. "She will get the goose bumps sensation when she hears your voice, and she'll be compelled to call you for a reading. Then, you can honor the spiritual contract you have with Claire."

I was getting a serious headache.

"What is my part of the spiritual contract with Kim?" inquired the young girl.

"To provide the catalyst for her to move forward with her channeling practice. Without you, even *I* could never have convinced her to channel on the radio. However, knowing it is the only way she will be able to reach your mother, she will feel compelled to do it."

"Why can't I just tell Kim how to reach my Mom?"

"How would you guess your mother might react to a phone call from a strange woman offering to provide psychic information about her missing daughter—*from* the daughter who is now deceased?"

"Okay . . . I get your point," responded Claire with a giggle. "My Mom is sort of . . . closed . . . just like you, Kim. She doesn't believe in *any* of this stuff. That's why I can't communicate with her myself right now."

"Both of you—hold on!" I insisted. "Stop making plans for me. I can't go on the radio!"

"Why *not*?" asked John peevishly. "In your advertising work, you frequently accompany clients to radio stations when they have appearances."

"But that's *different*. What would I talk about on the radio? I'm not an expert, or authority, on anything."

"You can tell the radio people that you're a psychic. You could channel for their listeners on the air," urged Claire. "Then my Mom could hear you and come to believe that psychic ability does exist! If you don't goof up."

I looked at John. He was trying to hide a smile.

"—then her angels will get her to call you, and I could finally speak with her. Please—Kim—*you're my only hope!*"

"Isn't there someone better," I asked them, "who knows what they're *doing*? I've just started channeling, and I don't know the first thing about—"

"This is the next step for you," John insisted. "Why do you always have to resist and make everything such a struggle?"

"What about the promise I made to David? I'm supposed to keep my departure from Advertising & Design, Inc. a secret."

"And so you will. You're simply going on the radio—you're not leaving town."

I sighed deeply. I had the distinct impression that I wasn't going to be able to wiggle out of this. "If I go on the radio, will you come along and give me the information for the people who call in?"

"I will go with you, of course; but the messages you receive for others will come directly from their individual guardian angels."

"How will I be able to talk with *them?*"

"Just like you're talking with *us,*" insisted Claire.

"You'll be able to hear them telepathically, inside your head," explained John, "and you'll also be able to hear their voices. Some of the angels will choose to materialize, like myself and Claire. There's no difference between communicating with us—and any other spirit."

"And, Kim," pleaded the girl, "you need to *hurry!* My Mom is crying all the time, and she's frantic about where I am. She keeps hoping that her intuition is wrong . . . that maybe I'm actually going to come home. But . . . I'm *never going home again.*" The young girl started to cry mournfully. "Mom keeps going into my room and looking at all my stuff . . . I just want her to know what happened."

I started to cry, too. It was all so sad—so tragically sad. I couldn't refuse her. With extreme misgivings, I agreed. I would honor my spiritual contract. I promised to meet with John and Claire the next day after I had the time to figure out how I was going to proceed with the new plans.

Chapter 14

Last Week I Couldn't Spell It and Now I Are One

I had to do some errands, so while I was out, I decided to pick something up for my allergies and stock up on groceries. It was already late Saturday afternoon by the time I got to the store, and when I reached the checkout line, I found myself standing behind an older lady who was extremely ill. She was very congested, looked feverish, had red, weepy eyes and a deep, rasping cough.

Suddenly, an angel introduced himself to me telepathically, and he began to quickly describe the poor lady's condition. He told me that he was one of her guardian angels, and he was asking me to give her a message. I hesitated. After all, she was a complete stranger, and this was a very public environment.

But you can help her, said the angel emphatically. *And you MUST because you CAN.*

Was this the process that John and Claire were just talking about, I wondered? With a nervous sigh, I lightly tapped the woman on the shoulder. She turned to look at me, and I whispered an introduction, hoping the other shoppers wouldn't hear our conversation. I asked if I could give her a message from one of her angels.

"What?" she replied with obvious confusion.

The checkout gal was working quickly, so while the sick woman's groceries were being rung up, I decided to proceed. I told her that I wasn't a physician but that I was "hearing" psychic messages that might possibly help her doctor treat her symptoms. I started to hurriedly pass along the health information her angel was sharing with me. I explained that she didn't have an allergy-type virus as her doctor originally suspected but, instead, a bacterial infection that she had picked up from her granddaughter who had just been visiting from out of town. She needed to get a prescription for an antibiotic, because Echinacea, her favorite homeopathic remedy, was not doing the trick. The angel told me to tell her that her mucous had turned a putrid green and she needed this antibiotic as soon as possible. She was advised to return to her doctor and that he would prescribe it right away. If she waited any longer, her angel cautioned, her illness could turn into something more serious—like pneumonia.

I repeated exactly what the angel told me in soft, soothing tones, hoping not to further alarm her about her health. As I spoke, her eyes widened like bloodshot saucers, and she kept stepping farther away from me as if *I* had some sort of disease that might contaminate *her*.

When I mentioned that her granddaughter had visited, she punctuated my channeling with a loud, "But how do you KNOW THAT?" Unfortunately, this attracted the attention of other shoppers around us, but I continued. After I finished, I gently placed my hand on her arm and told her that I hoped the information might help and that she would feel better soon.

"Don't touch me!" she cried, cringing, pushing my hand away.

With the other shoppers now curiously intent on what was causing the ruckus in the aisle three checkout lane, the sick woman grabbed her groceries and rushed away, looking back over her shoulder to make certain that I wasn't following her.

I felt awful! I certainly never meant to scare her. I just wanted to help her feel better. I blushed under the disapproving stare of the cashier as she rang up my groceries. I couldn't wait to get out of there.

When I got to my car, I summoned John and asked what had gone wrong. I was naturally concerned that I had needlessly scared the poor woman; but, all the same, I hoped that she listened to what I had told her.

He reminded me that I had passed along information at the request of her guardian angel with nothing but the most loving intent and the woman's reaction to the generous gift of psychic information had been regrettable. Although I wouldn't be privy to what happened next—as I had with Sam, the doorman—John reassured me that the unexpected experience would compel the sick woman to make another doctor's appointment.

John reminded me that life on the earthly plane is like climbing rungs on a ladder. I had climbed several rungs by making weekly overtures to my networking group; I had climbed still others by talking with Sam about his sister; sharing my plans with David; and I had just scaled several more rungs on my spiritual ladder by approaching a stranger in the grocery store to share vital channeled information about safeguarding her health.

John happily proclaimed that he could now help me transition to the next stage of our work together. I would no longer be faced with the difficult prospect of appealing to unsuspecting strangers. The radio appearance would motivate people like Claire's mother to come to *me* for spiritual messages. He suggested that once I got home with my groceries, I put on my thinking cap and consider how we were going to facilitate this next course of action.

After thinking long and hard, I was at my wits' end. It was so much more challenging to promote oneself than it was to market someone else. How would I entice a radio station to have *me* as a guest? At that time, very few folks in Houston even knew what the term *channeling* meant. Before the angel recently popped back into my life, I thought that a channel was something on a TV set.

John was surprised that, in spite of my experience in advertising and marketing, I was drawing a blank when it came to promoting my channeling practice. He pointed out that everything we do is preparing us for the next chapter of our lives, like so many small stepping stones that are leading toward a particular destination.

In a flash of awareness, I suddenly realized why I needed the advertising and public relations background and why it had been necessary to learn about the industry, as stressful as that experience had been. I would somehow utilize the modest expertise I had developed to promote myself as a channel. Ironically, I had never once considered how I could use my existing marketing know-how to establish this new enterprise. And frankly, I recognized that it was going to be a real uphill battle.

Although there was a small, burgeoning metaphysical community in Houston at that time, the vast majority of Houstonians were not aware of the spiritual renaissance that was sweeping other parts of the country.

In spite of the fact that I really didn't give it much thought—prior to reuniting with John—I assumed that angels were fat little cherubs who spent all of their time reposing on clouds in heaven. I thought that people who claimed to have visitations with deceased loved ones were misguided souls who were mentally disturbed—or just couldn't let go of the past. Little did I know!

As a child, I had dutifully attended catechism. I thought of the no-nonsense nuns who taught there. With a mischievous smile, I guessed what their reaction might have been if I had announced, back then, that I had been communicating with angels and deceased human beings, and having psychic dreams, as well. In the Catholic faith, unless you were a priest, it was considered very bad form indeed, if not downright blasphemous, to announce that one was communicating with spirits—even if they *were* guardian angels or loved ones who had passed on.

In addition, I wondered if people belonging to fundamentalist religions might be quick to assume that the messages were somehow the influence of a darker force? I realized that I had no way to dispel those notions except to continue channeling and helping people understand how the process worked. I reasoned that if folks learned to communicate with their own guardian angels and deceased loved ones as I had, then they would come to trust and benefit from the process.

John confirmed that an important part of my life's work was to teach others how to channel for themselves; therefore, folks would call upon me only if their own ability had become blocked due to stress or fatigue, or when they wanted to seek confirmation from another source.

I *loved* the idea of teaching others how to channel for themselves, as

John had taught me. I went at it full–steam ahead. From a marketing point of view, I began to consider what strategies I would adopt if I had a client who was starting a channeling practice.

I wrote a press release and sent it to a big, local radio station. When I called the producer to follow through, I was thoroughly surprised when he invited me to be a guest on the popular morning show. That appearance would allow me to honor the vitally important contract with my new friend, Claire. At the same time, I'd be climbing additional rungs on my spiritual ladder. It was now or never.

I was so nervous the night before my first big radio gig that I couldn't sleep a wink. I arrived at KRBE Radio at 6:30 a.m., utterly consumed with nerves. I knew that the station was taking a chance with me, and I didn't want to let them down. I couldn't let Claire down, either. I had to do a good job so that her mother would be inspired to call me. I was worried because I had never channeled for someone I couldn't see and I had no experience whatsoever with radio. I wished I had approached a smaller station so it would be less humiliating if I bombed.

The producer met me in the reception area and gave me a warm welcome. I was absolutely terrified, praying that he wouldn't notice how badly I was shaking. Too frightened to speak, I simply nodded in his direction. He gestured down a hallway toward what he called the "control room," and I meekly followed him through the hushed labyrinth of offices.

In my complete ignorance, I thought that there would be a small army of staffers required to put on the fast–paced, funny show, and I was surprised at how quiet the big radio station was at that time of the morning. There were only a handful of people there. The producer hospitably pointed out the location of the bathroom and the kitchen, and suggested I make myself at home. It was obvious that he somehow assumed that I was a radio veteran.

I'd be discovered as an imposter in no time at all! What was I *doing* there? *Maybe I should have told him that I'd never done radio? Maybe he'd take pity on me and give me extra help? What if I can't do it once I'm on the air and there are hundreds of thousands of people listening? If I live through this, I'm going to kill John! I must have done something unspeakable in a past lifetime to have to make up for it like this . . . oh my God, I need to throw up!*

The producer suddenly stopped at the end of the long hallway, indicating that we had reached the control room. Big windows allowed us to peer inside, and I was surprised to see such a compact, cluttered alcove. I learned that all the disc jockeys who worked at the station produced their shows in this one small insulated room.

From my vantage point just outside the control room, I could see the two on-air personalities sitting across a long desk from one another, laughing and bantering back and forth. I was surprised to see them casually dressed in T-shirts and shorts. And why *not*, I thought—the listeners can't see them. I felt ridiculously overdressed in my conservative navy business suit. I could hear what they were saying because the show was being piped throughout all the outer offices on a PA system. The disc jockeys announced a song, and the moment it began to play, the producer lightly tapped on the window. The disc jockeys waved us in, and the producer hurriedly swung open the heavy wooden door.

As we entered the inner sanctum, the producer excitedly announced, "Here she is!" Both disc jockeys came up to me, shook my hand, and warmly welcomed me to the station. I nodded and tried to muster a smile.

The control room was freezing cold and it had unbelievable energy—it was as if the whole space was supercharged with electricity. There was a long, wide desk that ran almost the entire length of the room. On one side of the desk was a huge panel of knobs and controls, and it reminded me of the gadgetry in the cockpit of an airplane. A new fear now gripped me. Since they all appeared to trust that I was a radio veteran, would I be expected to know how to work that thing?

"Hey, Kim," said one of the jocks. "We've been promoting you heavily all morning as our Psychic in Residence, and listeners have already begun to call in. Great, huh?"

I felt sick to my stomach.

"If this works," said the producer, "we're going to offer you a two-hour weekly guest appearance."

I didn't think it was possible, but I began to feel even sicker.

"Okay—twenty seconds," the jock announced, assuming his place behind the cockpit-like panel.

Oh, no! What am I doing here? I was told to sit in a chair across from the cockpit. I quickly complied.

"Kim, we want to keep this segment fast-paced, so you've got forty seconds per person. Give 'em all the information you can. We want to really light up the phone lines."

Forty seconds? To channel for someone? I don't know if I can clear my throat in forty seconds!

"Are you turned on?" he inquired.

I had no clue what he meant. Was he referring to . . . *my channeling ability?* For the first time since I arrived, I heard John's voice telepathically telling me to pick up the headset that was lying on the counter in front of me.

What's a headset, John?

It's the contraption that looks like earmuffs.

That big, heavy thing? Do I have to wear that?

PUT IT ON. NOW!

I grabbed it and awkwardly put it on. It covered my ears, and I could hear the same song that was playing out in the hallway.

"Turned on?" the jock asked again, now all business. We were only seconds to air time.

I finally understood what he was asking. I nodded. He smiled and gave me a thumbs-up gesture. The other disc jockey quickly took her seat and grabbed her headset.

My heart's going to explode! I need to go to the bathroom! I can't do this—

The song that was playing ended abruptly, and the jock feverishly twisted and turned the knobs on the cockpit panel in front of him. At the same time, he shouted into his microphone, "AND WE'RE BACK! As you know, we have a special guest with us in the studio today. It's the WORLD-FAMOUS PSYCHIC KIM O'NEILL. She's here for the MORNING SHOW. Say hello, Kim."

I was so terror stricken I was mute. My brain was going a mile a minute. *Why were they calling me "world famous?" That's not true! I hope no one thinks I'm promoting myself like that—*

"Say hello to our listeners, Kim!"

SPEAK NOW! shouted John telepathically. *Speak into the microphone in front of you and say "hello."*

"Hello," I squeaked obediently.

The producer and the two on-air personalities started to frown. This was not what they expected.

SPEAK! John commanded.

"It's . . . it's . . . great to be here," I lied, my voice cracking.

"Okay! Now we have Janice on the line." The producer and the two jocks stared at me expectantly.

Having no clue what to do, I quickly leaned toward the large, gray, spongy microphone and clumsily bumped it with my nose. A loud *thud* could be heard reverberating throughout the studio. Out of the corner of my eye, I saw the female disc jockey put her head in her hands. I had never spoken through a microphone before, and it felt awkward and artificial.

"JANICE . . . are you THERE?" I asked, as if trying to reach out to someone on the dark side of the moon.

The caller answered immediately. I could hear her voice through the headset. "YES! Kim, I'm so happy I got through. Can you please tell me about my marriage?"

"Your marriage," I repeated. *And from this ridiculously brief question, I'm supposed to provide you with all the information you're looking for?* But miracle of miracles, no more than a second later, I was telepathically bombarded with information from one of her guardian angels. I heard it loud and clear, and I passed it along to her without hesitation.

"Janice, your husband has not been committed to the relationship for a long time. And he has not been faithful. But let's talk about YOU. You're not getting what you need from the marriage, and you're lonely, depressed, and unfulfilled. Is that correct?"

"YES!"

"And you aren't in love with him anymore. Isn't that true, Janice?"

"YES! How did you KNOW that?"

"But you ARE crazy about your kids, and you're a wonderful, doting mom. You're going to muster the courage to get into therapy this year and really work on YOU! Then, it's very likely you're going to file for divorce. You're going to get a great job, and then you and the children are going to be just fine. And—"

Abruptly, one of the jocks cut me off. "WHEW! That's a lot of information! So, Janice, what do you think about Kim's psychic reading?"

"Oh, my God, she's absolutely right! Kim, how did you KNOW all that? That's EXACTLY what's been happening. You've just confirmed what I thought. You're a lifesaver! I REALLY mean it. Now I know what I need to do. Kim, you're incredible!"

The producer and the two on-air personalities were smiling joyously. The bile in my throat was starting to subside a little as we went to the next caller. *Maybe I would live beyond this . . .*

"Tom, you're on the air with the WORLD FAMOUS PSYCHIC Kim O'Neill!"

I winced again with embarrassment.

"Hi, Kim! How does my job future look?"

Again, I was inundated with intuitive information that I simply passed along exactly as I heard it. The two jocks cut me off after about a minute. "So, Tom, was Kim accurate?"

"Kim was great! She's the BEST. Starting my own business is JUST WHAT I WANT TO DO! I want to call her for a private psychic reading. What's her number?"

"Okay, morning show listeners, here's how you can get in contact with Kim O'Neill for your own personal, private psychic reading." And he proceeded to share my office telephone number. "The phone lines are all lit up! We have time for one more call. Suzie, are you there?"

"I'm here . . . " Suzie sounded as scared as I was.

I leaned toward the mic and said, "Hi, Suzie! This is Kim O'Neill. What is your question?"

"When am I going to do better financially?"

I took a deep breath to quiet my nerves, and the angelic information flowed again. "Suzie, your angels tell me that you work in a family business and the business isn't doing very well. You're not happy there and have been thinking for a long time about going off on your own. Is that correct?"

"YES!" Suzie burst into tears, sobbing over the airwaves.

"Are you *okay*?" I asked with concern. I had never had anyone react to information like that before. This was awful! *Did I say something wrong?*

"I'm fine . . . " She replied, sniffling.

One of the disc jockeys made a rolling hand gesture that I assumed meant *go on.*

"Suzie, what I hear is that you feel guilty about leaving—not only

because it isn't doing so well, but because you have a difficult relationship with your mother, who is your boss in the business."

"YES!" More sobbing.

"And your angels recommend that you simply tell her that you're not
happy and that you want to explore other job opportunities. THIS is the
time to finally leave the family business and become successful on your
own." I was now on a roll. "And another thing, Suzie . . . your Mom can
be really critical of you, and boy, does she have some control issues—"

The female disc jockey interrupted quickly. "That's all the time we
have! Suzie, what do you think about what Kim told you?"

Sniff . . . sniff . . . "Kim was right on target with everything she said. I
can't believe it! Thank you, Kim—I'm so glad I called. I just hope my
Mom wasn't listening." A loud CLICK reverberated in the headset as she
hung up.

"Kim, will you join us again next week?"

"I'd love to," I answered, shocked that they wanted me back.

My very first radio show was over as quickly as it had begun. The
on-air personalities introduced another song, took off their headsets,
and came over to congratulate me. Following their lead, I pulled off my
headset and carefully laid it back on the counter as if I was handling the
British crown jewels. I breathed a huge sigh of relief.

"You were really funny, pretending to be nervous. At first, we didn't
realize that you were joking, bumping the mic. No one's ever done that
before! Why don't we do that again next week?" And they laughed
raucously. "You'll come back next week, right, Kim?"

I nodded in dazed confusion.

They escorted me out of the control room and into the hallway,
thanking me profusely for appearing on their show. As the song came
to an end, they scrambled back inside the control room to do the news,
traffic, and weather.

Alone in the hallway, I just stood in a confused stupor. Peering down
the long corridor, I tried to remember where the reception area was. The
radio station was now a buzz of activity. Someone touched my arm,
making me jump. I turned to see a young woman who asked if I was
the psychic who had just done the morning show. I nodded. She said
that several people who worked at the station had listened to the show

and would love it if I could channel for them while I was there. I looked at my watch. It was still pretty early, so I agreed. This was such a dramatic turnaround from people running away from me in public places when I tried to offer information.

She escorted me to an empty office. For the next hour, I channeled for at least ten people. I finally had to leave. There were still others who were waiting for a mini-session, so I promised to channel for them the following week when I returned.

I left KRBE at nine and walked to my car. I felt as if I was floating. I got in, started the engine, and just sat there for a moment. I had climbed a big mountain! I was okay. And no one laughed at me.

"John, are you there?" In seconds, he materialized in the seat next to me. Claire appeared in the back seat behind him. She had a huge smile.

"So, how do you feel?" he asked with a huge grin.

"I can't *believe* it! We did it!" I squealed, and Claire joined me. John rolled his eyes at the two of us.

"*You* did it," he stated. "And it wasn't difficult, was it?"

"At first, I was *so* scared, I couldn't speak! Nothing would come out."

"Yes, I know. But you overcame—"

"And people called in! And they appreciated the information! I think they liked me. Do you think so?"

"That was rather apparent. They asked you back, didn't they?"

"Claire, do you think your Mom heard me?"

"She *did!* And her angels have told me that they're going to nag her until she calls you. I can't wait!"

"I can't believe I did it! And do you guys know *what?*"

"What?" they warmly asked, in unison.

"It was fun! I LOVE radio. I can't wait to go back next week."

"I hate to say I told you so," said John.

"Do you really think they'll have me back? Maybe they'll cancel my appearance? Maybe they'll change their minds. And if they do have me back, maybe I won't be able to do it again. Today might have been a fluke. Maybe I was just lucky, and next time—"

"You're starting to get anal."

"Okay. You're right! I just feel so emotional . . . "

I dug through my messy purse for a tissue. I sat there weeping, overcome with feelings of exhilaration. I had taken the biggest risk of my life, and it had worked out okay. I could feel a tangible shift, as if I had just jumped to a completely different chapter of my life.

When I returned to the office, Shirley was smiling. She handed me a number of messages she had taken. "People calling from the radio show," she explained.

I rifled through them to see if Claire's mother had called. She hadn't yet, but six other people had. Six people! I couldn't have been more thrilled. I had hit the big time!

Chapter 15

Connecting a Parent with Her Murdered Child

Weeks passed, and I hadn't heard a word from Claire's mother. I had continued as a guest on KRBE Radio as their world-famous "Psychic in Residence," and a handful of people were calling for private readings after every appearance.

John had advised me to do as many sessions as I could—without charging any fee—while I was still in the process of building my confidence and expertise. I was relieved at his suggestion because I continued to feel very insecure about my ability.

I discovered that channeling for other people was incredibly exhausting. John explained that producing the special energy with which to channel was like building strength and endurance at the gym. The more an individual worked out, the greater his strength and vitality.

While I was in the process of expanding my channeling energy, John suggested that I limit each appointment to half an hour. He also recommended that I offer clients a choice: they could ask about anything that was a priority to them; or they could choose to open the floor to their angels or deceased loved ones and allow the spirits to pass along whatever messages they deemed most important.

As I practiced my channeling, the information flowed faster and became far more comprehensive and specific. I quickly discovered that angels, like human beings, all have distinctively different personalities, but they all share one thing in common. They are all very anxious to help human beings discover the special path meant just for them and how they can move their lives forward with purpose and meaning.

I was struggling to get my new channeling practice off the ground, and David did everything he could to derail my progress. Although he never belittled my weekly radio appearances, he developed the obnoxious habit of knocking loudly on my door when he knew I was conducting a session—or worse, yelling embarrassing obscenities up and down the hallway when I was welcoming a client in the reception area. David and I quarreled about it repeatedly until John recommended that I ask the art director to create a small sign to hang over my doorknob that read *Angels at Work—Please Do Not Disturb!* Inexplicably, when I started using the angel sign, David stopped interrupting sessions and became as quiet as a mouse when channeling clients were present.

One Thursday afternoon in late May, a sudden storm blew in from the Gulf of Mexico. Winds picked up and the sky turned ominously dark. Torrential rains began to fall, accompanied by thunder, lightening, and large hailstones, making for a treacherous and unpredictable afternoon commute.

Shirley turned on the TV in the conference room, and we all gathered to watch the news coverage. A storm alert had been issued, advising everyone to stay at home if at all possible. Tornadoes were sighted in neighborhoods around the city, and dangerous flooding was occurring in low-lying areas. Motorists were warned to avoid taking risks with the rising water that had made many intersections completely impassable.

"Good thing I planned to stay late anyway," said Craig.

All the other staff members chose to wait out the storm, too. Shirley decided to explore what dinner options were available from the leftovers in the small refrigerator. I walked across the hall to David's office to warn him about the weather. He was already in his running clothes.

"David! You can't go running in Memorial Park. The sky is pitch black. There's a terrible thunderstorm!"

"So?" he tersely interrupted.

"Tornadoes are touching down—there's flooding everywhere."

"I'm not going to *miss my run*," he answered emphatically, as if challenging Mother Nature's faulty and inconvenient decision to produce a severe thunderstorm during the time he scheduled for his regular workout. Nothing *ever* caused David to miss his daily exercise.

"Excuse me, kids," said Shirley, poking her head into his office. "There's nothing in the fridge that I can identify, so—"

"What do you mean?" objected David, testily. "I just got my yogurt, and I saw plenty of food."

"Are you referring to all the containers of smelly carry-out that everybody throws in there and then forgets about?" answered Shirley. "If I pick up a package and look inside—and there's no telling if it's animal, vegetable, or mineral—it goes in the garbage. I know I'm not supposed to be making executive decisions, but—"

"Well, then, order out," he replied impatiently.

"Let me get this straight," said Shirley. "You want me to call Star during this terrible storm and ask some poor schlemiel to risk his life so we can have pizza pie for dinner?"

"If they won't deliver when we need it, then tell them they've lost our business. You'll work it out. Have a good evening."

And with that, he left. We both stared after him.

"I'd like to put him over my knee and give him a good old-fashioned spanking," said Shirley with a sigh. "Then . . . some serious drugs."

"I think he needs medication, too," I agreed.

"No . . . I meant for me."

"Hello?" a female voice tentatively called from the reception area. We couldn't imagine who would have braved the storm in rush-hour traffic to visit the agency. As Shirley walked back up front, I returned to my office. The moment I got there, Shirley buzzed me. "Kim . . . your five-o'clock is here."

I looked at my watch. It was 4:55. I couldn't believe my channeling client had arrived—right on time. How could she have done that with the gridlock of traffic all over the city? She hadn't called to cancel, but I had assumed that she was going to reschedule her appointment because of the horrendous weather. When I walked into the reception area, a pretty blond gal in her early forties jumped up from the couch and approached me. She looked familiar somehow, but I knew we'd never met before.

"I'm Kim O'Neill," I smiled at her. "You must be Mary?"

The woman nodded. She appeared extremely flustered, and she spoke very quickly. "I almost called to cancel, but I decided to try to get here. It was the funniest thing—and I know it sounds crazy—but it was like all the traffic just *parted* for me. In fact, I got here a little early, and I've been sitting down in the parking garage. I've really been looking forward to this appointment; I wouldn't have missed it for anything in the world. Normally I'm not this scattered . . . I'm just terribly nervous."

After offering her something to drink, which she declined, we walked back to my office. The client took one of the seats that flanked my desk and began to dig through her large purse for the list of questions that she had prepared at my request. I hung the angel sign, closed the door, and took the seat behind my desk. I pulled out a tape and placed it in the recorder.

"Today is Thursday, May 20, and we are in Houston, Texas, conducting a channeling session for Mary Franklin." I rewound the tape and then played it back to make certain that it was working correctly. It was time to begin the session.

"Mary, I'm going to be receiving information from your guardian angels, whom I call 'guides.' I can also receive messages from your family members and friends who have passed on. All information from spirit tends to be very frank and candid—is that okay with you?"

"Yes," she answered in a very quiet, hesitant voice.

"Good! Now, if anything I relay to you during this session doesn't make sense, for any reason—or if you need *more* explanation beyond what I've provided—I'm inviting you to interrupt me at any time. You will not be rude, nor will you derail the channeling process. I'm here to serve you, and I speak very quickly in order to get you as much information as possible in our time together. Interrupting me may be the only way you can get a word in edgewise!"

The client somberly nodded her head. She had just pulled several dog-eared sheets of yellow-lined paper from the recesses of her handbag and was tightly clutching them. She looked scared yet anxious to begin.

"In order to make our session as productive as possible," I suggested, "you may want to start by asking the most important questions *first*."

The rain began to come down in torrents, beating horizontally against my window. A flash of lighting and a peal of thunder made us both jump.

"You might find it hard to believe," I shared with her, "but this is my favorite weather."

"It's my daughter's favorite weather, too," she responded, her eyes filling with tears.

Claire immediately materialized in the chair next to her, and with a broad smile said proudly, "This is my Mom."

No wonder the client seemed familiar—she looked like a grown-up Claire! Neither Claire nor John had prepared me for this afternoon. I was glad they hadn't said anything to me. I would have been on pins and needles from the moment Mary Franklin had scheduled the session. I was thrilled to see Claire; but, suddenly, I was even more nervous than her mother.

Mary Franklin followed my gaze and looked at the chair next to her and obviously saw nothing. She looked puzzled by my behavior. I quickly realized that this was going to be, by far, the most difficult session I had ever conducted. Were spiritual contracts always this tough to honor, I wondered?

I took a very deep breath. Suddenly, I began to wish I had chosen some other kind of life's work. I was really scared, absolutely *dreading* what I was about to do—which was to tell this poor woman that her precious, beautiful daughter was dead. I prayed that she wouldn't ask too many questions about *how* she died.

An intuitive flash took me back to the forest preserve where I saw Claire tied to the tree, begging to go home to her mother—the woman who now sat directly across from me. My eyes filled with tears. I needed to gather some strength and get my feelings under control. As an emotional and sensitive person, I could easily extend sympathy, compassion, and support to the folks for whom I channeled; however, I was discovering that it was a battle for me to maintain a neutral, passive, and detached manner, as John had told me I needed to, when the topic of conversation became as heart-rending and gut-wrenching as this. I quickly excused myself, telling the client that I needed to use the restroom. I dashed up behind Shirley, scaring her.

"Quick!" I said. "I need Kleenex!"

She took one look and handed me the box. "Anything else?" she asked kindly.

I shook my head, holding a tissue to my eyes. It wasn't going to take much for me to break down and start wailing. That's all I needed to do just before a session! A client was seated in my office . . . and I'm out in the hallway crying! *What am I doing? I'm so incompetent!* In a moment I would have to go back in there. I had to collect myself and somehow get my emotions in check.

Shirley was regarding me with an expression that said, "Are you *sure* you want to do this?" *No, I definitely wasn't sure*—but I had already made a commitment. The client was cooling her heels in my office, waiting for me to tell her that her teenage daughter had died hideously at the hands of a rapist and murderer. What's more, she had braved a terrible storm to do so. I took several deep breaths, nodded to Shirley, and returned to my office. I mustered a constipated smile as I opened the door.

"Thank you for your patience," I told Claire's mother, a little too cheerily, trying to overcompensate for all the painful emotions that were churning inside of me.

"That's okay," she hesitantly responded, clearly noticing my reddened eyes and sniffles.

"Allergies," I lamely explained, pushing the buttons that activated the recorder. "Where would you like to begin?"

The client dug through her purse for a tissue. "I'm so sorry!" she apologized. "It's just that . . . well . . . I have to ask about my daughter . . ."

My heart was pounding, and I felt sick to my stomach. John appeared to my right and stood with his hand on my shoulder.

Steady . . . steady, he said telepathically to reassure me.

"Mary, what would you like to ask?" I gently inquired.

She burst into uncontrollable, wrenching sobs. She bent over and I could see her whole body shaking. I started to get up and go to her, to offer some kind of comfort, but John held his hand on my shoulder and strongly recommended that I stay put. I just sat there in silence until she recovered enough to speak.

"I'm so sorry! It's just that . . . well . . . Kim . . . do *you* have any children?"

"No . . . I don't."

"Oh . . . then you might not be able to imagine what it's like . . . to lose . . . "

Your only child, Claire said, finishing the sentence for her mother.

"Oh, my God, Mary—Claire was your only child?"

Mary Franklin's eyes shot open in astonishment. "How did you know?"

Tell mom I'm right here. Tell her I'm okay.

"Claire is right here, Mary. And she wants you to know that she's okay."

"She's *here*? How can she be *here*?" Mary Franklin turned in her chair and searched the room. Seeing nothing, her eyes returned to mine, hurt and questioning.

"She's sitting right next to you."

Mary looked at the chair to her right and saw nothing. She was quiet for a moment, deep in thought. I prayed that she was hearing something telepathic. Brow furrowed, she mustered the courage to ask, "Does that mean she's *dead*? That Claire's *spirit* is here? Is *that* what you're telling me?"

"Yes," I quietly answered, my tears welling again. I reached for a tissue from the box I kept on the floor behind my desk. John's hand remained firmly on my shoulder.

"I *knew* it! I just *knew* it! Her father keeps insisting that she'll come home—he just won't face the truth! I just *knew that something happened.* She would *never* have just run off—we were so close—I would have *known* if she was planning something like that. She told me *everything* . . . we were best friends. She had just turned sixteen, and we had a big birthday party for her right before she disappeared." Then she started to sob again. I dabbed at my eyes and remained in my chair. A minute or so—which seemed like an eternity—ticked by.

Tell Mom I'm in heaven with Grandma Helen and Uncle George.

I repeated Claire's message to her mother. Mary Franklin abruptly stopped sobbing and looked at me with surprise.

"How do you know about my mother-in-law? And my brother?"

"Claire just told me."

"She's really *here*?" Mary turned to the chair next to her. "But I don't *see* her! And I don't *hear* her?"

MOM! MOM! IT'S ME, CLAIRE! I'M RIGHT HERE!

Her mother remained oblivious to her daughter's presence, in spite of the fact that Claire sat immediately to her right and was yelling quite loudly in an attempt to get her attention.

Tell her what I had for lunch! A grilled cheese, with Vlasik baby dills, and cheese Doritos—and a glass of chocolate milk! Then I had some Oreos.

I smiled. Only a teenager would eat that combination of foods. When I repeated what she said, her mother began to chuckle through her tears.

"That *was* her favorite lunch! Is it *true*? Can you *really be speaking with her*?" Her tears were pouring down her cheeks. "I guess now I know that when I go to the grocery store—I won't be buying any of the pickles that she loved—or the Doritos—or the chocolate milk—ever again!" She put her head down and sobbed. She quieted after a few moments. "I didn't tell her father I was coming to see you. He doesn't believe in any of this."

Claire laughed raucously. *Of course he doesn't, Mom! He's so stubborn that you can't tell him anything. He never listens! Remember the ice cream trip right before my birthday when I tried to give Dad directions?*

When I repeated Claire's statements, her mother smiled and shared the memory with me.

"Claire heard about this ice cream place that had just opened, and she asked me to take her. It was a Sunday and her father was home, so, as usual, he insisted on driving. Before we left, Claire had the presence of mind to call and ask for directions. When she tried to give them to her father, he told her to pipe down—that he knew full well where he was going and that he didn't need any help from her. So she sat quietly in the backseat with her arms folded, just looking out the window. After we had been driving and driving and driving, her father turned to her in the backseat and said something like, 'Are you sure this place has even *opened* yet? Where the hell *is* it?' And she told him, 'You told me to 'pipe down,' so I did. We passed it about ten miles back."

Mary Franklin and I both chuckled.

Her mother's eyes looked haunted again. "Please, I have to know—how did she die? She told me she was going to the store for some doughnuts before school . . . right around the corner. We never saw her again. *What could have happened?*"

My stomach started to churn and my heart began to race. This was what I had dreaded most. *What would I tell her?*

Steady . . . steady, said John. *You can do this.*

Tell her I was kidnapped, Claire said. *And forced into a van by this guy I didn't know. Tell Mom he just grabbed me and threw me in. It was nobody from school. This was an older guy . . . a stranger.*

I repeated word for word. Mary's eyes widened in horror and her hand flew to her mouth. Claire seemed eager to continue.

Then he drove for a long time—I couldn't tell where we were going because he made me lay in the back so I couldn't see out the window. I thought of jumping out, but there was no door handle! He finally turned onto this bumpy road, and branches were hitting the side of the van. Then he stopped, came around to my side, and pulled me out. He dragged me into the woods and tied me to a tree.

"Then what happened?" asked her mother frantically. "Did he *hurt* you? Did he *touch* you? What *happened?*"

He killed me, her daughter replied.

"But *how?*" Mary beseeched her daughter to share everything that had happened, but Claire was reluctant. She didn't want to subject her mother to more trauma than she had already sustained.

He raped me, and then he stabbed me.

For her mother's sake, I was incredibly grateful that she didn't go into any more detail.

"OH, MY GOD!" the mother screamed. "My *child!* I was always worried about someone grabbing you when you were little, but—"

MOM! I'M OKAY!

"Where is she buried?" Mary asked me. "Will we at least recover her body?"

I thought of what John had shared earlier about what the killer had done to her teenage daughter's remains. I wondered morosely if a burial could still take place if a family only had little pieces of a body . . . or maybe none at all?

No, Mom, you won't get my body back. But it doesn't matter—that was only my shell. The guy who killed me has already moved—he's in Florida now. He's done this to other girls, too.

"What?" said Mary. "That's *terrible!* He has to be *stopped*—so that other families don't have to go through this. Is there anything I can do?"

No! answered Claire. *The cops are already looking for him . . . the body of another one of his victims was just found this morning. They're doing the best they can.*

What a diplomatic way to tell her mother that he'll never be caught, I thought.

Kim is going to help you become psychic so we can communicate whenever we want. Okay? I miss talking to you!

"That would be wonderful!" answered Mary Franklin. "But I can't do that! I don't see how it's possible?"

"Babe Ruth had to hit his first baseball," I pointed out, parroting what John had said to me so many months before. "Julia Child had to cook her first soufflé. Channeling just takes a little practice. There's no reason why you can't stay close to Claire. We talk all the time."

"You *do?*" she said wistfully. "I would love that more than anything in the world!"

"Then let's plan another session for next week, and I'll go over the basics. In no time, you'll be talking with Claire—and your angels—and Grandma Helen—"

"Do I have to speak with *everybody* over there?" she asked, mischief in her blue eyes. Claire burst into a peal of giggles.

Grandma was always telling her what to do—and it drove her nuts!

I repeated her statement, and Mary smiled, rolling her eyes.

And you could channel for Dad! Claire and her mother had a big laugh at the thought of Mr. Franklin eagerly receiving psychic messages from the beyond.

"I'm absolutely devastated but relieved to know what really happened," she told me. "I just knew *in my heart* that Claire was dead. I think somehow it's worse not knowing. Always wondering what has become of your child. Claire *must* be here—otherwise you would have never known about the grilled cheese sandwiches—or the ice cream trip. *Thank you* for telling me what happened. I'll never stop missing my darling baby."

Several minutes later, after giving me a warm hug, Mary Franklin left my office. I went back to my desk and sat crying for a little while. Thanks to Claire and her mother, I suddenly lost the fear of the clairvoyant dreams that had haunted me since childhood. Although I knew they would occur again, I finally understood that they had an important purpose. The nightmares would allow me to better relate to the families for whom I would channel after such a tragedy had taken place. I had the distinct feeling that there were going to be many more victims like Claire from whom I would channel messages. It fueled me with a sense of purpose . . . knowing that, in some very small way, I could help their families.

The raging summer storm had blown through, and the night air was warm and humid. A rainbow stretched across the sky in hues so breathtaking that it didn't look real. I hoped Mary Franklin had noticed it. Claire must have been the artist responsible.

As I left the office, I was inspired to stop at the store for groceries. When I got home, I donned my nightshirt, fed Winston, made my dinner, and settled in front of the TV. I feasted on a grilled cheese sandwich, pickles, cheese Doritos, and a large bag of Oreos for dessert. It was the best meal I ever had.

Chapter 16

Earning My Transition

It was Thanksgiving weekend, and I was decorating my Christmas tree in a corner of the living room. I had a hot chocolate and some homemade cookies on the end table. The old movie channel was playing *It's a Wonderful Life*, and John was seated in his favorite chair opposite the couch. Claire was helping with the ornaments. When I took the lid off the box that held all of the lights, they were in a tight, snarled ball. No matter how carefully I packed them away each year after the holidays, the lights always became tangled while stored in their plastic container.

"Look at these damn lights!" I cried with frustration. "This happens every year."

"If you get some long pieces of cardboard," John advised, trying not to chuckle, "and gently wrap each string of lights on a single cardboard, *then* lay it in the box—one on top of the other—you wouldn't have the tangles."

"That happens to my Mom every year, too," Claire sympathized. "She and my Dad always get into a big fight about who's gonna untangle. Then she goes Christmas shopping and comes home when she knows it's done."

"That sounds like a great idea to me," I said, looking at John expectantly.

He shook his head. "There are some feats even an angel cannot perform."

"Didn't you tell me that you worked as a guardian angel for members of the French Resistance during World War II?"

"Trust me—that was simpler."

"It's because he's a man," explained Claire. "My Mom always says that men hate three things: being asked to paint, being asked to untangle Christmas lights, and being bothered when they're reading on the toilet."

"And how right she is," acknowledged John. "A very wise woman, your mother."

"Yeah . . . but she always does all three with my Dad anyway."

"There's something I'd like to watch on another station," asked John suddenly. "May I?"

"Sure," I answered, concentrating on all the tangled lights. It was going to take me hours to unravel the mess. *Maybe I should just go to Target and buy some new ones and pack these away for next year.*

"Thank you for watching Eyewitness News! All of us here at Channel 13 want to wish you and yours the happiest of Thanksgivings. And don't forget to watch *Good Morning Houston* on Monday, when our guest will be Ed Jones, author of *The Guardian Angel Myth—Debunking the Existence of Spirits.* Good night!"

"Did you hear *that?*" I angrily asked them.

John nodded.

"But it's not true! We *do* exist!" insisted Claire. "What if people, like my Mom, who have lost someone, watch the show and get the wrong idea?"

"Everyone is entitled to their beliefs," John observed.

"But it's hard enough for us to try and make contact," Claire complained. "Kim, what are you gonna *do?*"

"Me?" I asked. "Nothing. What can I do?"

"You could go on that show and prove that we do exist. You already are on the radio—so TV would be easy. You *have* to!"

I looked at John, who had returned the TV to the old movie channel using his own special method of remote control. He pretended to be very engrossed in *It's a Wonderful Life*. I had now known him long enough to recognize when I was being maneuvered.

"*Kim!*" cried Claire. "*Please!*"

"But honey, I'm sure someone else will offer to dispel—"

"No, they won't," piped John, without taking his eyes off the TV screen. "No one else will come forward."

"You just *have* to do it," pleaded the young girl, who had become one of my best friends.

"Why not allow people to believe whatever they choose?" I asked them.

"How can people make informed decisions if they don't hear *both* sides?" Claire responded. There was no arguing with that logic. "Isn't it your life's work to teach people about spirits and stuff? Isn't that what you're committed to do?"

She was right. I did enjoy channeling on the radio very much, after I had stumbled through the first program. So that very day, after we finished with the tree, I sent a press release to the producer of *Good Morning Houston*, the most popular TV morning show in the city.

The following week when I called to follow through on the release, the producer penciled me in as a guest for the special show on New Year's Eve. She asked me to make local, national, and international psychic predictions for the coming year, as well as discuss how others could recognize and build their own psychic ability. Then, I'd take calls from viewers. She also told me that the show was "live," which meant nothing to me. I agreed. Claire was delirious with joy.

However, this proved to be a tremendous amount of work. It took John and me hours to access all that information, and then I decided to memorize it. I didn't want to spend my first television appearance with my head down reading notes in my lap. As the date loomed ahead, I got a little nervous, but John kept insisting that it would be successful. After all, I had ten months of radio appearances under my belt. I trusted John's judgment and actually looked forward to the experience.

When I arrived at the big station for the scheduled appearance, I was greeted by the producer who led me to the homey little set. I met the two well-known hosts, and they were very gracious to me. However, as we started to discuss all the information I had so painstakingly prepared, the male host told me that he was going to play "devil's advocate" and challenge me on what I was going to predict. *Challenge me? What does that mean?* I didn't like the prankster gleam in his eye. I began to hope that he hadn't had a fight with his wife that morning. The female host told me that he was teasing, and she brushed off his comment with a wave of her hand. But I started to fret.

The female host then told me that I was going to be the first guest interviewed on the show that morning and that she was very excited about communicating with angels and family members who had passed on. She invited me to sit down at one end of the sofa, and she took a seat toward the other end. She told me that I would have about twenty seconds to answer a psychic question from each of the viewers who called during my segment. I would have only twenty seconds to listen to a question from a viewer and then to answer it? Was she kidding?

As she gathered her notes, she began to speak about an angelic encounter she had experienced, perhaps to assure me that her interview was going to be friendly and that she, like me, was sensitive to communication from "the other side." I began to get even more nervous, however, because I was distracted by all the peripheral noise and excitement.

I noticed all the big TV cameras. I saw all the camera men and women working to position their cameras. I saw numerous staffers scampering about in a very no-nonsense fashion doing their particular jobs. I saw the other guests they had scheduled for the program waiting for their turn in front of the cameras. *This is not going to be as simple as radio!*

Then I heard someone mimicking the theme from the *Twilight Zone*, followed by the sound of laughter. I wasn't a paranoid person, but somehow I knew they were laughing at me. *I was being laughed at! Why would anyone laugh at me? I was asked to be a guest on the show like everybody else. And I had worked so damned hard to compile the information . . .*

Suddenly, my heart started racing, my mouth went completely dry, my tongue felt as if it wouldn't move, my breath came in shallow gasps, and I couldn't remember what the dickens I had prepared for the show. It was all gone . . . as if I had Alzheimer's! My face started to burn, so I knew that it had turned crimson–and worse, I could feel hives popping out like huge, angry mosquito bites on my forehead and chin. I told myself to GO! NOW! I wanted to get up and flee the TV station, but my body wouldn't budge. I was so frightened that I was literally frozen on the sofa. All the while, the charming, friendly female host was patiently explaining what we were going to do in my segment, which was going to last for nine minutes.

I didn't hear most of what she said. *I can't do this! I'm going to make a fool of myself in front of the entire city. But . . . it's nine o'clock in the morning, so maybe a lot of people are at work already and won't see the show. This is not warm, friendly RADIO! How will I ever show my face at the ad agency again?*

At that very moment I fervently wished I was back in the office work-ing on one of the boring annual reports for one of our advertising clients in the energy industry. *At least that was safe. What am I doing here? Why am I putting myself out there like this? For public ridicule? I could have stayed at the office and been ridiculed—in private—by my ex-husband.* I was shaking and perspiring, but now I had no choice.

Suddenly, a cameraman standing across from us held up ten fingers. I could see him silently mouthing the word "ten." Everybody silenced on the set. The male host ran over and jumped into the chair next to me. The hosts smoothed their clothing and began to smile at the cam-era. The *Good Morning Houston* theme song began to echo throughout the large studio. I was panic stricken. The cameraman silently counted back-ward with his fingers: nine . . . eight . . . seven . . . six . . . five . . . four . . . three . . . two . . . one.

"Welcome to *Good Morning Houston!* We have a great show for you today . . . "

I thought my heart was going to explode out of my chest. I couldn't breathe, and my mind was an absolute blank. *Oh God, why am I here?*

The camera remained focused on the hosts as they excitedly intro-duced the topics they were going to cover that day. Not knowing what else to do, I, too, looked toward the camera, and I caught sight of my image in a little monitor. It was a mistake to have looked.

Early that morning, I had been concerned that my face would look washed out if I wore my normal make-up, so I applied a bit more to give me what I thought would be adequate color and help me look a little glamorous. On the set under all the bright lights, my make-up appeared so heavy that it made me look like a man in drag! The dark business suit I had so carefully chosen made my milky–white skin look embalmed. And my long nails, painted a bright red, looked like talons. My bleached–blond hair, however, was the big problem. I had painstakingly arranged it into what I believed was a stylish mass of messy curls. I winced when I saw my reflection on the monitor. I was a 1980's country music queen wannabe, only without the guitar. It was apparent that I had lived in Houston long enough to have contracted—besides an allergy to pollen—the insidious affliction commonly known as Texas Big Blond Hair. I appeared downright scary in comparison to the professionally groomed and coiffed female host. Nothing I could do about it now! This made me love radio even more. *Nobody can see me on the radio.*

I suddenly heard my name. They were introducing my psychic segment. I could see from the monitor that the camera had focused on me.

"And this is psychic Kim O'Neill, who has an office in the Galleria area. We're so excited to have her in the studio for the show today."

My frozen expression made me look like a deer caught unaware during hunting season. My eyes were huge with fear. I couldn't speak and I couldn't smile.

The female host continued cheerily, "Kim is here to share all kinds of interesting information about what we Houstonians can expect in the New Year. She's also going to answer your personal questions, so CALL NOW."

As she spoke, I wanted to respond, but in my near–hysterical state, my eyes kept darting back and forth across the set as if I was watching a tennis match. My brain had gone to mush. I couldn't think of anything to say. And there were four cameras, and I didn't know which one to look at. Did it matter, I wondered?

Speak! Now! John demanded. *Just get through with this! You can do it!*

I managed an anemic smile, and in a squeak of a voice, I somehow remembered several of my local predictions. Then the host decided to "go to the phones" and take personal calls from viewers.

"Hi, caller—what is your question for Kim?"

"Are you talking to me?" asked a disembodied voice that echoed through the studio.

"Yes, caller," confirmed the host. "Do you have a question for Kim?"

"Yes."

There was dead silence . . . and I realized that half of my twenty seconds had already expired for this caller. Somehow, I found my voice. "Hi! This is Kim O'Neill. And what is your name?"

"Are you talking to me?"

I wondered if the caller was more mentally challenged than I was at this moment. I pressed on. "YES, caller. What is your name?"

"Sheila."

"Hi, Sheila. Thank you for calling. And what is your question for me?"

"Uhhmm . . . I have so many . . . "

"Your time is running out," I told her.

"My time? You mean I'm going to DIE?"

"No! I mean for this call."

"Oh. Okay—how about telling me if I'm going to win the lottery?"

"No, you're not. And if I may continue?" I posed this question to the female host, who nodded her approval. The angelic information started to flow fast and furious.

"Sheila, you must move on with your life. You have to get a job and move to your own apartment. Your family is really worried about your drug use—"

CLICK. The phone line went dead.

"Oh, what a shame," the male host smoothly announced. "We lost Sheila. Let's go to the next line. Caller, are you there?"

"I'm here!" answered a bubbly female voice dripping with a Texas twang. "My name is Kathy, and I had to call y'all because I recently heard Kim on the radio. She's great! I *thought* she'd be a blond. Kim, I LOVE your hair!"

The male host had to turn away to keep from breaking into laughter. My first television experience was not going well.

"Hi, Kathy. What is your question for me?" I asked, while at the same time looking confusedly at all the different cameras. The cameramen were all motioning to me with hand gestures that I couldn't understand. I had no idea what they were trying to tell me.

"Kim, do I know my soul mate now?"

"What I'm hearing from your angels is that you will meet him in two years."

"Oh, *no!* Then . . . what about my fiancé? We have a wedding date set for February."

"Well, Kathy, your angels are telling me that you don't love your fiancé and that you are marrying him because you're afraid that nobody else will ever come into your life. Is that correct?"

"Yes . . . " and then there was the unmistakable sound of muffled crying. The caller loudly blew her nose. Not knowing what else to do, I continued. "Your angels recommend that you call off the wedding. Wait for a Mr. Wonderful who can offer you what you need and want most—a heart, mind, body, and soul relationship."

"But what if Mr. Wonderful never comes along? And all the wedding plans? My fiancé will be so disappointed—"

"He'd be more disappointed with a divorce." I quipped. "Won't it be easier to break off an engagement—than it would a marriage?"

"I guess so . . . it's just that I'm four months pregnant and—"

"Well!" quickly responded the male host. "Then . . . congratulations are in order. We certainly wish you the best. Have a great day, Kathy. Now, let's move to the next caller. We have Bubba on the line!"

"Yeah . . . this is Bubba. And I don't believe in this psychic stuff. It ain't natural."

"Do you have a question for Kim?" asked the female host.

"Yeah . . . I want to ask about my Sadie, my dead grandma. What does she have to say to me?"

"I can't answer that question, Bubba," I responded.

"See! I was RIGHT. Some psychic. I KNEW all this was just a bunch of hooey!"

The male host laughed and said, "Bubba, I'm with you! All this is a little too far out for me," and then he began to whistle the *Twilight Zone* theme. Staffers could be heard softly snickering from behind the scenes.

"Why can't you answer that question, Kim?" interrupted the female host.

"Because Bubba doesn't have a grandma named Sadie," I said. "But—he *does* have a deceased grandmother named Myrtle. She wants him to know that he'd better stop fooling around with his secretary, or his wife is going to find out and take the kids back to Pennsylvania where all of her family is."

"Holy crap!" replied Bubba.

"*Now* what do you think of psychic ability, boys?" the female host asked, obviously enjoying herself. She smiled at me and I smiled back. *So this was live TV? I was in desperate need of some chocolate.*

"Bubba . . . do you have any other questions for Kim?" she asked, still smiling.

"Yeah. Okay . . . what should I be doing to make more money? And maybe to improve my marriage, besides leaving my secretary alone?"

"It's your destiny to own your own business, Bubba," I told him. "And to make a positive difference in other people's lives. You can begin to accomplish a lot if you quit fooling around and mature a little bit. The drinking and the carousing must stop."

"Yes, ma'am," he answered solemnly. "That's what my wife says."

"You'd really enjoy owning your own auto mechanics business—"

"That's what I do now. I hate it!"

"What your grandmother Myrtle is telling me, Bubba, is that you hate your *boss*, not the business. You enjoy working with your hands and fixing things, and you're really good at it. If you opened your own garage, you'd be making the money you're worth, instead of seeing your boss get richer and richer from all of your hard work."

"Yeah . . . that's right! I do hate my boss, that sorry son-of-a—oh! Excuse me."

"That's okay," I replied. "Now . . . let's talk about your marriage. If your wife felt heard by you—"

"Say *what?*"

"Your wife feels that you don't listen to her and that her feelings aren't a priority to you."

"That's just what she says! Hey, is she on the other line or somethin'?"

Everyone laughed. The female host jumped in, "Well, we all learned a lot about psychic ability this morning. I'm so sorry that we have to say goodbye. Thank you, Kim, for joining us."

"Yeah . . . thanks, Kim," Bubba piped in. "Hey, can I talk to you in private? Do you only do this on TV?"

"I almost forgot," replied the male host. "If you'd like a psychic reading from Kim, you can call her at her office." He held up my business card and read my telephone number. "Please stay with us. Next, we're going to interview a man who talks to plants. Discover his secrets to a more beautiful winter garden. Don't go away!" He kept smiling at the camera until the cameraman made a hand gesture. Suddenly, the monitor was showing commercials.

This was their break between segments. The next guest, the plant man, was ready to take the seat I was eagerly vacating. The hosts graciously thanked me and promised to do another psychic segment. *That will be a cold day in hell, I thought. What a disaster.*

I was so shell-shocked I needed to spend some time alone. I didn't even want to talk to John or Claire. I left the television station feeling completely demoralized. I was far too depressed and embarrassed to return to the office, so I went shopping and bought a pound of my favorite chocolate and a black cocktail dress that I knew I could return, unworn, in a couple of days when I was feeling better.

Several hours later, I sheepishly went back to the agency. I had work to do that couldn't be put off any longer. Shirley started waving frantically the moment she saw me. She had been on the telephone nonstop after my *Good Morning Houston* appearance.

To my complete shock, the phone line had rung off the hook with people wanting to schedule a private session with me. The calls were still coming in, one right after the other. I simply couldn't believe it. She winked at me as she picked up the line again. "Yes, this is Kim O'Neill's office. Yes, she's the psychic who was on the show . . . "

I picked up a big handful of messages that had been stuffed into my message box, and I walked back to my office reeling with confusion. I thought the TV appearance was horrible. I hadn't realized how badly I needed a makeover. And those callers! Couldn't the universe have had more positive people calling in? And the host making fun of my profession in front of all the viewers. It was like a nightmare. If I ever had my own show, I decided, I'd welcome my guests with open arms—I certainly wouldn't ask them to block out time from their busy schedules to appear and then treat them disrespectfully. What kind of person makes fun of someone else's life's work?

Both John and Claire materialized in the chairs across from my desk. They sported huge grins. John started to whistle the theme from the *Twilight Zone.*

"You think that's funny?" I asked him angrily. "The show was awful!"

"I thought it was too cool!" announced Claire. "You did great! I'm so glad we're friends."

"I'm proud of you, too," John said. "You've climbed some *big* rungs on the ladder this morning. What did you learn from the experience?"

"That I *never* want to do TV again!"

"Oh, but you will," the angel casually replied. "Your phone is going to ring consistently now. And, it's time to start charging a nominal fee. I suppose the next step is to start looking for office space."

My mouth dropped open. "Are you kidding?"

"Certainly not . . . you've earned it."

"You mean that I can leave here . . . now?" I asked, not believing my ears. "For good?"

He nodded, smiling at me. "Look at all of those requests for appointments. And there will be many more to follow in the next few weeks. You've done it. This is the moment you've been working toward."

Instead of screaming or jumping up and down, I just sat quietly. I couldn't believe that I was finally going to make the jump away from David and all of the melodrama that I had experienced with him and the ad business. I had *earned* the opportunity to move on—plus, I had been honest with him all along about my intentions. I had actually started a business that made my heart and soul sing—and it was becoming successful. David had been all wrong about what I could accomplish. And so had I. If only I had chosen to enjoy the journey.

"Divine timing of the universe," squealed Claire, who was jumping up and down and clapping her hands in excitement.

John and I went out the next morning, and he led me to a very modest, older, two story office building in the Galleria area. When the building manager showed me the only suite he had available, I thought it was perfect. The office was on the second floor, and it had sage green walls and matching sage green carpeting. The reception area was the size of a postage stamp, and the inner office where I would conduct the channeling sessions was also tiny, but it was lined with windows reflecting lots of natural light, with a view of the parking lot in the back of the building.

The building manager, who I discovered was also the owner of the property, asked what kind of business I was in. My heart caught in my throat.

"I'm a channel."

"Huh?" he responded, cigar clenched between his teeth.

"I'm a psychic," I explained in a squeak of a voice.

"The kind on the phone? In that network?"

"No!" I answered, perhaps a little too emphatically.

"Okay," he said casually, with a small shrug. That was all the convincing he needed. I got the distinct feeling that he might have considered renting the office to me if I had told him I was an executioner and was going to do my work on the premises. He seemed a little amused that I was so thrilled with the space. The rent was $204 a month, and I was scared silly about being able to pay for it.

Within a matter of two days, I was the proud tenant in the miniscule suite on Fountainview Avenue. My landlord was even kind enough to put my name among all the others on the signage in front of the property, in spite of the fact that I occupied the smallest office in the building.

David never showed up on my moving day—to help or to wish me good luck. After saying a tearful goodbye to the Advertising & Design, Inc. staff, I loaded the furniture from my office into a rented trailer.

Overwhelmed with excitement, I arrived at my new building and set up my office. I had opened my very own business as a psychic channel. I had declared myself, and I knew there was no going back.

Part Three

Slowly Building a New Life

Chapter 17

Taking a Huge Leap of Faith

"You're running late!" urged Maria, the girlfriend who had volunteered to help me with my first speaking engagement. "You *have* to go in there."

The two large wooden doors that led to the ballroom of Houston's Adam's Mark Hotel were slightly ajar, enabling me to take yet another squeamish peek at the people who had assembled for my very first angel seminar. The audience was getting restless. I could hear the hum of quiet conversations, light laughter, sporadic coughing, and the rustling of paper as they perused the handouts they were given when they arrived. It had taken much longer than expected for Maria and my Mom, who was pitching in, to get everyone registered. It was already well past 7:00 p.m., the time the presentation was supposed to begin.

There were 143 people waiting for me to stride into the room and begin a confident and invigorating discussion about guardian angels. I, however, remained in the corridor, pacing back and forth in front of the registration table, anxiously reviewing the numerous small, lined index cards that held my notes. The seminar was scheduled to last three hours, and with the exception of a short break, I was to hold the floor all of that time.

According to John, hosting seminars and workshops was the next vital step in conducting my life's work. I had asked him about enrolling in some type of public speaking course, like Toastmasters, but he immediately rejected that idea. He argued that I would never trust that I was good enough to stop taking the classes. He promised that my professional speaking ability would blossom as time went on and that experience would be my best teacher.

Prior to my first public speaking event, he had instructed me to mention the workshop to all of my channeling clients, as well as during my regular gig as KRBE's "Resident Psychic," but I was still surprised by the turnout. Secretly, I had hoped that no one would come so I wouldn't have to do it at all—but no such luck.

"I *can't do it!*" I whined, skittishly approaching the two large doors as if they led to the gallows. I peered inside the cavernous room where the audience was beginning to fidget impatiently.

"I've only been channeling for a few years," I said to my girlfriend. "Maybe I don't know enough about angels yet! People traveled from out of town to be here. What if they think I'm *boring*? They're going to be *so disappointed*. What if I can't channel in front of a group? What if—"

Maria swiftly approached from behind and pushed me through the two large wooden doors. I literally stumbled into the small ballroom. I had to catch myself from hitting the floor. I turned to see the doors close silently behind me.

The room began to quiet down as people saw me standing motionless by the entrance, wide-eyed, flushed, and shaking so badly that I was convinced my legs would give out. I scratched at the hives that were blooming all over my face and neck, and felt sick to my stomach. It was beyond my ability to comprehend how some people really *liked* to speak in public. How I envied them!

It took no more than a few seconds before all eyes were focused in my direction. I regarded the audience with dread as if I were being confronted by an angry mob intent on lynching. Apart from some isolated whispering, there was an excruciating silence. With all the strength I could muster, I somehow put one foot in front of the other and made it to the front of the ballroom. I climbed the two stairs leading to the large stage platform and made my way to the lectern, clutching my precious note cards so tightly that my knuckles were white. My heart beat furiously, and my mouth was so dry I found it impossible to move my tongue. Then I realized I had forgotten to place a glass of water on the stage. The ballroom remained in a deathly hush as the audience stared up at me. I *knew* they could see me shaking.

I looked down at my index cards. As John suggested, I had prepared a speech that included a warm welcome and then a funny anecdote to help the audience relax. Unfortunately, in my case, it wasn't the audience who needed to relax. I decided to begin as quickly as I could, praying that once I launched into my material, the task at hand would get easier. Because of my nerves, I spoke in a speedy staccato that made me sound like a seasoned auctioneer at a Ft. Worth cattle sale.

"Uhhh—Hi—Hello—Good Evening—I'm Kim O'Neill—tonight—I want to welcome you—to my angel workshop—I'm so happy—to be able—to spend—this time—with you—here in Houston—isn't it—a beautiful—time of year—"

"Excuse me—" someone interrupted from the very back of the room. "Could you please speak up?"

Now I realized why the hotel's event planner had been unconvinced when I told her I didn't need a microphone. Oddly, the room didn't seem as big when it was empty.

"Sure! No problem." I answered loudly, before breaking into a nervous, high-pitched, hysterical giggle. The audience started to murmur. I had gotten through the welcome part of my introduction, but I knew I was much too terrified to attempt my clever opening joke. Instead, I decided to begin with a discussion of how angels communicate with human beings.

With shaking hands, I placed the tall stack of index cards on the sloping lectern. The pile of meticulously organized cards began to slowly slide, and I watched this happen as if it were occurring in slow motion— in much the same way as witnessing one's own serious traffic accident. I clumsily tried to catch them, but it was too late. They fell to the floor of the stage with a loud *slap* and scattered everywhere. All my notes! I couldn't conduct the seminar without them.

The audience watched as I hastily got down on my hands and knees to retrieve them, which wasn't an easy task dressed in my fitted navy blazer, tight skirt, and high heels. In the few harried, adrenaline-packed moments it took me to gather all the cards, I could hear someone whispering loudly, "What is she *doing?*" followed by the awful sound of muffled laughter.

As I tried to stand up, I realized that the left knee of my expensive Donna Karan pantyhose—which I trotted out only on special occasions—had been caught by a splinter on the floor of the stage. Still down on my hands and knees, I clutched the index cards with a death grip in one hand and tried to gently disengage the knee of my stocking with the other . . . but the sturdy silky fabric remained stubbornly attached to the floor. I had no choice but to give it a swift yank. There was a loud ripping noise as it tore away.

I stood back up—faced the audience with a huge hole in the knee of my stocking—and reluctantly took my place back at the podium. It felt like a bad dream. The evening was out of control, and I hadn't even started yet. This was *not* what I had planned.

To my further dismay, I discovered that the notes I had so painstakingly assembled were now all out of sequence. I had forgotten to number the cards! I frantically rifled through them, but I was so flustered that they no longer made any sense. It was like trying to decipher Egyptian hieroglyphics. Should I try to reorganize them while everyone watched? *What was I going to do?* With my overwhelming shyness, it was painfully obvious that I simply wasn't cut out for public speaking. This made television look easy! At least when I was a guest on a TV program, there was someone sitting across from me asking questions. Even if they were hostile, I wasn't all alone . . . with 143 people expecting me to be lucid, intelligent, and clever, while waxing poetic about the whole angelic realm. *Why am I here? I don't know anything! I have nothing to share with all of these people. What a waste of time for them—*

Kim . . . focus! John cried telepathically. *Anal moment! Anal moment! Ask for questions!*

But won't that seem strange? I queried back telepathically. *I haven't even started the lecture yet!*

No stranger than what you're doing. Ask for questions! DO IT NOW!

"ANY QUESTIONS?" I barked at the attendees like a Marine drill sergeant, causing many of them to jump in their seats, startled by my unexpected tone.

The audience was clearly taken aback. They looked at one another with obvious confusion. I surmised that this might be the first event that any of them had ever attended at which they were asked for questions from a speaker who hadn't even started speaking yet. Not knowing what else to do, I just stood there with a desperate, pleading expression.

I saw a lady's hand go up in the middle section of the audience. I nodded in her direction. She stood and smiled at me. She had dark hair, was beautifully groomed, and looked to be in her early forties.

"My name is Carolyn Grace, and I've been so excited about this seminar. I'm very happy to meet you," she said graciously, in a calm, modulated tone. "I've heard you on the radio, and I think you're terrific. Kim . . . did someone tell me that this is your first public speaking engagement?"

"Hard to believe, isn't it?" I responded, and everyone laughed. I was relieved now that the audience knew that this was my very first public speaking event. Some members of the audience were now smiling at me. I started to feel a tiny bit better.

I slapped my forehead with my left palm, feigned a confused expression, and quipped, "Even with my amazing psychic ability, I've never been able to figure out why I was kicked out of Toastmasters!"

The audience roared with laughter. I was so thankful to the pretty gal who had raised her hand. I didn't know why, but she seemed eerily familiar to me.

"I have a question about the direction my business will take this year," she ventured, when the laughter had died down.

A guardian angel appeared and told me, *I was hoping to get the chance to speak with her tonight. That's why I asked her to come! Okay . . . here's the lowdown . . .*

"Carolyn," I said, repeating verbatim what the angel was telling me. "You have a very important life's work. You are meant to be a shining light on this earthly plane, assisting people as they resolve issues in the present by healing from the past. Does this make sense to you?"

The lady beamed and responded, "I am a licensed psychotherapist with a specialty in the use of hypnosis. An amazing number of people, while in the trance state of hypnosis, move back into past life experiences during the age-regression segment of hypnosis. I have found that, in many instances, the source of a client's current challenges can be traced to traumas or struggles experienced in a previous life. When a person can heal the past, it can have a remarkable effect on the present."

I continued with her angelic information. "You have a guardian angel by the name of Martha, and she goes on to say that you will be authoring a number of books. You will also be speaking in front of big groups. She wants you to know that writing and speaking are two of your greatest gifts. What's more, you are very tolerant and non-judgmental. You're a wonderful therapist because you have a great deal of empathy for others—you help them triumph over adversity."

"Well, thank you very much!" she replied with a huge smile. "I already speak on a regular basis . . . and I've been sensing that I will write some books based on what I see in my practice. Kim, you're *very* good at what you do. I'm *so* glad I came tonight." With that lovely recognition, she nodded to me and resumed her seat.

Tears welled in my eyes, and I had to fight the impulse to run to where she was sitting and throw my arms around her. I was so grateful for her kind words! Martha was certainly right. The lady had apparently understood *my* pathetic struggling and hadn't hesitated to step up to the plate and provide a shining light for me. I guessed that she could be one of the guardian angels in human form that John was always talking about.

"Any other questions?" I tentatively asked the audience. All at once, half of the attendees eagerly raised their hands, and I spent the next three hours channeling for as many people as time would allow.

Toward the end of the evening, several of the angels referred to me as their "opening act" and told me that I needed to resolve "a couple of things" before they would consider hiring me on permanently to work in front of groups like this one. As I shared that with the audience, they laughed along with me . . . but I certainly recognized that I desperately needed help. I just wasn't sure what *kind*. I was such a terrible speaker and so miserably uncomfortable in front of an audience that I didn't know where to begin.

It was close to midnight when I finally got home from the seminar. I was exhausted from all the gut-wrenching stress, and I had scheduled early sessions the next morning, so I went straight to bed. I tossed and turned all night long, suffering terrible nightmares in which I was locked up in some kind of prison . . . cold and hungry . . . hunted like an animal . . . and threatened by big snarling dogs.

I woke up with a start—and then gasped upon seeing the shadowed silhouette of a man sitting on the end of my bed.

"It's only me," said a familiar voice.

"John . . . what a horrible night!" I sat up, smoothed the curly hair away from my face, and groped for the glasses on the nightstand. I was so nearsighted that I truly believed if it wasn't for "second sight" I wouldn't have any sight at all. I squinted toward the bedside clock. It was just after five. "I have a splitting headache," I complained, rubbing my forehead. "I had nightmares all night long that didn't make any sense."

"Yes, they did," responded John.

"*What?* How?"

"As you discovered long ago, dreams occur to convey necessary information. With the exception of those reflecting mental fears and concerns, dreams not only spotlight the present and future—like all the clairvoyant images you receive so frequently—but also provide awareness about the *past.*"

"The *past?*" I repeated dumbly. I was never at my best first thing in the morning.

"After witnessing what happened last night at the seminar, and then being privy to the dreams that followed in the wee hours, I'd say that you're in dire need of some work involving—"

"—I *told* you that I needed some kind of classes! You never listen to me. Last night was so humiliating. I'm just not cut out to speak in public. We're *not* all Winston Churchill."

"If I hadn't put the thought in Maria's head and you weren't pushed, you'd still be pacing in the hotel corridor," said John, trying to suppress a smile.

"I should have known that you were responsible! Why can't I simply channel for people in my office and conduct my life's work without speaking? Is it the end of the world if I don't do it?"

"Actually, yes. You planned for speaking to be an integral part of your life's work to allow you to interact with many more individuals than you ever could in your office. And, at the same time, it's going to be therapeutic and allow you to conduct some very necessary healing."

"Healing? I still have healing to do? From what? My marriage? The advertising agency? My childhood?" I was puzzled because I thought I had finished with all that work.

"No. You have some healing to attend to from the traumas you experienced in your last lifetime."

"You're joking!"

"Hardly. And I would recommend that you hop to it so you don't have another repeat of what happened last night. What you're experiencing is much more serious than a simple case of stage fright. A part of you is still locked in the past. Your subconscious is unable and unwilling to face the challenges and adversity you are encountering in the present. You must retrace your steps and go back to find the key. Your whole future depends on it."

"*Huh?*"

"You must retrace your steps by revisiting the life you had on earth before this one," John explained patiently. "You must return to Germany in 1944. All the answers to your current challenges will be there waiting for you."

"What? I was in *Germany* in 1944? That was during World War II." The goose bumps sensation washed over me like a torrent of electrical energy, but this time it felt like a dire warning of some kind. "I have to go back there? How the hell do I do *that?*"

"Past-life regression therapy conducted through hypnosis."

"*Hypnosis?* I'm not going to do that!" I chortled. "I've seen hypnosis on TV. I saw a guy on a talk show make people from the audience act like they were drunk. They barked like dogs and danced all over the stage like ballerinas. How is *that* going to help me?"

"I assure you," John explained with a long suffering sigh, "that there are many different ways to conduct hypnosis. How would you like your channeling practice to be compared to a Madame-Lagonga-type psychic who sells magic potions and demands thousands of dollars to bury packets of animal by-products to ensure good fortune?"

"I see your point. But if I'm hypnotized back to a past lifetime, could I get *stuck* in World War II? What if I can't come back?"

"That's an impossibility. What you'll be doing through the process of regression therapy is exploring the *memories* of a past life . . . stored within your soul."

"Hypnosis can allow me to review my own spiritual photo album?"

"In so many words, yes."

"Can't *anything* in my life ever be *simple*? Are you sure I can't just take public speaking classes?"

"When you planned your destiny for this lifetime, you obviously didn't have 'simple' in mind. One of your objectives was to fully heal from the trauma you experienced in that past life."

"I was traumatized?"

"Yes, you were. A great many souls were traumatized during that period."

"Can't you just *tell* me about it—describe it to me—and I could heal that way?"

"It won't work unless *you* go back and see it for yourself."

"So . . . how long will this take? How much hypnosis will I need to go back and . . . see things?"

"I'm guessing that you'll be successful in one or two sessions."

"Oh! Then it's not going to be a long, drawn-out ordeal?"

"No, indeed. And I'll be right by your side."

I was quiet for a moment. "But, John, where will I find someone who can help me go back in time?"

John smiled at me. Suddenly, in my mind's eye, I was back at the seminar providing channeled information to the lady in the audience who was the first one to ask a question. *What was her name?*

"Carolyn Grace," John answered, reading my thoughts.

"But won't she think I'm nuts to want to return to 1944?"

"Are you falling back into an issue you've already resolved?"

"What do you mean?"

"Caring about other people's approval. Don't you remember what you shared with Ms. Grace last night? I assure you, she will not think that you are 'nuts.' At least . . . not in that regard," said John, clearly amused.

"I can't believe you're talking me into this," I agreed reluctantly. "Will it really help make speaking easier for me?"

"Immeasurably. I recommend that you call her as soon as you get to the office this morning. She's going to have a cancellation for next Thursday. I want you to have that appointment."

I didn't need any more convincing. Later that morning I left a message at Carolyn Grace's office, and she called back, penciling me in for a session the following week. She had sensed the evening before that the universe had deliberately intended us to meet so that we could offer assistance to one another. When she disclosed that I seemed very familiar to her, I told her that I had felt the same way. It had to be destiny.

Chapter 18

Reliving the Holocaust

I arrived at Carolyn Grace's high–rise Galleria office a little early, checked in with her secretary, and took a seat in the reception area. Soft music was playing, and a small bubbling fountain sat on an end table in a corner of the room. It was a very hushed, soothing environment, but I found it hard to contain my restless energy. I had absolutely no clue about what to expect because I had never been exposed to hypnosis before, nor did I know anyone who had. Was it really going to help me with my public speaking? I figured that it couldn't make it any *worse*. But what if I couldn't be hypnotized? Could she really help me go back to Germany in 1944? What if I saw something scary or negative? How was that going to help me heal? If I was frightened by looking into the past, wouldn't that create even more healing that I'd have to do? Consumed with second thoughts about the appointment, I distractedly flipped through all the magazines on the coffee table.

Fifteen minutes later, the door to the inner office opened abruptly, and a young woman in her twenties gave me a shy nod as she hurried out of the suite. Carolyn Grace then appeared and with a warm welcome invited me to follow her into the large inner office. She closed the door behind us and offered me a seat on the couch as she settled into an armchair nearby.

I took a quick, tentative look around and discovered that she, like me, did not believe in the decorating philosophy *less is more*. Although her furniture was rather formal, she had created an inviting cocoon that was extraordinarily comfortable. Soothing music was playing. Books, photographs, and whimsical objects lined all of her bookshelves, diplomas shared wall space with beautifully framed prints, and a huge giraffe held court in a corner. Natural light filtered in from the windows that lined the far wall, and from the vantage point of her fourth floor office, one could see lush green treetops swaying in the soft fall breeze. It was like visiting a very luxurious tree house.

"I enjoyed your seminar," she said kindly. "Tell me why you're here. How can I help you?"

"I'm really nervous," I stammered.

"Yes, I can see that," she responded gently. "Confronting fear can be like jumping off a cliff into the unknown. You don't know what you're going to encounter until you've taken that first leap of faith."

"Well . . . I'm not sure how this process works," I shared with her uneasily. "I need to do some healing work to help with my public speaking."

"Speaking in front of a room full of people isn't easy, is it?"

"It's the most difficult thing I've ever done."

"Kim, rather than focusing on a more conventional approach to your therapy, I've been sensing that we might want to consider hypnosis. How do you feel about that?"

"That's *exactly* what I want," I answered assertively, looking at my watch. "We have forty-five minutes. Is that enough time for you to get me back to 1944?"

"Excuse me?" she responded with a chuckle. "That's not quite how this works. However, with your psychic ability and your knowledge of a specific period in which you experienced trauma, your age regression may be a more brief process than it is for other people."

"Something happened in my last lifetime that was so troubling that it is affecting me now with my public speaking. If you can get me back there, maybe I can see what it was . . . and then I'd be able to confront it."

Carolyn didn't waste time asking how or why I knew that. I guessed that after I made the appointment the previous week, she had been intuitively guided by her own angels to suggest hypnosis as the best way to facilitate my stroll down spiritual memory lane.

"Well, then, if you're ready, I suppose we'd better begin," she said with a smile. "I'll tape the session for you. Might I suggest that you lie down?"

I kicked my shoes off and awkwardly stretched out. I felt uncomfortable lying down on a sofa in a business office. I wondered what would happen next. I tried to picture what my clients would do if I suggested they repose on a couch for a channeling session.

Carolyn put a tape into her recorder and depressed the button. My first encounter with hypnosis was about to begin. She started to speak in the most soothing, modulated, melodic voice I had ever heard.

"All right . . . I want you to just look above your head at the ceiling. Find a place somewhere up there where you can keep your eyes focused. Take a series of really slow deep breaths . . . fill your lungs all the way up . . . and hold it . . . hold it . . . and then let it go . . . very slowly."

I did as she directed. It made a surprising difference. I hadn't realized that my physical body was so tense.

"That's right . . . fill your lungs up all the way . . . and then release . . . just as slowly."

As I concentrated on breathing, my apprehension disappeared. I started to relax. In fact, the sound of her voice was so tranquil that I had to suppress a yawn.

"One more time now . . . breathe in . . . very slowly . . . and now . . . slowly release. Just let your eyes close . . . now that they're blinking."

I found myself actually getting sleepy. Normally, I could never nap during the day, no matter how tired I was. I was now very comfortably stretched out on her sofa. It felt like the most natural thing in the world.

"That's right . . . .close your eyes," she suggested in a soothing whisper. "And now . . . with your eyes closed . . . slow your breath down twice as much as it was before. Inhaling . . . and as you inhale . . . you're bringing in relaxation. Do it very slowly . . . hold it . . . that's right, Kim."

I modulated my breathing. Slowly inhaling . . . and exhaling. Inhaling . . . and exhaling. Inhaling . . . and exhaling.

"Give your body the message that it's okay to release and relax . . . and just let go. Releasing and relaxing . . . allowing your breath to bring in relaxation. And then allowing your breath to release all of the tension . . . and stress . . . of this day."

Already, the hypnosis was accomplishing what I would have considered impossible . . . I felt a complete and total level of relaxation for the first time in my life. I had let go of my anxiety, and an inner peace began to wash over me.

"And now I want you to imagine yourself out in the countryside . . . there's an old house sitting on top of a gently sloping hillside. Do you see it?"

I silently nodded. I envisioned an old farmhouse with open windows and curtains blowing in the light breeze of a summer afternoon.

"Make your way to the back side of this house. There's a long open porch running the full length of the home. Imagine yourself on this porch. Take in the feeling of peacefulness . . . the feeling of relaxation . . . the feeling of gentle warmth."

I loved standing on the porch that I was seeing in my mind's eye. It was as if I were really there! I could feel a light, caressing breeze that carried the captivating scent of blooming flowers, fresh-mowed grass, and the promise of long, lazy summer days.

"Notice that at the bottom of this hillside there is a meadow. And notice how inviting . . . and safe . . . and relaxing . . . this meadow is. When you reach the bottom of the hillside . . . in a few minutes . . . and you arrive in this meadow . . . you will find yourself in a deep . . . safe . . . state of total relaxation."

Now smiling, I hung on Carolyn's every word as I stood on the rough-hewn timbers of the porch, gazing down at the bountiful meadow.

"And as you stand in the middle of the porch, I want you to become aware that there are a set of steps going down. Do you see them?"

I silently nodded, affirming the existence of the stairs in my mind's eye.

"Good. In a moment I'm going to count from *ten* down to *one*. As I do . . . I want you to begin to make your way down this hillside. Making your way closer . . . and closer . . . to the bottom as I count back. And when I get to *one* . . . you'll be all the way down in the peaceful, relaxing meadow . . . with its trees . . . and shade . . . and wild flowers. And when you are in this meadow, you will be in a total, deep, safe state of relaxation."

I nodded again.

"Good. Now I'm going to begin to count. *Ten* . . . just starting to make your way down the steps . . . easily and gently. With each step you take, finding your body becoming more . . . and more . . . relaxed. Moving on down the stairs."

I could easily visualize my descent.

"*Nine* . . . *eight* . . . you're going deeper . . . and deeper . . . into relaxation . . . into calm. *Seven* . . . *six* . . . *five* . . . you're half way there now. Moving down . . . calm . . . feeling your body getting heavy with relaxation . . . letting go."

With each step I took, I reached a deeper level of inner peace.

"*Four* . . . *three* . . . moving down. *Two* . . . getting closer and closer to a total deep, safe state . . . in your body and in your mind. Feel your body so heavy now. Feel your muscles loose like noodles. Releasing . . . and relaxing . . . and just letting go. And, finally . . . *one*. Moving on off into this meadow. Now . . . what do you see?"

Suddenly, the peaceful meadow disappeared and I could no longer hear Carolyn's soothing, reassuring voice. All at once, I was at the center of a dark, swirling vortex of energy, as if I had been sucked headlong into a raging tornado. Muffled, unfamiliar sounds in the distance were getting louder and coming closer. In no more than a few moments, the swirling energy abruptly stopped, and I felt my physical body violently jump like it did sometimes when I slept. I had traveled to another place . . . and to another time. I was no longer Kim O'Neill . . . and I was no longer in my current lifetime.

I was an inmate of Bergen–Belsen Concentration Camp. My name was Sabine, and I was eight years old. I wore a filthy, striped cotton shift that was far too big for me, and I shivered with cold . . . and fear . . . and hunger. I was on my stomach, unseen, huddling under a cot in the corner of the big, dimly–lit medical facility. The building stank of human waste, blood, decay, and death. Since my arrival several months before, my large dark eyes had become hollow from starvation; and I was haunted by the spectacle of horrific medical experiments conducted on a succession of small children who had been ripped from the arms of their parents—and forced into this desolate place where hope and faith did not exist.

The double front doors to the medical barracks burst open and two soldiers hurried inside, letting in a blast of frigid air. The doors swung shut behind them as they laughingly brushed snowflakes off their heavy woolen overcoats. They remained just inside the doorway for a few minutes, talking and sharing a cigarette.

There was a sudden commotion on the other side of the room. From my vantage point under the cot, I could see a redheaded little boy being lifted onto the surgical table. He spoke loudly in a language I did not understand, obviously pleading to be left alone. The boy was naked, and I could see him struggling with the orderly who was attempting to hold him down. The camp doctor approached, carrying his large tray of steel instruments. He set the tray down and began to examine his new patient. I turned away and covered my ears, but nothing could drown out the sound of the boy's piercing screams and the doctor's voice shouting in German. As the boy continued to shriek—and it seemed to go on forever—I prayed that he would die quickly. And then, finally . . . as always . . . the pitiful screams were followed by deathly silence. Mercifully, the child struggled no more.

I knew that in a few hours, or in a few days, the mangled, lifeless body of the redheaded little boy would be carried out—like a piece of rotting garbage—and casually thrown onto the pile of decomposing corpses in the large pit at the rear of the barracks.

As an inmate of the Nazi extermination camp, I had become accustomed to hearing the tortured cries of many girls and boys. I instinctively knew that my time would come, too; but like a trapped animal, I discovered that I could delay the inevitable by hiding as best I could. I had learned *not to speak*, or cry out, or try to escape, or do anything that would call attention to me. I quickly understood that there was no place to run to, and that there were no adults who could—or would—protect me. No one was going to come to my rescue. I was completely on my own.

To survive, I had to hide . . . *disappear* . . . so that the camp doctor wouldn't notice me. I lived in dread of the inevitable moment when it would be *my* turn, when he would point his finger at me and I would be stripped by the orderly and lifted onto the tall table . . . held down . . . and then he would approach carrying his tray, and I would suffer helplessly like all of the previous victims of his gruesome medical experiments.

There were times when I thought I couldn't bear any more and my heart would beat so fast from fear that I thought it would explode. I learned to remove myself from what was happening by pretending to be back home in France, before the war . . . and before the Germans came.

My mother, father, and I lived in a small farmhouse just outside a beautiful forest. We observed the Sabbath every Friday night at dusk, and I found it comforting to remember how my mother would carefully place the veil over her dark hair, light a candle, and say prayers as she swept her hands in a circular motion. Then we would eat dinner, as my Papa told stories that always made me laugh. My Papa and I were very close, and I was immensely proud of him. In the village, it became common knowledge that he had joined the French Resistance, and he was highly respected for his bravery. Unlike many others, he was taking a stand against the Nazis. One day, he failed to come home. He seemed to vanish into thin air. I *knew* something had happened to him. I was certain he would never willingly leave my mother and me. As the family of a well-known Resistance fighter, we were left completely vulnerable and unprotected.

The Nazis were storming toward our little town, and my mother was terrified about what they might do to us. We were Jews, and they didn't like us for reasons that I couldn't understand.

One day, German soldiers banged at the door. My mother hid in the attic after telling me to let them in and explain that everyone in the family—but me—had already gone. Wide-eyed and shaking, I did what she asked. The Nazis rushed past me and started to ransack the house. One of the soldiers dragged me to the waiting truck and threw me into the back along with others from the village. Another soldier drove us to the train station where we were herded into a boxcar.

Men, women, and children were squeezed in so tightly that, in order to rest, we had to lay down in shifts. Some were old and sick, and one lady actually died right after we pulled out of the station. We were given no food or water, nor did the train ever stop. Day turned into night . . . and night turned into day . . . and day tuned into night . . . and still, we continued on our journey. The other children, accompanied by their parents, endlessly asked, "Where are we going? When are we going to get there? Why couldn't I bring my dolly? I want to go back for her. I'm hungry! Why can't I have some milk? I have to go to the bathroom. Why can't we stop? I feel sick from all the motion . . . "

To quiet the children, mothers sang lullabies, and I pretended that I could hear my Papa's voice singing to me, as well. None of us knew where we were headed, although the grownups prayed we were being sent to a labor camp—rather than destined for any of the Nazi extermination facilities that we had heard about. Since I could remember, there had been stories that circulated, always in whispered tones, about the hideous atrocities being inflicted upon Jews in the German and Polish camps. The stories were so unbelievable that many of the grownups speculated that they were nothing more than exaggerated rumors.

The train finally started to slow down, and then it came to an abrupt halt. Gasps could be heard from the grownups who peered from the slats of the boxcar. "We're at Bergen–Belsen. They've taken us to Germany! We're all going to die!"

Everyone began to cry and pray. Moments later, the big doors lurched open and we were blinded by the huge floodlights. The scene was pandemonium. Soldiers screamed at everyone to get off the train, and when they didn't do so fast enough, the Nazis climbed aboard and began to throw people from the cars. Thousands of people were everywhere. The noise was ear–splitting. Huge, snarling German shepherds were leashed, but the soldiers allowed them to maul anyone they chose, including children and old people. I was lifted from the train by a kind man who had ridden in the same boxcar. He gently placed me on the platform . . . and disappeared. I was left there all alone—more frightened than I had ever been in my life. My eyes began to water from all the smoke in the air . . . it carried an awful, permeating smell.

All of the people who had just gotten off the train were directed to stand in a line. The first line was made up of healthy men, women, and teenagers. The second line consisted of pregnant women, women with small children, old people, and the sick or injured.

A soldier shoved me into a small group of children who stood apart from everyone else. I saw that many of them were twins. We were quickly herded into the medical infirmary where we were stripped, showered, given a thin, dirty, striped uniform meant for a grownup, and each assigned a small cot. We were then handed a small crust of bread and some thin, watery soup.

In rapid succession, each child met his cruel fate at the hands of the doctor on the surgical table. I witnessed it all. As the days unfolded into weeks, I mustered the courage to remain alive by fantasizing that my parents were going to come and get me, and I prayed that we would return to our happy life in France.

As I daydreamed about life before the war, I was spied hiding under the cot. Someone was suddenly grabbing me by the arm! I was being pulled out from my hiding place! It was the orderly. He roughly yanked me to my feet and shoved me toward the table where the redheaded boy had been a short time before. His body was gone, but the table was still covered in a sheet saturated with his blood. The orderly gestured for me to remove my over-sized striped uniform. Instead, I glared at him and screamed at the top of my lungs. Outraged by my disobedience, he attempted to tear off the ragged garment, but like a cornered animal, I fought ferociously with strength far beyond my weakened physical state.

The doctor approached with his tray and saw what was happening. He scowled at the disturbance I was causing, and he tersely yelled at his assistant. The orderly abruptly let me go. I stood absolutely still, my chest heaving from the exertion and fear, as I stared up at the doctor with unmasked hatred.

He calmly placed his tray on the surgical table and then reached for the pistol at his hip. Smiling, he held it in front of my face. I didn't flinch. I had already seen so much death that I accepted what lay in store for me. I quickly decided that it would be much less painful to be shot where I stood than surrender to being brutalized with his razor-sharp instruments. *I was not going to get on that table.*

The doctor was still smiling, and I could tell that he enjoyed playing with me—much the same way a rat greedily toys with a scrap of food right before he devours it. Never taking his eyes from mine, he pulled back the hammer. I had nothing more to lose; in open rebellion, I spat on one of his shiny black boots and defiantly looked back at him.

Without hesitation, he placed the cold steel barrel against my forehead. I kept my eyes on his. He pulled the trigger. There was a loud *click!* but nothing else happened. He frowned and looked at the gun. He pulled the hammer back again and placed the end of the barrel to my forehead. He pulled the trigger . . . there was a loud *click!* but it still failed to fire. In a fury, he viciously slapped my face, knocking me to the ground. He threw the gun at me and shouted something in German to the orderly. Then they both strode away.

I couldn't believe my good fortune! I scurried to find another hiding place. Without making a sound, I rolled under another cot in the back of the room. On my tummy, I huddled against the wall. I wanted to make myself *invisible.*

Right next to where I hid, my eyes fell upon a large, frayed calendar page that had been discarded, featuring a photograph of a blonde, blue-eyed, cherubic little boy with a milk-white complexion made ruddy from playing outdoors in the brisk, Teutonic winter. The calendar read November, 1944.

Moments later, I saw the orderly assisting another girl—obviously more compliant than I—to the surgical table. The girl and her twin sister had just arrived at the infirmary the day before, and they spoke a language I couldn't understand. The girl obediently took off her uniform and allowed the orderly to lift her onto the big, filthy table. I wanted to shout *NO! GET DOWN! REFUSE TO LET THEM HURT YOU!* But I was too afraid to let out a sound.

My heart began to pound as I watched the doctor approach and set about arranging his steel instruments for the surgery. The girl's eyes widened with alarm when she saw the medical tools. Tears flowed from the corners of her eyes, but she remained absolutely still. Once his tools were organized, the doctor began to examine the girl's abdomen, all the while reassuring her in a tender, fatherly tone that I had heard many times before. He nodded toward the orderly, who grabbed the girl's arms and held them down.

I quickly turned my head and covered my ears. Seconds later, the girl began to shriek so loudly that I was certain the inmates from outside *must* have been able to hear her. I couldn't imagine why all the grownups who lived at Bergen–Belsen ignored the screaming children in the medical barracks. *Why didn't anyone ever come? Did no one care? Where was my Papa? Why was God allowing this to happen?*

I came out of the hypnosis with a start. I sat up, feeling incredibly dizzy and discombobulated.

"You might want to be still for just a minute," Carolyn Grace softly suggested.

I was so overcome that I burst into wrenching, uncontrollable sobs. I was grieving for my lost childhood and the horrible cruelty I had been forced to witness. I had endured the degradation of living like an animal in a place where human life had no value, and where the ongoing struggle to survive was a minute-by-minute ordeal. I had waited in desperation to be rescued by parents who would never come to save me.

By returning to the past, I experienced what it was like to be persecuted for who I was and what I believed in. How many countless people fueled the holocaust by standing by and *allowing* it? How could people know what was going on and make the conscious choice to sit by and do *nothing* to stop it? What about all the innocent children, like me—and the little girl—and the redheaded boy—and the others who suffered untold agonies?

"Is there some connection between these memories that you've just reclaimed and your reactions and decisions in this present life?" Carolyn asked quietly.

I suddenly realized why I had always sought other peoples' approval in my current lifetime. The approval issue emerged during World War II when I learned that it was crucial to one's *survival* to be approved of and accepted. If someone was outside the acceptable norm—like being Jewish at the time of the Third Reich—to *be seen* . . . meant certain death. That's why I was so afraid of public speaking! I would be *seen* by others when I got on the stage. That fear had been hardwired inside of me . . . until now. I started to cry again.

Carolyn waited patiently all the while I sobbed. I was embarrassed to discover that I had used her whole box of Kleenex.

"No worries," she said with a little smile.

I sat very still, looking down at the wet tissue I was holding. "It was so terrible, I don't know where to begin." I felt numb and shell-shocked.

"Do you think that you revisited a past life?"

"Oh, yes."

"Was it the one you wanted to visit? Did you return to 1944?"

I nodded mournfully.

"How do you know?"

"I saw a page of a calendar: November, 1944. I saw . . . I saw . . . " I couldn't go on. I started to cry again.

"Do you know what part of the world you were in?" inquired Carolyn.

"Germany."

"Were you male or female?"

"I was a little girl. I had brown eyes . . . and dark, curly hair. I was eight years old. I was Jewish."

"Were you . . . in hiding?"

"Yes . . . but not in the way that you mean. I was locked up in the medical infirmary of Bergen–Belsen Concentration Camp. The doctor was conducting medical experiments on children. I stayed alive by hiding so he couldn't find me . . . I was hoping he would forget I was there. There were so *many* children."

"I'm sorry," replied Carolyn in a small voice.

I nodded, still looking at the wet tissue.

"How did you survive?" she inquired. "What did you have to eat?"

"Very stale bread and some kind of thin, watery soup. I remember how hungry I was. I was starving."

"Did the doctor conduct experiments on you?"

"Not that I know of. He tried, but I wouldn't let him."

"I beg your pardon?" she asked, brow furrowed. "Did I understand you correctly? You were an eight-year-old little girl, and you wouldn't '*let him*'?"

"It's true," I said. "He put a gun to my head and I still wouldn't do it. Then I spat at him."

"You did *what*?"

I chuckled through my tears. "My papa had taught me to speak up for myself and not allow anyone to bully me."

"Kim, I think that referring to the Medical Commandant of a Nazi concentration camp in World War II as a 'bully' is redefining the word."

I chuckled again. "You know, when I went back, I learned that my father had been a very courageous man. He became a member of the French Resistance." I took a deep breath; then I shared the whole story of what I had seen when I returned to 1944. When I finished, Carolyn and I sat in silence for a few minutes.

"So now it's easy to understand why you were so reluctant to speak in public—to have attention focused on you," observed Carolyn. "When that happened at Bergen–Belsen, it meant certain death."

"When I was going to speak last Thursday at my seminar, my heart was pounding . . . I was shaking . . . and I experienced the exact same physical sensations that I did when I was terrified of being singled out in the concentration camp."

"The soul has a very clear, distinct memory," the therapist stated. "It records everything that occurs in each of your earthly lives. All of your experiences are there, like a giant computer file, just waiting to be tapped. You can retrace your steps to understand why you have certain fears and phobias; and, at the same time, you can go back and obtain insight into your gifts, talents, and abilities."

"You're saying that each individual is a spiritual composite of all of his past lives?"

"Exactly. The more we learn about who we've *been*, the more we can understand about who we are *now*. I've conducted hypnotherapy for other individuals who have discovered that they experienced the holocaust."

"*Really?* There are others like me?"

"Yes," she nodded somberly.

"Do they have challenges as great as mine?"

"Some people have come into this lifetime with holocaust issues so debilitating that they have a hard time *functioning*."

"Oh," was all I could respond. Carolyn's statement reminded me of one of my channeling clients who was so afraid of flying that nothing on earth would get her *near* an airplane. She lost out on some wonderful opportunities to travel because she simply refused to fly.

Then I thought of the seminar I had conducted the week before that

I had considered such a disaster. I had to admit that although I was scared to death, I *was* able to plan the event. And I *was* able to get myself there. With a little help from Maria and John, I *was* able to find my way, however clumsily, onto the stage. I *was* able to speak, however badly. And, most importantly, I *had* been able to channel. So perhaps my predicament wasn't as bad as I thought. Although I was terrified when I had to face the audience, I had chosen to move forward in spite of it. My thoughts then turned to Sabine. She fought the Nazis—as an eight-year-old little girl! That made my current challenges pale by comparison. It occurred to me that if I had the same soul as I did when I was Sabine, then I must have the identical strength and courage in this lifetime, too. I quickly decided that, in the future, when I was confronted by something that I believed to be too much to handle, all I had to do was remember Sabine, and I'd have an instant reality check.

"Courage is being scared to death and saddling up anyway," shared Carolyn, as if reading my mind.

"Who said that . . . George Washington?"

"John Wayne," she answered, with a twinkle in her eye.

"I *am* feeling better," I realized. "I'm so proud of what I did as that little girl. I want to review what I saw and think more about it."

"You should," Carolyn advised. "And now, because you have the tape from our session, you can go back any time you wish and revisit your life as Sabine—or continue the process by investigating any other past life you choose. You've probably had thousands of prior incarnations on this earthly plane. There are times when an individual has to look *back* before he can see the present and future more clearly."

"I wonder how many other past life traumas are derailing my forward movement?" I asked, my head swimming with questions about my spiritual history. Before the session, I had hoped that hypnosis might allow me to begin taking a few timid baby steps toward a better understanding of why I had such a problem with public speaking. Instead, I found myself catapulted into a brand new level of self-awareness and enlightenment. I felt myself letting go of the need for other peoples' approval. Carolyn Grace had initiated the first glimpse inside my soul, and I was wildly curious to explore what other mysteries it could reveal . . . about me.

Chapter 19

Occupational Hazards

Five years had passed since I had left Advertising & Design, Inc. My channeling practice had become increasingly secure and established, in large part due to my weekly radio gig, local television appearances, and hosting of the monthly seminars. I had also begun to receive numerous referrals from existing clients, for which I was very appreciative. I had moved to a nicer building with a first-floor office suite with a large reception area, a separate room for all my filing cabinets and office equipment, and a good-sized inner office with windows that offered a view of the small park across the street.

Like most people in any profession, I was often faced with occupational hazards that were unique to my business. Following all the exposure on radio and television, the tables turned unexpectedly, and now it was a host of strangers who would approach *me* in public places and say, "You're Kim O'Neill . . . the psychic! Can I just ask you one question?"

It was not uncommon for me to get requests for channeled information while getting my teeth cleaned, working out at the gym, or shopping. People even made requests in the ladies' room of restaurants, on the street, in elevators, and even in the same grocery store where, years before, the sick woman had run away from me.

On a Friday in October, I underwent a lengthy gum surgery that required general anesthesia because I needed some deep tissue grafts. After the procedure was finished, I remained quite woozy and terribly sore because of the extensive number of stitches in my gum. There was a big, gaping hole in the roof of my mouth where the surgeon had harvested the necessary tissue for the grafts. My mouth was raw, throbbing, and quite bloody, and I remained hooked up to a machine that was monitoring my vital signs. Suddenly, a young nurse wheeled her small chair up to where I lay, bent down, and stared into my eyes. After a few moments, she placed her hand gently on my arm and softly inquired, "Are you Kim O'Neill . . . the psychic?" I nodded groggily. She looked around to make sure no one was listening, leaned down and whispered, "Then, could I just ask you one psychic question?"

When I returned to the office the following Monday after the surgery, I sat behind my desk preparing for what I knew was going to be a rigorous day of channeling sessions. First, I was going to conduct a reading for an astronaut who was training for an upcoming shuttle mission; then I was going to provide information to the family of a murder victim in the hopes of helping the investigation; and the next client was an aggressive female criminal defense attorney who was going to inquire about the nefarious activities of *her* colorful clients. After a short lunch, I was going to act as a medical intuitive, providing patient diagnostics for a doctor with a thriving practice in the medical center; and my last channeling client was the owner of an oil company who wanted me to provide specific numbers relating to energy stocks.

My girlfriend Maria had graciously volunteered to work my first day back from the surgery to assist with secretarial work. She knocked lightly on the doorframe, and I waved her in. She entered carrying a tablet and a pen and a cup of the cinnamon coffee that she had brewed. With her hip, she closed the door behind her, placed the steaming mug in front of me, and took a seat in one of the leather chairs that flanked my desk. Maria was frowning, and the day hadn't even started yet. Without wasting any time, she launched into an impromptu meeting holding pen to paper.

"Kim . . . a woman from San Antonio called last night and left a message asking if you sacrifice chickens as part of the psychic services you provide. When I call her back, what do you want me to tell her?"

"Tell her only on Fridays—during a full moon—that is, if I have any time left after I've finished sacrificing all of the goats."

Maria stared at me blankly. She was not amused.

"You're kidding me, right?" I asked her.

She pursed her lips and slowly shook her head to the contrary. I wondered if Maria wished that she had pitched in for a girlfriend who was a CPA.

"Animal *sacrificing?*" I was incredulous. "Why are so many people calling and asking about that cockamamie stuff? Curses, magic potions, blessed rice, prayer candles with supernatural powers, burying packets of animal by-products to ensure good fortune—"

"I keep *telling* you that you're missing the boat as an entrepreneur," she responded wryly. "The armoire in the reception area would make a big, impressive display cabinet, stocking all sorts of goodies that you could swear have special woo-woo powers."

"Perfect to impress my conservative clients," I said. "And members of the media when they visit the office."

"You could sell a liquid curse-remover—that could also be used to take stains out of carpets," she suggested, now smiling. "Or you could offer magic packets of herbs, like garlic powder, specially formulated to ward off evil spirits—that could also be used to make a great pasta sauce."

"Go ahead and laugh," I told her. "But you'd be amazed at how many people are convinced that all of their problems are a direct result of a curse that somebody has placed on them. I hear it over and over from people who find themselves taken in by that kind of senseless baloney. I can only imagine how much money folks waste on useless junk that they're manipulated into buying."

"I think some of the psychic hotlines promote those things."

"But when phony psychics *do* manage to provide some information that *is* on target," I lamented, "they start building credibility with the poor schlemiels who want to believe in them. I've heard of people spending thousands of dollars for some of that stuff."

"There was a woman operating in the southwest part of town that advertised readings for five dollars," shared Maria. "My friend Stella visited her once, just for fun."

"What happened?" I inquired.

"Well, Stella is no dumbbell—did I ever tell you that she is a tenured college professor?"

I shook my head.

"From the get-go, she assumed that this psychic was a fraud. After all, how could anyone remain in business doing readings for *five dollars?*"

"Why did Stella go to her if she thought she might be a fraud?"

"I don't know—she was bored, I guess . . . wanted something different to do. Even though she was broke, she knew she could scrape five bucks together."

I rolled my eyes and took a careful sip of coffee. My mouth was still sore from all the stitches.

"But the moment Stella sat down, the woman was able to tell her things that she couldn't possibly have known, proving that she *was* psychic. Then, after a few minutes, she got all excited, and she told Stella that she could "see" an old curse that was interfering with her abundance. The psychic explained that although Stella had a good job, the curse would ensure that she'd always have money problems."

"Stella didn't believe that, did she?"

"The psychic told her that the curse could be removed but only if Stella returned the next day with four thousand dollars. The woman told her that she needed to place the money in a special bag and then bury it in her backyard under a statue of the Holy Virgin."

"But if Stella was having so many money problems, where did the woman think she was going to get the four thousand?"

"The psychic told her to get an advance on one of her credit cards or borrow from a family member. The woman advised Stella that in order to start attracting more money . . . she had to spend more money."

"*What?* That's absurd!"

"So Stella knew she was a con artist and figured that a lot of other people had been cheated by her, too. Stella went to the police, but when they arrived at the woman's home the next day, she had disappeared."

"That really makes me angry!" I said, truly upset. "So this woman undoubtedly took a lot of other people's hard-earned money with her when she went on the lam. She'll set up someplace else and start stealing all over again. Con artists like her are the reason that psychics and channels are looked upon with so much suspicion."

"There are unscrupulous people in *every* profession," Maria reminded me. "Mechanics, attorneys, physicians, CPA's—"

"I *know*. It's just that I worry about people being swindled by the con artists who claim to be in *my* profession. The public needs to be informed, or educated, in some way."

"You could give people tips on how to find a reputable psychic tomorrow when you're on the radio."

"I've offered to do that several times, but the DJ prefers that I take calls from listeners."

"Then why don't you write a book?" offered Maria. "You were an advertising copywriter . . . how hard could it be?"

"Are you *kidding?* Do you know how many angel books are already on the shelves?"

"Have you read any of them?"

"I've seen a couple," I answered sheepishly.

"You should read what other people have written," she advised. "I think you could add something to what's available out there. You don't have to think of your book as better or worse . . . just different."

Maria looked at me with a secret smile, and I knew *exactly* what she was thinking. Just a few weeks before, I had gone to a large New Age conference that featured a number of lectures and workshops conducted by authors of metaphysical-type books. I had never seen another channel at work, so I registered to attend a lecture hosted by a man who had become well-known in the field.

I arrived early and sat in the first row of seats. A few minutes later, a young woman sat directly to my right, which I thought a little strange considering that we were the only two people in the huge meeting room. I smiled at her and she nodded back at me. She held a spiral-bound notebook on her lap. She flipped to the first page and began to review what was written there. A man who looked surprisingly disheveled approached her. His hair was uncombed, and he wore a wrinkled shirt and a rumpled pair of pants. He looked like someone who had climbed out of bed several days before and hadn't bothered to shower or shave since. I couldn't help but hear their whispered conversation.

"Are you all ready?" he asked.

"Yes," she answered.

"You sure you can read my writing?"

"We've been over and over this," she replied in a lecturing tone.

"Do you know what to do?"

"*Yes*," she hissed. "*Hello!* I think it's pretty simple! Whaddya think . . . I'm *stupid?*" It was clear that she thought he was micromanaging.

The man hurried away. The gal sitting next to me took one last glance at her notes and then put them aside for a paperback romance novel she pulled out of her purse.

Over the next forty minutes the lecture hall began to fill up, and the time finally came for the big presentation. I was incredibly eager to see another channel at work—and from the perspective of *my* public speaking history, I was speculating that he might have butterflies at the thought of facing such a large audience. I wondered if *he* had ever needed hypnosis?

A woman took the stage and proudly introduced the channel and author we had all come to see. Amid thunderous applause, a man stepped out from behind the curtains that adorned the stage and shyly approached the microphone. It was the same man who had spoken to the girl sitting next to me. I was a little surprised that he had done nothing to spruce himself up before facing his audience.

After a few brief introductory remarks, he said, "I will take questions now."

Hands sprang up from every corner of the room. He nodded toward a woman in the back.

"What is my life's work?" she asked eagerly.

She's going to be a plastic surgeon, I heard John tell me telepathically. *You're going to find this very interesting.*

The channel put his fingertips to his forehead as if in deep intuitive concentration. After a few moments he replied, "You must look inward . . . and all of the answers will come to you."

The woman furrowed her brow, clearly not understanding what she had just been told. She politely sat down.

Why didn't he tell her about her life's purpose? I asked John inside my head.
Shhhh! he replied.

The channel then chose another audience member, who asked about his missing daughter.

The eighteen-year-old daughter wasn't kidnapped—she ran off with her boyfriend . . . and is living in Mesa, Arizona, John said to me.

The channel put his fingertips to his forehead, and after a few moments replied, "You must look inward . . . and all of the answers will come to you."

The man looked puzzled and surprised by the lack of information. He took his seat with a look of genuine disappointment.

Why does he keep saying the same thing? Why doesn't he answer their questions? I asked John.

Just listen! he said.

Another member of the audience was chosen.

"Can you tell me if I've already met my soul mate?" asked a young woman.

It certainly isn't the guy she's dating now, shared John with a naughty chuckle. *Her Mr. Wonderful isn't due to arrive for another three years . . . but she will eventually have a very happy marriage.*

The channel placed his fingers back to his forehead, concentrated, and then replied, "You must look inward. All of the answers will come to you."

I don't understand what's going on? I said to John.

You will, he replied. *Just wait.*

The young girl was undaunted. "But I asked you a simple question," she loudly complained. "Can't you just tell me if the guy I'm dating—"

"Look inward . . . and all the answers will come to you!" he repeated.

"But can't you answer my question?" she demanded.

Ignoring her, the channel began to search the room for another audience member to call upon. I literally had to fight the impulse to jump up and shout out the intuitive information John had shared with me. The poor gal had taken the time—and spent the money—to attend the lecture because she needed direction in her personal life. I had what she was looking for at my fingertips.

Don't you dare! John warned, interrupting my thoughts. *Where are your* manners? *It's very, very bad form to interfere with someone else's lecture. How would you like it if someone did that to you?*

He was right, of course. With mounting frustration, I continued to sit quietly.

The gal directly to my right began to frantically wave her hand. The channel motioned to her. "And what is your question?" he asked, deliberately giving the impression that he didn't know her.

"Should I stay in the house I'm in now . . . or move elsewhere?" she inquired.

Take a peek at the questions she has written in her notebook, suggested John. I glanced down at the yellow-lined pad, and sure enough, the question about moving was there. I didn't understand what was going on.

The channel put his fingertips to his forehead, and in a moment replied, "You should stay right where you are. It's . . . it's . . . 123 Maple Street!"

"That's exactly *right!*" the girl gasped. "You're *amazing*. How did you *know?*" She dramatically pulled her driver's license out of a pocket of the notebook, stood up, and held it in the air.

The audience murmured their approval. *This* was more like what they came to see—and what they expected from a professional, well-known psychic.

The channel was clearly buoyed by their positive response. "Do you have another question for me?" he asked the same girl.

"Should I stay at my present job?"

He put fingertips back to his forehead, hesitated a moment, and then declared, "Yes. You have a good job at Remarko Steel Company—you recently got an award, didn't you?"

"Oh, my God. I *did!*" she cried, pulling an official-looking certificate out of the notebook and holding it up. The audience applauded. As far as I could tell, I was the only attendee who was in muddled disbelief. *How did she just happen to have that piece of paper with her? Who carries something like that around with them?*

Now it was my turn to gasp. I finally understood. They had it all planned before he came out on stage. He obviously wasn't going to *really* channel for anyone that day. But *why?* Didn't the audience deserve his best effort? If he was the real McCoy, wouldn't he be able to do it without all the trumped up shenanigans? I remembered that there were no accidents in the universe; so why had the gal sat right next to *me*? I realized that if she hadn't, I would not have had as clear a picture of what was going on.

This speaking engagement was to be an important reality check for you, John explained. *So you could compare your ability to someone else's—and learn what never to do at your own seminars.*

I would never do anything like that! I told John telepathically. Then I asked, *When this guy is really channeling . . . do you think he's better than I am?*

That isn't the point, Kim. There will always be someone better . . . and there will always be people who do not have your ability. You and he are just . . . different. Here's another reality check: there were several people directed to attend your first seminar to learn what not to do at their own speaking engagements.

I winced with embarrassment and then laughed. I had always liked reality checks—until then.

"I can take one last question," the channel grandly announced, directing his statement once again to the gal on my right.

"My grandmother recently passed away," she declared. "Can you tell what particular item of Granny's that I'm carrying right here in my purse?"

Fingertips flew to the front of the channel's head. As if pulsating with intuitive energy, he jumped up and down and shouted, "Her reading glasses!"

"That's *right!*" the girl screeched, producing them for all to see. "Look! Here they are."

The audience gave the channel a standing ovation. I watched as he thanked everyone for coming and beat a hasty retreat. I turned toward the gal who had been sitting next to me . . . but she was gone, too.

Maria and I heard the outer door open, and my thoughts returned to the present. My first client, the astronaut, had arrived. It was time to go to work. Later that afternoon, I planned to follow my trusty girlfriend's advice and visit Barnes & Noble. Maybe she was on to something—and I *did* need to share some of my experience with others.

I could write a book detailing how to find an ethical psychic who wouldn't waste an individual's time or money with nonsense like curses, voodoo hexes, or magic potions. Better yet, I could offer suggestions on how people could learn to communicate with their guardian angels themselves. After all, I was already providing information about chan-neling in my seminars. I really *liked* the idea. Not because the book I'd write would be better than anyone else's—just different.

Chapter 20

My First Book

It was only a little after 6:00 p.m., but there was already a small crowd waiting to be seated in the busy Chinese restaurant just down the street from where I lived. I had become a regular takeout customer because the food was great, it was fairly inexpensive, and because I believed that cooking just for me was a colossal waste of time and energy. No matter how many times I came in and routinely ordered the same meal, the petite Asian hostess with the heavy accent always treated me like a stranger.

"I'm here to pick up the carry-out order for O'Neill," I told her. "Chicken with vegetables—and would you include some extra fortune cookies, please?"

"You picking up *call-in* order? Only for *one dinner?*" she asked in a loud businesslike tone. She had no time for pleasantries.

"Yes," I replied.

"The order is just for *one?*"

I nodded.

"*Only* for *one?* How come? You not married?" she inquired aggressively, as if demanding an explanation.

"No, I'm *not*," I answered peevishly. Why did *she* care if I was single and dining alone? Italian restaurants never asked that question when I'd order only a small pizza.

"You order chicken with vegetable, right?" the hostess asked, completely ignoring my piqued tone.

"That's right."

"D3—CHICKEN WITH VEGETABLE!" she bellowed into the kitchen. "O'NEILL ORDER—JUST FOR *ONE!*"

I wondered why the restaurant didn't replace her with someone who demonstrated better people skills. Maybe she was a family member? There was no doubt that having the food delivered would have been the most convenient option; in fact, the week before, I had the bright idea to order two separate dinners so I could meet their minimum delivery charge, with the intention of saving one for the next night. However, I discovered that Chinese leftovers didn't always keep well and it took me two full days to get the smell out of my refrigerator.

While I waited for my food, I stood in front of the massive fish tank by the bar.

The hostess bellowed again to the kitchen staff, her voice echoing throughout the small restaurant. "D10—GENERAL TSAO CHICKEN! ROSENBERG ORDER—JUST FOR *ONE!*"

It was easy to spot the Rosenberg customer—she was the red-faced gal, cringing with embarrassment, standing next to the diminutive hostess. I returned my gaze to the exotic, multicolored fish.

"D12—CHICKEN WITH GINGER! MARTINEZ ORDER—JUST FOR *ONE!*"

"D4—CHICKEN HAPPY FAMILY! SMITH ORDER—JUST FOR *ONE!*"

Did every unmarried woman in the area stop by for carry-out on her way home from work? I was glad that everyone seemed to be ordering chicken, because invariably, the kitchen packaged the wrong meal. Although I requested chicken with vegetables every time I placed an order, I hadn't yet been graced with that particular dish. I didn't complain because I had actually liked every chicken entrée they had given me.

"O'NEILL!" the hostess summoned, like a drill sergeant taking roll call. I quickly approached her.

"You O'Neill?" she asked brusquely.

"Yes!" I answered emphatically. I was starving.

"Here your dinner—for *one*," she said loudly, thrusting the steaming plastic bag in my direction.

"Chicken with vegetables?" I asked her. "Extra fortune cookies?"

"Chicken with vegetable!" she assured me. "Only for *one*!"

I took the bag, hurried to my car, and drove home. I had recently given up the small apartment I had been renting since my divorce, and had moved to a much bigger one-bedroom condo nearby—for almost the same rent. I parked my car right below my new unit and climbed the two flights of stairs to the back door. I smiled and waved to Winston, who was gazing out from his perch just inside the bedroom window. I fumbled with my keys, opened the sliding glass door, and closed and locked it behind me.

As I walked into the kitchen, Winston was immediately underfoot wanting to be fed. I felt something warm and wet on my ankle. I looked down and saw that the bag from the Chinese restaurant was leaking.

A thick, dark brown liquid had spilled onto my pant leg, my suede shoe, and all across the kitchen floor. I gasped, still holding the bag as it continued to leak—now all over Winston's thick white fur. He made a hump and scurried into the bedroom. I yelled at him to come back before he smeared the smelly sauce all over the apartment, but, of course, he ignored me.

I quickly placed the messy bag into the sink, drizzling sticky brown liquid on all the lower cabinets in the process. I hoped that the bag hadn't started to spew the sauce until I had removed it from inside the car. I quickly peered out the patio door, which was also streaked with sauce, and saw a brown trail leading all the way down the stairs. Then it occurred to me that chicken with vegetables wasn't supposed to have a brown sauce.

I threw my clothes into the dry cleaning bag, snuggled into my robe and white crew socks, cleaned my suede shoes, pulled Winston out from under the bed, bathed him, and returned to the kitchen to clean up the mess in there. I fed the cat and then was finally able to eat.

I had no clue which chicken entree it was, but I loved it. I'd just have to make certain that, in the future, whatever I got from the Chinese restaurant was double-bagged. I wondered if the other customer, who had unknowingly gotten *my* order, was as delighted with the chicken and vegetables and the extra fortune cookies.

It was a little after seven–thirty when I sat down in front of the computer that I had set up on my small dining room table. Spurred on by my friend Maria, my guardian angel John, and my spirit buddy Claire, I was going to start working on my first book. I had lots of paper, Post-it notes, several pens, a new cartridge in my printer, and my trusty *Thesaurus*. I also had a reference book on hand that John had told me I would need, entitled *How to Write a Book Proposal*, by Michael Larsen. Winston jumped up on the table, wrapped himself into a tight ball, and went to sleep.

"Are you ready to begin?" asked John, who materialized and sat in the chair next to me. "This is going to be jolly good fun."

"I'm here, too," said Claire. "I'm ready to help."

"I have no idea if I can do this," I said to them.

"You can't be confident about something you haven't done yet," John reminded me. "And you haven't yet started this writing endeavor."

"I don't know where *to* start," I said. "I have no clue as to what I want to say."

"Do you have any thoughts about what you *don't* want?" John asked.

I was surprised by his question. I had to think for a moment. "I know that I don't want it to read like a spiritual textbook. I don't want to write in such esoteric terms that people have a hard time digesting it. There are some channeling books out there that you need a degree from MIT to figure out."

Then, suddenly, I had a flood of ideas. "I want the book to be user-friendly and easy to read. I want to explain how simple channeling is and how good *anybody* can be with just a little practice. I want people to know that they don't have to meditate or be fearful of accessing information that isn't correct. People need to understand that they can receive information as good—if not better—than any professional channel or psychic, because they all have their own guardian angels."

"Well . . . that's an excellent start," John observed. "The book might also allow you a platform from which you could share your opinions about magic potions, curses, and the like."

"That's right!" I said, now enthusiastic. "I could devote a whole chapter to cautioning people about baloney like that so they don't waste their time or money—and they don't get caught up in believing that anyone else has any impact on their lives but *them*."

"What if you called the book *How to Talk With Your Angels?*" asked Claire. "How does that sound?"

"I like it!" I responded. "It's simple. And from the title, you can understand just what the book is about. Claire—you have beauty and brains."

"I agree on all counts," John chuckled. "*How to Talk With Your Angels* it is."

Now my ideas were coming fast and furiously. "I need to explain that, along with communicating with their angels, people can also learn to speak with their deceased loved ones."

"Like you do for my Mom when she wants to talk with me," said Claire.

"Exactly! People need to realize that they can easily maintain a relationship with loved ones who have passed, and talk with them whenever they want—without having to invest their time or money in visiting with a professional channel. I'd also like to help people understand that there is always a tremendous amount of valuable angelic information available to them that they can tap into at any time."

"Like people who come to your office and are all confused about what direction they should take," offered Claire. "And then, after you've channeled for them—they know what to do, where to go, and how to get there."

"Yes," I confirmed. "I want people to be able to do that for themselves. Claire, I keep telling your Mom that she is fully capable of talking with you completely on her own."

"Yeah . . . but she doesn't have the confidence. My Dad thinks she's crazy . . . and she listens to him."

"But *why*? She doesn't listen to him about *other* stuff? Didn't she just tell me that they went shopping for a new sofa? He wanted brown . . . but instead, she went right ahead and picked the soft yellow that she loved—"

"Kim, it is *so* gorgeous," said Claire. "And my mom also ordered these two arm chairs and matching ottomans that haven't been delivered yet . . . my dad doesn't know about those . . . and they're the same pale yellow and this cool turquoise—"

"Oh . . . I'd *adore* that. Your mom is so creative . . . maybe I could do something like that in my office?"

"It would be perfect with all your pine furniture."

"Ladies—may I interrupt? Kim has a book to write."

Duly chastised, Claire and I shared a conspiratorial smile. "We'll discuss that later, alligator," I said to her.

"In a while, crocodile!" she answered, and we laughed together. I turned my attention back to John.

"I want you to study Larsen's book on proposals," he instructed.

"I wondered why you wanted me to buy it," I said, distractedly flipping through the paperback reference book. I casually tossed it back on the dining room table. "What do I need that for?"

"Because, dear one, it's what I consider one of the most definitive guides to completing a book proposal worth submitting."

"What's a book proposal?"

"For a work of nonfiction, you'll need to complete a proposal. It will provide an agent and a publisher the blueprint for *How to Talk With Your Angels.* I'm going to guide you through the process of securing a literary agent, who will sell your manuscript to a publisher."

"That sounds very complicated," I sighed.

"On the contrary . . . it's very simple."

"Why do I have to produce a proposal?" I whined. "Why can't I just write the book and submit that? Isn't that *enough?*"

"No, it's *not.* Agents and publishers like to review a blueprint, rather than having to wade through an entire manuscript. It includes an introduction, your bio, a detailed outline of all the chapters, and—what's more—you need to provide a list of other books comparable to yours that are already out on the market. The proposal will also give them an idea of when you'll have the project finished. After you finish the proposal, you'll write a one–page query letter to literary agents, telling them about the manuscript and offering them a read of the proposal."

"How many pages will the proposal be, do you think?"

"All told . . . about eighty pages."

"*What?* That's like a whole book in itself! You must be *kidding.* I don't want to do that. And, John, there *aren't* any other books out there that are comparable to the one I'm going to write, so I can't—"

"If you want to engage a publisher, then you must abide by their rules. Are you interested in getting published . . . or not?"

"But . . . how can I give them an estimated time when I'll have the book finished? How can I possibly gauge that?"

"They understand that you're giving them your best guesstimate."

"So . . . this 'simple' process involves writing the cockamamie proposal, and *then* writing the book, and *then* writing a query letter, and *then* contacting literary agents, and *then* waiting to hear from them. Do I have that straight? And it's all going to take so long that—*then*—I'll be going through menopause!"

"Hardly," said John in a lecturing tone. "You'll write the proposal, which should take several weeks, and then you'll create the query letter to send out to the agents. Once you've sent out the query letter, you'll work on the manuscript itself."

"Oh . . . so I don't have to wait until everything is finished before I contact literary agents?"

"No, indeed, although some authors choose to do that. In the end, it might be less stressful if—"

"I'd rather make things move forward as quickly as possible."

"After working with you for all of these years, that's exactly what I surmised," he said with a sigh.

"How will the agents contact me?"

"You'll send them a self-addressed stamped envelope with the query letter, and they'll respond by mail or possibly by telephone."

"Will I get rejections?"

"Of course."

"Many rejections?"

"Yes—most of the agents you query will reject your idea for one reason or another."

I frowned at the angel. "But if I take the time to go through this entire process, I will *eventually* get an agent? Right?"

"Yes."

"And a publisher?"

"Keep in mind that getting published is part of your destiny. If you do the work, then it *is* going to happen. Part of the process is for you to approach a handful of literary agents who have a spiritual contract with you in order to provide them the opportunity to rise to the occasion and recognize, intuitively, that they're meant to work with you."

"But if I have only a 'handful' of agents with whom I share a spiritual contract, then why don't you just tell me who they are, and I could send a query only to *them*? Why do I have to send the query letter all over?"

"Because, as you know, some people fail to rise to the occasion and honor their spiritual contracts. So, if you want to get published before you reach menopause, then I suggest you blanket all of the agents who handle your genre."

"My *what?*" I asked.

"Genre," John repeated. "It refers to the kind of book an agent handles. There is horror, science fiction, romance, self-help, cookbooks, biographies."

"Oh . . . I see. What is my genre?"

"Your genre would be described as nonfiction, New Age, spiritual, or self-help."

I sighed heavily. "So after I've finished the proposal and the query letter, how long do you think the manuscript will take to write?"

"Of course, you'll have to work around your existing schedule of channeling sessions," John conceded. "But if you muster the perseverance and discipline to work nights and weekends, the entire project will take about eight months."

"Sort of like giving birth to a baby," said Claire, bubbling with optimism.

"Sort of like," answered John with a smile. "Now, Kimberly . . . open Larsen's book to the part on the chapter-by-chapter outline . . . we'll begin there."

It took three long weeks to finish the proposal. During that time, I learned valuable lessons about two of my biggest issues: patience and learning how to pace myself.

I discovered that if I remained focused strictly on what I was accomplishing *at the time*, rather than reviewing *everything I had yet to do*, I was able to get through the process much easier. I learned to focus on the *moment*, which was a very different way for me to look at my life and all the dynamics on my to-do list. Instead of singly concentrating on *what was left to achieve,* which always made me feel impatient, frustrated, and depressed—I concentrated instead on the immediate past and present to maintain an awareness of what I *had already completed* and what I *was in the process of completing.* By doing so, I was able to develop an unwavering, consistent sense of accomplishment as I slowly navigated this unknown path.

After I finished the proposal, John directed me to write a one-page query letter to literary agents all over the country, in which I briefly described *How to Talk With Your Angels* and the fact that I was looking for an agent to represent it. I felt butterflies just writing the letter. Although I sent the same letter to every literary agent, I still had to personalize each one with a different heading and its own envelope, along with a self-addressed stamped envelope. That task took a full Saturday; and it wasn't until after 8:00 p.m. that I reached the post office to drop off over seventy separate query letters.

As it turned out, that Monday I became ill with a very bad head cold that I was certain I picked up from a client who had come to the office quite sick the week before. Not only did I feel physically miserable, but I was completely stressed out because of all the commitments I was forced to cancel, including my radio gig and all the private sessions I had scheduled.

I had no choice but to lie on the couch with a pillow and blanket all week—and sleep or watch daytime TV. Winston remained curled up at my feet, and I kept a cup of hot tea and a box of tissues at hand on the coffee table. I was so congested my head was in a fog and I couldn't think clearly. Late Thursday morning, the phone rang and I assumed it was my mom calling to see how I was feeling.

"Hello?" I croaked pathetically.

"May I speak to Kim O'Neill?" asked a cheery female voice.

"Speaking," I croaked.

"This is Pat Teal."

I had no clue who Pat Teal was. I assumed she was a telemarketer, and I was just about to inform her that I wasn't interested in whatever she was selling.

"I'm with the Patricia Teal Literary Agency in Fullerton, California. You sent a query letter recently?"

OH, MY GOD! *It was a literary agent calling me.* My heart started to beat out of my chest. "Yes!" was all I could think of to say in response. Hives started to bloom. I was thankful she couldn't see me. I sat up on the couch. My head was splitting, but I didn't care.

"I'm interested in reviewing your proposal for *How to Talk With Your Angels.* It sounds like an interesting project."

"Great," I mumbled. "I'm sorry I sound like this . . . I have a cold." And with that, I suddenly sneezed loudly, right into the receiver. I grabbed a tissue and blew my nose. *What a great impression I'm making.*

"I hope you're feeling better," she said cheerfully. "Do you want to get back with me?"

"No! Thank you . . . I'm fine. I'm fine." Sniffle . . . sniffle.

"Well, there are a lot of angel books out on the market, but I think it's really compelling that you are a professional channel conducting readings full time."

"Yes . . . I am . . . I do." Besides being sick, I was so nervous I could hardly string words together.

"As soon as you're feeling better, would you send the proposal so I can review it?"

"Yes . . . I will. Right away!" I sneezed again, right into the receiver.

"I'll be looking for it. Feel better!"

"Bye," I croaked, hanging up the receiver. *A literary agent had just called me. She's interested in my idea. A real literary agent!* I was so happy that I started to cry. I blew my nose for the hundredth time. Winston looked up at me, bleary-eyed, from the end of the couch. All the hubbub was disturbing his sleep.

The next day I was feeling a tiny bit better; I wrote a brief cover letter to Pat Teal that I included with the proposal. I dropped the package at the post office and went back home to continue recuperating.

I was able to finally return to work the following week. Between my channeling sessions, I obsessively checked my messages to see if the agent had called. She finally called late that week to tell me that she loved the proposal and was interested in representing *How to Talk With Your Angels.* She was going to send a contract for me to sign and return to her, and then she would go about trying to sell my proposal to a publisher.

It was no more than two weeks later when Pat Teal called again to share the wonderful news. She had an offer from Avon Books in New York! Was I interested? I assured her that I was, and she handled all the rest.

Shortly thereafter, I received a contract from Avon. Carrie Feron was assigned to me as my editor, and she called to discuss my book's cover design. She also asked me to provide her with a date by which I thought I could deliver the finished manuscript. I had never written a book before—so I literally had no clue about how long it might take me. I committed to six months. With that commitment from me, Avon was then able to project a publication date for *How to Talk With Your Angels*, which was approximately one year from the time I promised the manuscript.

I sat in front of my computer at the dining room table reviewing the contract that was signed, sealed, and delivered from Avon Books. I had legally promised something that I wasn't certain I could do. I put the contract aside. My fingers moved to the keys, and I typed *How to Talk With Your Angels*. Chapter One. Page One. I was consumed with nerves. I was going to be a published author. I suddenly understood why John had tried to explain why some authors wait until *after* they've actually completed a book project before they attempt to sell it. Too late for those thoughts now!

With a full roster of sessions five days a week, plus a weekly radio show and no vacation planned in the foreseeable future, I had a scant six months to write a whole book.

Chapter 21

National TV and a Near Plane Crash

The flight departing California and bound for Texas was completely full, and I shoved my small carry-on under the seat in front of me as I nodded a hello to the couple directly to my left.

"We're just back from our honeymoon!" announced the young woman by the window. Her new husband sat between us. She began to rub his fuzzy forearm as he leaned toward her and they kissed. I decided that this was going to be a very good flight. I could relax and read the new book I had just bought without someone talking my ear off or—worse—asking for psychic information once they learned I was a channel. I buckled my seat belt and reached for the in-flight magazine. The last four days had been a whirlwind, and I was anxious to get home.

"Good afternoon, ladies and gentlemen. Welcome to the flight. We want to make your flying experience as comfortable as possible."

The pilot's monotone voice was very soothing, masculine, and authoritative. I wondered why American pilots never seemed to speak with regional accents. Did they all go to some kind of voice training school? Not that I was a seasoned traveler, but I couldn't ever recall hearing a pilot from New Jersey, saying, "Yo! I'm Captain Vinnie. So how yez all *doin'*? Ya wanna go to Vegas? You got it! Durin' the flight, ya need anyting—jus' ask one of da goils—dell take good care a yez. An' don worry about nuttin'—anybody up dere gives us a hard time—dell get a piece of Vinnie! Tanks for flyin' wid me—I appreciate da respect!" Or a pilot from New York City, announcing, "I'm Captain Irving. So . . . what do you want from me? Okay . . . *okay* . . . we'll go to Florida. Oy . . . I hope we don't hit any wind sheer . . . last week it almost killed me! I asked my co-pilot to bring me some good deli food for the flight—but what does a guy named Hank know about food? My Aunt Ida—now *she* knew food!" And what about pilots who were raised west of the Pecos? "Howdy! I'm Big Tex . . . yer Captain! Wer gittin' ready to straight'n up— an' fix'n to fly right. But furst, ah'm askin' ya'll to mind the purty lil' blond-headed gal who's gonna show ya'll how to buckle up, 'for we take that mighty long ride up north to Pittsburgh. Ya'll be careful and keep 'em covered in Yankee land." It was a curiosity.

The plane taxied down the runway and we were airborne; and I was on my way back to Texas. My thoughts turned toward everything I had encountered the previous few days as a guest on *Leeza* and *Gabrielle*, my first nationally syndicated TV program.

The producers of both shows invited me to discuss my new book, *How to Talk With Your Angels*, following its release in bookstores across the country. Traveling to Los Angeles on business was a brand new experience. When I had arrived in LA a few days before, I had been met at the airport by a cab driver who was leading-man handsome.

"Welcome to sunny Los Angeles! I'm Lance . . . and I'm happy to serve you." He grabbed the two suitcases and threw them into the trunk. He then opened my door with a theatrical flourish, and I hopped in. Lance jumped in the front seat, and we quickly left the LAX airport terminal.

"Did you come to California for business . . . or pleasure?" he asked in a resonant voice.

"Business," I answered, gawking out the window.

"Are you in town for the big AMA convention?"

"No . . . I've written a book about channeling, and I'm here to appear on *Gabrielle* and the *Leeza Gibbons Show*."

"Leeza's *fabulous*. Everyone thinks she's the greatest. And you're a *chan-*

nel? That's fantastic! I *adore* my channel. I don't know what I'd do without her."

"You have a channel?"

"Everyone out here does. Honey, in LA, channeling is considered a mainstream occupation. Where are you *from?*"

"Chicago, originally . . . but now I live in Houston."

"*Houston? As in, Texas?* Why do you live *there?*" Lance rolled his eyes as if I just told him that I lived on the dark side of the moon. "Isn't that an outpost of civilization? Isn't it all *redneck?*"

"It's the fourth largest city in the country," I answered with a little indignation in my voice. I adopted a Texas twang and said, "We just got them new-fangled 'lectric lights—an' next year, Mayor Billy Bob even promised indoor plumbin'!"

"Well, you're not in Kansas anymore, Dorothy. You belong out *here.* What's the name of your book?" he asked excitedly.

"*How to Talk With Your Angels,*" I answered.

"Oh . . . I've never heard of it," he shrugged in obvious disappointment, quickly deciding that I wasn't a prestigious fare. "There's the sign," he announced casually, pointing to a hilltop on my right.

I eagerly peered out the window and saw the letters spelling H-O-L-L-Y-W-O-O-D. I was excited to see the historic southern California landmark in person.

"I'm just doing this waiting for my big break," he shared. "I've written a screenplay, and I've got it in front of several people."

"Good luck," I said to him.

As he drove, I could psychically "see" that his real name was Clarence and that he would likely decide to give up his dream of screenwriting and return to his hometown of Sioux Falls the following year, tired of all the struggling. He was a very good writer—it was just that he hadn't hit upon the idea that would help him establish his career. Should I mention that to him, I wondered? I decided to go ahead.

"You know, Lance, you might want to consider writing a story about a cab driver who has all of these really funny experiences—"

"You mean write about what I do *now?* But who would want to see *that* on the screen?"

"Maybe the average person could relate to what you're doing now," I argued. "The driver in your screenplay could offer all kinds of sage advice to his fares—like a guardian angel who changes peoples' lives when they get in his cab. Did you ever wonder about *why* you're driving? How you ended up doing this . . . instead of all the other things you could be doing?"

"I didn't want to wait tables, and I needed the money."

"No . . . I mean the *spiritual* reason."

"Bad karma?" he chortled.

"Okay," I said quickly. "It was just a thought."

We pulled up to the ornately scrolled, glamorous entrance to Paramount Studios, and I sat staring in awe while Lance checked in with the guard at the gate. I pictured all the film stars who had reported for work throughout the years right here on the Paramount lot, where they had created an unforgettable magic that still breathed a luminous life of its own. Olivia De Havilland . . . Gary Cooper . . . Claudette Colbert . . . Audrey Hepburn . . . Grace Kelly . . . William Holden . . . Katherine Hepburn . . . Anthony Quinn . . . Gloria Swanson . . . and directors Billy Wilder, Cecil B. DeMille, and Alfred Hitchcock! They all arrived for work at this very studio and had to pass through the same gates that stood in front of me now.

We were flagged in, and Lance drove down a small street and up to a nondescript doorway. I had hired him for the day, so he was going to wait for me to finish my appearance on *Leeza* and then he was going to take me to my hotel. The *Gabrielle* taping wasn't until the following day.

"I should be out in a little over an hour," I told the driver.

"Aren't you a featured guest on the program?" he asked quizzically.

"Yes. But the show is only an hour long."

"So you figured that the taping would last an *hour*, right? You'll be in there at least three, probably four hours. Is this your first TV appearance?"

"No . . . I've done a lot of local stuff in Houston."

"This is going to be very different. They'll do your hair and make-up, too . . . so don't worry."

"Oh, they don't have to go to all that trouble. I've already done it." My voice trailed off as I saw him critically appraising my blond curly hair, my make-up, and even my suit.

Although I had really wanted to create a hip *I just threw this together* kind of look for my TV appearances in Los Angeles, I was never cool enough to be able to pull that off—it was much too complicated for me. So after a lengthy deliberation, I chose my favorite bright pink blazer and skirt, silk blouse, and pink suede shoes. I liked wearing black, but I could hardly appear on national television as a psychic wearing black to talk about angels. My profession spooked some people as it was, and I didn't want to make things worse with my wardrobe. I frowned, looking down at my hot pink ensemble . . . thinking about all the money I had invested in my recent makeover in Houston.

"You'll knock 'em dead!" said Lance, who unfortunately added, "You've got a nice smile—so people will see beyond the way you look. Break a leg!"

I opened the door and walked inside where I was met by a gal in her mid-twenties wearing jeans and a *Leeza* sweatshirt. She was carrying a large pad.

"And you are . . . ?"

"I'm Kim O'Neill!" I announced with perky excitement. I still couldn't believe I was really there. "I'm a guest on the *Leeza Show.*"

"Come with me," she said simply.

I followed her down a long hallway flanked by offices. Staff members were everywhere, and the place was a hub of activity. "First, we'll go to hair and make-up, and then I'll bring you to the Green Room."

"The what?"

"The place where you'll wait to be called onto the set."

"Oh." My eyes were like saucers as I followed her. We arrived at "hair and make-up," which was a large room set up with hair salon–type chairs, bright lights, and a wall of mirrors. The long counter that ran the length of the room held every hair and make-up product imaginable. A woman immediately approached me, took one look at my hair, and—without speaking a word—attempted to put her comb through it. She recoiled when she felt how stiff it was.

"What's *that?*" she asked accusingly.

"You mean . . . my hairspray? If I didn't use some spray, my hair would be an absolute disaster."

"I don't have enough time to fix it," sighed the make-up gal to her colleague, and I saw a look pass between them. Evidently, I didn't make the grade as their idea of camera-ready. "Just take her down the hall."

"Okay, Kim . . . this way." With that, the girl sped away, and I scampered behind her. We arrived at the Green Room, where I was told to make myself at home. It wasn't painted green, and I wondered where the name came from. There were lots of people milling about. Along one wall was a long table laden with fruit, bagels, sweet rolls, cookies, water, coffee, and soft drinks. A large TV in a corner of the room was playing what I assumed were previously recorded *Leeza* programs. I saw my client, Linda, who rushed up to hug me. She had been invited as a guest on the show, and the network had flown her in from Houston to appear with me and explain how the channeling process worked.

I looked at my watch; I had already been there forty-five minutes. I was beginning to understand what Lance had meant when he told me that I'd be at the studio for at least three or four hours.

Another *Leeza* staff member appeared in the doorway, and in a no-nonsense tone, called everyone to the set. We all dutifully followed her through another labyrinth of offices, into a dark backstage area, and finally onto the brightly lit set. Four chairs were positioned on the stage, and I was offered the one farthest to the right. I had never been a guest on a show with a studio audience before, and I wondered what the experience would be like. Linda was escorted to a chair in the audience. I stared out at the people who had assembled, and they were smiling, whispering, quietly laughing—obviously excited to be there. The energy in the room was very positive and upbeat, and I remembered how Lance had spoken of Leeza Gibbons in such glowing terms. I felt honored to have been invited as a guest on her program.

Just before the taping was to begin, Leeza appeared to welcome us to her show. I was astonished by how young she was. She was very slender and had flawless skin. Her blonde hair was stunningly sleek, her make-up was perfect, and she had one of the most genuine, radiant smiles I'd ever seen. I guessed that we were somewhat close in age, but I wanted to be *her* when I grew up! After warmly greeting each of us and thanking us in advance for our participation, she quickly disappeared offstage to prepare for the taping.

A young guy in jeans and a T-shirt approached to "wire me." He handed me a long thin wire with a small microphone at the end, instructing me to snake the long cord up from the bottom of my skirt and up into my blouse, where the mic would pop out at the top and attach to the lapel of my blazer. That way, the long, black unsightly cord would be invisible—hidden inside my clothing.

"I've written a screenplay," he explained, as I was fumbling with the cord. "And I want to direct."

"Good luck," I replied with a smile. I had lived in Houston for years; yet very few friends or acquaintances—outside of channeling sessions— had *ever* discussed their private goals or dreams with me. In Los Angeles, it appeared to be the main topic of conversation—even between strangers. A small battery pack was hooked to the back of my skirt, which created an unsightly bulge under my blazer, but I was to remain seated, so it would never be seen. The other guests on stage had also been wired, and we were ready to begin taping. I felt myself getting a little nervous, so I visualized the old house with the porch and the peaceful meadow that Carolyn Grace had taught me to do in my hypnosis session, and I was able to calm my nerves. I was actually going to appear on television without the dreadful hives!

The program's theme song began to play, and Leeza Gibbons swept onto the set holding a microphone. "Hello!" she said, with a big smile, facing the big TV camera. "Welcome to the show! Today we have some very special guests . . . " She suddenly stopped and said something to the effect of "I'm going to do that again" and strode back out of the room again. She repeated this several times until she got her opening just the way she wanted it.

"Welcome to the show! Good to see you! I'm glad you're watching today. We're doing a show on angels . . . and you're going to hear amazing stories about angelic encounters. Next, you're going to meet Linda, who believes that her two children, who were brutally murdered seven years ago, are still with her. People Whose Lives Are Touched by Angels. Stay with us!"

I finally understood the difference between "live" and "taped" television. In live television, if you said or did something that was unfortunate, offensive, or idiotic—too bad! There's no way to edit. With a *taped* program, however, time permitting, you could redo things until you had the end result that was most to your liking. Considering my previous camera faux pas, I had an immediate appreciation for the taping concept of television producing. But I acknowledged that even if I wasn't pleased with my appearance on *Leeza*, I'd have absolutely zero control over the finished product; nevertheless, it was reassuring to know that if something tragically embarrassing were to occur, they had the *option* of editing me out.

When the taping began again, Leeza introduced the four of us who were seated on the stage. We had each written a book about angels, and all of our books were presented and briefly described. Leeza then interviewed a woman who shared, at length, how her deceased son and daughter remain in communication with her. The audience appeared fascinated by her story. Then we went to break again.

During that time, off camera, the show continued as Leeza engaged the audience in a discussion about angels. I happened to mention that in my private practice, I spoke with clients' angels every day. The moment the commercial break was over and we started taping again, Leeza asked about that.

"Welcome back! We're hearing stories about people whose lives have been touched by angels. During the break, we asked the audience if they wanted to ask their angels a question—because Kim—you tell us that you can get the *answers*? How does this work, and what kind of information can you *get*?"

"This is a process called channeling," I responded. "It's the process by which we communicate with our guardian angels."

"So you can talk with *their* angels?" Leeza asked, gesturing toward the audience.

"Absolutely . . . anyone can learn how to do this."

Leeza went out into the audience and asked a young gal to stand.

"Do you think *you* have angels?" Leeza asked the girl.

"Yes," she replied with a big smile.

"Have you ever talked with them?"

"I was in a car accident about five years ago," she shared. "And as the car was rolling, my spine just tightened right up and I said, 'please, God, no,' and all of a sudden the pain just evaporated. So . . . I believe that God *told* my guardian angels . . . or *sent* a guardian angel . . . to help me.

And I've always *wondered*—why am I not in a wheelchair? I must have a purpose that God wants me to do . . . but what *is* that?"

"We have to ask why some people become so terribly injured in accidents," I said, grasping the opportunity to bring up the topic of destiny. "And then . . . why are some people spared? What *is* your life's work—and *what are you here to do* . . . and why were *you* meant to be uninjured? We can get very specific information about what your life's work *is*, and when you're meant to get into it . . . from your angels."

"Do you want to *know* that?" Leeza asked the gal, who nodded eagerly. Then the TV host turned back to me, "Can you tell her that right now?"

"What is your first name?" I asked the gal.

"Beth," she answered.

"Beth . . . you are here in this lifetime to be a *teacher*," I told her, thankful that her angels started to provide channeled information right away. "Your angels are telling me right now that you are going to be working with children. And, in the future, you're going to be writing children's books."

Beth broke into a wide grin.

"You're smiling," I observed. "Is this something that you've thought about?"

"I *am* a teacher . . . I've graduated college, and I *do* want to write children's books! I've already written a couple."

The audience broke into applause.

Leeza approached another lady, and she stood to ask a question.

"Kim, I'm in the process of a career change. Will I complete the nursing program for an RN when I go in September?"

"What's your first name?" I asked her.

"Lucille," she answered.

"Yes, you will complete the nursing program. But you've got one little stumbling block . . . I hope you don't mind if I'm candid?"

She shook her head. Lucille certainly wasn't inhibited—she was willing to have her life opened like a book on national television.

"You don't realize how incredibly smart you are. And you're very self-critical—"

She started to laugh.

"So, you're already aware of this?" I inquired, laughing with her.
She nodded.

"Not only will you complete the RN program," I informed her, "but you're supposed to become a healer."

Lucille beamed and put her head down.

I continued relaying what her angels were telling me. "You're going to finish the RN work and then study to become a doctor. That's what you're here to do. You're meant to be a physician."

Lucille's hands flew to her mouth and tears started to flow.

"Now wait a minute," Leeza asked her. "Is that what you want to do?"

"What she said is *true*," confirmed the lady, nodding emphatically. "*Very* true!"

"You already *have* this awareness," I pointed out to Lucille. "So that, *in itself*, allows you to know how well you're hearing your angels. How *aware* you are about what you're supposed to be doing. And this is one of the biggest questions most people have: what is my purpose?"

"Thanks, Kim!" said Leeza graciously. "And thank you, audience. We'll be right back with . . . "

I was startled back to the present by a tap on the shoulder. A pretty flight attendant was smiling down at me, offering something to drink. I asked for an orange juice and some black coffee. Although I wasn't crazy about sugary nuts, I took the small bag she handed me and began to eat them ravenously. I never understood why flying always made me so *hungry*.

The plane vibrated sharply from some turbulence, and I glanced nervously at my seatmates. They were kissing and murmuring sweet nothings to each other. Although the shade partially concealed the small window, I could see that we were flying through some heavy clouds. I hoped that we weren't going to encounter any bad weather.

Recently, I had the misfortune to see a TV documentary about a plane that crashed, killing everybody onboard, because of wind sheer, and I wondered if the pilots had any instruments that helped them steer clear of such potentially lethal weather patterns. If we were forced to land in uncertain conditions, how could the pilots avoid tornadoes that could instantly spawn from a brewing storm? And I wondered if commercial aircraft had special protection against lightning strikes.

The plane shuddered again, rocked by turbulence. I grabbed the armrests that flanked my seat and gritted my teeth. I *hated* feeling so helpless and vulnerable. Driving was statistically proven to be much more dangerous than flying—but at least in a car, I was on the ground. And I didn't always trust statistics.

To my intense relief, the rocking abruptly ceased, and the flight became smooth as glass again. I loosened my grip and drank some juice. My thoughts returned to my recent trip to California—and the disastrous taping of *Gabrielle.* I had arrived at the studio and was already seated in the Green Room ready to go onstage when I heard someone mention that the topic for that particular show was going to be *Stop Seeing Psychics!*

Had I *heard* correctly? The national TV talk show was obviously going to put a negative spin on channeling. No one had disclosed that to me before! I wouldn't have considered going on the program. I was told that it was going to be a show about angels.

The other people in the Green Room were laughing and casually talking . . . obviously unconcerned about the taping that was scheduled to begin momentarily. Should I walk off? Should I *leave?* Would that be ethical? Was I crazy to stay if they were going to belittle my profession?

It quickly occurred to me that I, too, lambasted the con artists who swindled an unsuspecting, trusting public. Maybe this was a wonderful opportunity for me to explain how people could find an ethical professional to channel for them or—better still—learn to channel for themselves. I was just about to ask John when a *Gabrielle* staff member poked her head inside the doorway.

"Okay everybody—it's show time!" There were about seven of us following the gal who led the way to the set. I had the uneasy feeling that I was about to navigate a field of land mines.

When we reached the stage, I was astounded and unnerved by the behavior of the studio audience. They were in an absolute *frenzy*—cheering, hooting, and yelling up at us as we got wired and seated on the stage.

Rock music started to *blare,* and Gabrielle bounced into the studio and stopped right in front of the live audience. When she began to enthusiastically dance, they shrieked even louder. The music stopped, and she grabbed a mic and stood in front of the TV camera. She breathlessly introduced the show.

"Welcome to *Gabrielle!* The show today is *Stop Seeing Psychics!* We're going to talk with people who are addicted to the psychic hotlines—people who can't make a decision without getting feedback from psychics—and people who spend so much money seeing psychics that they can't pay their rent! We're going to talk with guests who have been cheated by psychics—and we're also going to question psychic Kim O'Neill about her business practices. All coming up. So don't go away!" And the audience screamed, clapped, and howled as if they were attending a raucous sporting event.

Question me about my business practices? I was incredulous! I had never been unethical; nonetheless, it appeared as if they were planning to hold *me* responsible for all of the deceptive, unsavory things that took place in the psychic world. On *this* program, channeling was not going to be celebrated; it was going to be crucified. If I was given the chance to explore and outline my honorable sensibilities, would anyone believe me? If I protested too much, would that appear defensive—as if I had something to hide? My eyes widened with fear.

There I was—captive—in front of a large studio audience, fully aware of the unblinking TV cameras that were recording every glance, gesture, and utterance from moment to moment. Should I get up and leave in front of all of those people before the situation got any worse? Or would the host criticize me after I left, insinuating that there was something unscrupulous lurking in my professional background that I didn't want revealed or exposed before the studio audience and all the viewing public? Could this one national TV appearance ruin my reputation and destroy all my knee-buckling, gut-wrenching hard work? I certainly didn't want to continue just sitting there like a dummy and have my character assassinated in front of millions of people—but I truly didn't know what else to do! I prayed that I was wrong.

Although I wasn't hearing anything from John at that moment, I speculated that perhaps this appearance was supposed to help me with my issue of wanting other people's approval; if so, wasn't that like learning how to swim by being thrown into the middle of the Atlantic Ocean? Waves of nausea threatened to make me sick—right there on the stage—

and the dreaded hives began to bloom. Stricken with nerves, I swallowed hard and tried valiantly to smile so that at least I wouldn't look as terrified as I felt. Then, Gabrielle, mic in hand, began to speak again in front of the cameras.

"I'm going to introduce a tape we've put together for today's show—a tape that you won't *believe!*" Gabrielle announced to the studio audience and all the viewers at home. "Watch this!" And we all looked at a huge monitor set up beside the stage.

In order to demonstrate how easily the public could be hoodwinked, the show had arranged, somewhere off a busy Los Angeles street, for an imposter to pretend to be a professional psychic. A hidden camera revealed how the fraudulent channel guessed—and hemmed and hawed—his way through each short reading for a steady stream of unsuspecting but satisfied customers. Once they stepped away from the phony "psychic," all of the customers were accosted by a microphone-wielding representative of the show, deliberately embarrassing them by calling attention to their gullible naiveté and demanding to know what they thought of being so easily duped.

When the short tape concluded, Gabrielle summarized that literally anyone could set up a psychic practice to extort money from people, and the studio audience laughed and booed.

"Now I'm going to introduce Tony from New York," said the host, gesturing to a thirty-something man who occupied one of the chairs on the stage. "What do you have to share with us?"

Tony went on to vividly describe how his wife had spent all of his hard-earned money on psychics who were meddling in their marriage and who had bilked her for every last dime they could get. He spoke very angrily about his wife's addiction and stated very plainly that he believed all psychics were unscrupulous vultures.

Then, one by one, each of the guests shared a horror story about how they had been tricked and fleeced by one psychic after another. One guest claimed to have lost her life savings; another, her marriage; and yet another described how a psychic threatened her with satanic consequences if she didn't get a loan on a credit card and return the following day with thousands of dollars.

Throughout the entire taping, I sat on the stage, in full view of the cameras, listening to the process of channeling being misrepresented, mocked, dishonored, and scorned. The show deliberately neglected to present any opposing or balancing view, and it became obvious to me that they believed their ratings were going to be higher if the program was derogatory and sensational. Evidently, they weren't concerned about psychics coming forward to challenge them once the inflammatory show aired. In spite of the fact that there are unscrupulous individuals in every profession, I guessed that *Gabrielle* was unlikely to produce a similar, obviously biased program depicting doctors, lawyers, teamsters, pharmaceutical companies, or corporate executives in such a negative light.

I was finally introduced toward the end of the show, and by that time, I thought the studio audience was going to lynch me. To tell the truth—I was more than a little frightened. The audience had turned into an unruly, angry mob; their worst suspicions had been ignited about how people in my profession manipulated the public without facing the appropriate consequences for their misdeeds. They booed and hissed at me as if I were a villainous scoundrel.

"Wait, now, everybody . . . let Kim speak!" said Gabrielle. "Why don't we give her a chance?"

A young guy raised his hand in the back of the audience. The talk show host called on him.

"Hey, Kim . . . I'd like to ask you a psychic question," he challenged belligerently.

Answering his question was the last thing I wanted to do, but I didn't know how to refuse without fueling the negative impression the show had already created about the process of channeling. Hoping to redeem the dignity of my life's work, and with serious misgivings, I agreed to channel before the studio audience and the entire viewing public. If I could offer valid intuitive information that could provide this audience with another perspective, perhaps they could somehow feel intrigued about channeling and all of its potential.

He stood, took a few swaggering steps, and laughingly posed his question. His tone was mocking and his manner self-important. "So tell me about my girlfriend." The two guys on either side of him were snickering and playfully punching him.

"Well . . . " I began. It was hard to listen to his angels with all the distracting catcalls and loud horseplay coming from the audience, but I was somehow able to get the information. I figured that this crowd was not going to respond well to subtlety, and I had the distinct feeling that they would accuse me of *guessing*—-like the fake psychic we had all seen earlier on the tape. So I decided to be brutally candid. I was just hoping that the girl he asked about wasn't sitting in the studio because I didn't want to hurt her feelings or embarrass her in front of everyone.

"You don't really *like* this girl," I told him. "You're just *using* her—so you won't be dating much longer. But your angels are telling me that you have to be careful about pregnancy because you're certainly not going to marry her. In fact, you're going to date a lot of girls who could get pregnant if you're not more careful—"

I wasn't finished, but the whole audience broke up into derisive peals of laughter and looked back at where he stood. I didn't expect that . . . and neither did he.

"Hah! I fooled *you!*" he exclaimed defensively, his face now red as a beet. "Some *psychic!* I'm not even *dating* anybody right now! Hah!"

The audience hooted even louder and immediately turned their attention expectantly back to me.

"*You* may not refer to it as dating," I answered, "but the poor girl in question does. You two are having sex and you'd better be careful."

Like they were watching a tennis match, the audience swiveled their attention back to the young man.

"She's *right!*" loudly called his two pals, laughing uproariously. The young man's face was crimson. He took several swaggering steps, opened his mouth to challenge me again . . . thought better of it . . . and sat back down.

At that moment, Gabrielle closed the show, completely ignoring the intuitive information I had just presented. I got to my feet and unsteadily started to make my way off the stage. I felt as if I had been emotionally, spiritually, mentally, and physically battered. I was too stunned to even think about approaching Gabrielle or her producers to confront them about the show. I acknowledged that it was her program; and therefore it was her decision to present any topic exactly as she wished. Moreover, I knew before going out on stage that the program was going to have a negative spin; after all—it was called *Stop Seeing Psychics!* I had wrongly assumed that the program had asked me to be a guest to share my experience to provide a more insightful, balanced discussion.

Tony, the guest from New York, quickly approached me, and I shrank back when he touched my arm. During the three-hour-long taping, he had professed so much rage that I was unnerved by him.

"Hi, Kim! I thought you did great," he announced with friendly enthusiasm.

"I beg your pardon?"

"No kidding—I was really impressed with you. Do you have a card? I'd *love* to have a reading with you."

"*What?* I thought you *hated* psychics! You've just spent the last couple of hours saying the most hateful things—"

"Hey—I meant no offense. I have psychic readings all the time. I'm an *actor* hired by the show to pretend."

"Then all of what you said was just . . . *bogus?* You made up those bad experiences?"

He smiled and shrugged. "Some of the talk shows hire actors. Didn't you *know?* I thought *everybody* knew that. So . . . you haven't seen me on anything else?" he asked, rather crestfallen. "I've done a lot of these shows."

"So what's the point of doing the show if it isn't *real?*"

"Ratings! People are more prone to watch if they think there's going to be a good, juicy fight. This is really going to help your career. Everybody watches *Gabrielle*—and you were awesome! Now . . . how about a card? Hey—maybe you'll give me a deal because we were on the show together? I need to find out if the screenplay I wrote is going to sell while I'm out here, and . . . "

My thoughts were once again jarred back to the present when the flight began to encounter more turbulence. I tightened my seat belt, looked at my watch, and guessed that we were only about forty-five minutes from Houston's Intercontinental Airport. I glanced at all of the people around me, but they seemed happily unconcerned. Maybe I was overreacting and needed to visit Carolyn Grace to help with my persistent fear of flying.

I always felt that it was a gigantic leap of faith to board *any* commercial airliner, and every time I flew, I became anxious and insecure. I really, *really* didn't like to fly because I could never get my brain around how such a massive multi-ton vehicle could become airborne and safely stay that way. No matter how many times the *theory* of flight was explained to me, it just wouldn't compute. Plus, there were so many other alarming concerns when the big jets were aloft—like poor weather conditions, pilot sobriety, other planes coming too close, leaking fuel, mechanical failure, doors inexplicably disengaging in mid-flight and sucking passengers out, explosions in the baggage compartment, and even birds getting caught in the engine and causing crashes. What if the pilot had a heart attack or stroke? Or what if there was a faulty decision made by an air traffic controller?

As a World War II history buff, I had unwavering respect for the military fighter pilots who not only went up into the wild blue yonder, but risked getting shot down every time they flew. I couldn't begin to imagine the courage required to fly thousands of feet above the ground and not only deal with turbulence, but dodge lethal enemy fire at the same time!

The pilot spoke over the intercom in a soothing monotone. "Uh . . . this is your Captain speaking . . . we're expecting to encounter some turbulence in the next few minutes . . . so I'm going to ask you to fasten your—"

At that moment, the aircraft fell from the sky as if it were an elevator hurtling toward the ground. It didn't nosedive—the huge plane remained horizontal—but we were free falling—plummeting—seemingly out of control! The engines began to roar—but *nothing was happening.* We were falling—and falling—and falling! It seemed to go on *forever.*

In a split second, there was utter pandemonium as passengers were caught completely by surprise. Cups and trays became airborne, smashing against the ceiling of the plane, falling back down, spilling food and drinks everywhere. The overhead luggage compartments flew open, and the contents tumbled out on top of the people who sat beneath them on the aisle. I had to put my arms over my head to protect myself from the heavy, falling debris. Then the plane stopped plummeting just as suddenly as it had started.

"FASTEN YOUR SEAT BELTS!" the pilot screamed over the intercom. His voice wasn't monotone any longer. "HOLD ON! IF YOU'RE IN THE BATHROOM—STAY THERE. STAY THERE! FLIGHT ATTENDANTS—TAKE YOUR SEATS AND BUCKLE IN. NOW. *NOW!*"

One of the flight attendants who had lost her balance, when the plane suddenly dropped, landed on the floor of the aircraft close to where I was sitting. She sprang to her feet, leaped over all of the debris in the aisle, jumped into her small seat by the kitchen galley, and quickly buckled herself in. I'd never seen such a look of fear on anyone's face before. She made the sign of the cross—which I did *not* find reassuring.

As the airliner suddenly plummeted again, I screamed along with all the other passengers. My stomach lurched into my throat. The wild hysteria escalated as we kept falling . . . and falling . . . barreling toward the ground. Passengers—men, women, and children—shrieked and cried . . . and I could hear people praying out loud, "Hail Mary, full of grace—"

I grabbed the beefy arm of the newlywed next to me and held on for dear life. My fingernails were digging into him, but he was so scared that he didn't seem to notice.

"We're going to crash and burn!" I cried. "We're all going to die!"

He was obviously very frightened, but to his great credit, he tried to calm me at the same time he was supporting his new wife. His head swiveled back and forth between two completely unstrung females.

"It's going to be okay," he said with a strong but quivering voice. "Try to focus on something else." The plane steadied again, but now it was convulsing with rough turbulence. I fully expected that, at any moment, the huge airliner was going to nosedive and rocket straight down—crashing to the ground in a ball of flames.

The cabin was now in so much chaos because of the roaring engine noise and passengers crying and screaming that we had to yell.

"WE'RE ALL GONNA DIE!" I cried again.

"FOCUS ON SOMETHING POSITIVE. LIKE WORK. WHAT DO YOU DO FOR A LIVING?" he hollered.

I clung to his arm with both hands. If I could have climbed into his lap, I would have. "YOU MEAN—WHAT IS MY *PROFESSION*?"

"YES! YOU'D BETTER KEEP TALKING, MA'AM—YOU LOOK LIKE

YOU'RE HYPERVENTILATING. WHAT DO YOU DO BACK HOME?"

"I'M A CHANNEL."

"YOU'RE A *WHAT?*"

"A PSYCHIC."

"A *PSYCHIC?* HOLY SHIT! WE'RE ALL GONNA *DIE!*"

His alarming proclamation caused even more screaming, and now the newlywed was holding *my* arm for dear life. I could feel tears falling to my cheeks, my heart was beating out of my chest, and my mind was racing: *so this was the nightmare that people experience before a disaster! We all know what's happening, but there isn't a damn thing any of us can do about it. What is it going to feel like to crash? Are we going to burn up—helplessly buckled in these small seats? I don't want to die this way! Will the plane shatter in mid-air? Will the doors blow open and suck people out still buckled in their seats? What about all the children—*

No one is going to die! bellowed John telepathically. *I'm right here! I swear on my soul that no one on this flight is going to die! Trust me! The plane isn't going to crash! The pilot will regain control!*

The plane plummeted again, and it felt as if we were free-falling out of the sky. I cowered in my seat, burying my head against the newlywed's shoulder. His shirt was stained with my mascara. *How long are we going to be suffering like this?* I feared that it was going to get much worse.

You are NOT going to die! cried John. *The plane isn't going to crash!*

Suddenly, to my immense relief, the plane stopped plummeting and resumed a normal flight pattern. Everyone was crying and moaning, and I could hear a few people vomiting.

John motioned to Claire, who was standing next to him in the aisle. She reached over and firmly put her hand on my shoulder.

Kim—the plane isn't going to crash! Claire assured me.

"It's *not?*" I said aloud, not caring who heard me. "Claire . . . are you sure?"

Positive! They're just having some engine problems.

"They must be pretty serious—we're falling out of the sky!"

This isn't your time to pass! It isn't the time for any of these people to die!

"How come you guys didn't *warn* me about this?" I demanded angrily. "I would have taken a different flight."

John thought it would help you with your fear of flying, responded the teenager, who brightly added, *Once you get through this, you'll feel that you can get through anything!*

"What?" I replied. "Won't this make me *more* scared to fly in the future?"

No! Turbulence will no longer bother you. You're going to be desensitized by this experience.

"You mean if I live through it! What about all the *rest* of these folks?"

John explained, *Once you've all faced the possibility of death and have survived, very little frightens you after that. When you release fear . . . you can accomplish anything.*

"Jesus! Couldn't I just have gone for some *hypnosis?*"

Some things have to be experienced in 'the now' to have a lasting impact.

"Are you *positive* that we're not going to crash? No one is going to die?"

You have my word, swore John.

I felt certain that if anybody was going to die, John and Claire would have told me; they were always so frank about everything. I squeezed the newlywed's arm to get his attention.

"Don't worry!" I told him, wanting to offer solace to him and his new wife. "We're *not* going to crash."

"How do you *know?*" he asked, his face now a mask of fear.

"Because my angels just told me."

"*Angels* are talking to you? Holy shit! We *are* dying!"

"No! It's okay! I talk with them all the time. This is happening to erase fear from our lives."

He stared at me as if I had gone stark raving mad.

The plane strained against another shock wave of blustering turbulence. The Captain's voice came over the intercom; his tone was now controlled and composed, but it *wasn't* calm.

"Uh . . . ladies and gentleman . . . we're on approach to Houston's Intercontinental Airport. We might continue to experience more turbulence . . . so please remain in your seats with your seat belts fastened. If you're in the bathroom, please remain there and hold on. Flight attendants—please stay seated."

For the duration of the flight, the only reassurance I received was from John and Claire. We heard nothing more from the pilot or anyone else in the cockpit. I normally wouldn't have given that a second thought, but after what had just transpired, the silence was deafening. Did that mean that the flight crew wasn't certain that the aircraft was fully under control? Was it a weather problem? I didn't see any rain on the windows, but that didn't necessarily mean anything. Had there been some serious mechanical failure or malfunction that they couldn't fix or overcome? Perhaps it was best that we didn't know what was transpiring or how serious our situation might be. The flight attendant, who minutes before had made the sign of the cross, remained seated and tightly buckled in. I don't think anything could have roused her from that small jump seat. Her petrified expression said, *I knew this stuff happened—I just didn't think it would ever happen to me! I should have become a dentist.*

The big jet started its descent. All of the passengers remained cowering in their seats, now quietly praying and talking in subdued tones. The Captain had not needed to mandate that we all remain seated and buckled up because there wasn't the remotest possibility of *anyone*—including the flight attendants—getting up and roaming around. The entire cabin was littered with debris: plastic trays, the remnants of the food and drinks that had flown through the air during the first drop, and small pieces of luggage, department store bags, big satchels, and other personal paraphernalia that had tumbled out of the overhead bins. We all remained very still, and the only sound that could be heard in the cavernous jet was the roar of the engines as the Captain and the cockpit crew struggled to get us safely on the ground. It was now dark outside, and the cabin lights flickered eerily.

The big craft rocked and shook, but there was no more plummeting. John and Claire stood in the aisle by my side, offering comfort, but I remained utterly panicked. I was trying my hardest to let go of fear. I kept shaking at the thought that—*at any moment*—the plane was going to explode into a ball of flames, consuming us all as we fell from the sky in dismembered pieces. It was as if we were suffering a near-death experience that was continuing on . . . and on . . . and on. Due to my work as a channel, I had absolutely no fear about what was going to happen *after* I had passed—I was just terrified about what my physical body might experience *during the process.*

"Seventy-five percent of all crashes take place during landing," loudly announced one of the male passengers. No one contradicted him. I guessed that he was voicing the concern many of us had. We all just sat in silence, listening to the steady roar of the jet engines.

Meanwhile, I continued to cling to the newlywed, with my head on his shoulder, as we descended through the dark night sky. Lights looked bigger now that we were getting closer to land. If we were spared, what would I do with the rest of my life?

I wanted to continue channeling, I wanted to write more books, I wanted to get married, and I wanted to have children. I fantasized about buying a home and having a cozy life with my soul mate and my babies. I wanted to visit France to see where Sabine had come from. I wanted to play in the snow again. I wanted to learn to speak Italian.

I remembered that I had left my apartment in a mess, and I wondered—if I was killed—who would have the awful responsibility of packing up all of my belongings? My mother, I guessed. I thought of the pain that my mother and brother would feel if I died. I couldn't make my transition *now* at such a young age—I had far too much left to do!

But then I thought of all of the spirits I had spoken with in my work as a channel—including Claire—who felt exactly the same way right before their young deaths. They certainly didn't want their entire futures mercilessly stolen from them at such a young age! But that became their tragic fate.

I peered out the window, and the blue runway lights were in clear view. The jet engines howled, and we were jostled by still more turbulence. I couldn't take my eyes away from the approaching runway and all of the promise it held; still gripping the newlywed's arm, my knuckles white, I tried to prepare for what might happen next.

Several long minutes later, we hit the ground—*hard;* the engines screamed as the huge jet slowed its roaring momentum. There was no clapping, cheering, or outward celebration of any kind; the cabin remained very still, except for some crying and praying.

By some miracle we had landed safely, but I assumed that there must have been some injuries sustained by the passengers and crew caught unaware during the first plummet and when free-falling luggage crashed heavily from the overhead compartments. I felt certain that the crew had somehow pulled a rabbit out of a hat and saved the lives of everyone onboard.

As we taxied, I looked around at my fellow travelers. Like me, they had tear–stained faces, and many were covered in splashes of coffee, soft drinks, juice, food debris, and vomit. Everyone remained very quiet; I guessed that they were either in shock or lost in their own thoughts. I wanted to acknowledge the kindness of the man seated next to me, but the newlyweds were whispering to one another and remained locked in a tearful embrace. Sharing my grateful thanks would have to wait.

I believed that none of us would ever forget what had happened on that flight. We had faced the harrowing moments that might have led to a traumatic and violent death. We were all spared because it wasn't our destiny to pass at that time and because each one of us still had necessary contributions to make on the earthly plane in the days, weeks, months, and years to follow.

Chapter 22

Hopelessly Single

It was after seven when I arrived at Carrabba's Italian Grill. Parking looked impossible, so I handed my keys to the valet and struggled through the throng of people standing outside. The casual restaurant was one of the most popular eateries in Houston, so I wasn't surprised to see that every table out on the covered patio was already occupied by happy diners—in spite of the fact that the early evening temperatures hovered in the sweltering mid-nineties. The humid air was perfumed with a captivating combination of blooming flowers that grew in the large pots flanking the heavy wooden front doors, as well as the garlic, tomato, and basil aromas that wafted from the busy kitchen.

Once inside, I had to squeeze through the congested entry to make my way to the crowded bar. Although Carrabbas was family friendly, it was also a great place for singles. I searched the crowd for my two unmarried girlfriends and found them seated at the end of the bar with drinks already in front of them. We hugged, and I apologized for being late. The cute bartender approached, and I asked him for a glass of wine. He placed it in front of me with a saucy wink.

"There's only a thirty–minute wait for a table," said Drew. "And a lot of good looking men in here tonight." She was a very attractive brunette in her late thirties who was a partner in a busy law firm. Although confident, and brilliantly assertive in the courtroom, she was perpetually confused and uncertain about her personal life.

Diane, my other girlfriend, had just turned thirty–five, looked twenty-something, and had a thriving pediatric practice that she loved. As a physician, she possessed the courage to diagnose and treat children who, at times, had life–threatening illnesses; but, romantically, she was clueless and frightened about whether she'd ever meet and marry her soul mate.

Ironically, as a psychic, I held the record for the worst dating experiences of all my girlfriends. It was true that I was perfectly capable of accessing intuitive information about a perspective date—I just didn't always *listen* to it. I had gotten weary of waiting for my elusive Mr. Wonderful.

"So . . . Kim! How do things look at the end of the bar?" inquired Diane, enjoying her apple martini. That was my subtle cue to psychically analyze a particular man she had her eye on.

I took a sip of my white wine and glanced in the direction she was indicating. I saw the guy in question right away. Brown eyes. Dark curly hair. About 6'2". Gorgeous smile. Beautifully dressed. No wedding ring.

"Gay," I disclosed.

"No! Are you *sure*? Damn! I should have known! Okay . . . what about by the telephone?"

I looked to the far right side of the big room and saw a tall, distinguished, handsome man of about forty–five.

"Married," I declared. "And looking for a one night stand. His better half is away on a business trip."

"But he's not wearing a ring," Diane argued.

I looked knowingly at her. She had just broken off a relationship with a man who was separated but never could find the courage to go through with his divorce. He had recently moved back in with his wife. Diane had been heartbroken.

"What about over there . . . seated at the table?" asked Drew, who was nursing a strawberry Margarita.

"He's single," I told her. "But he's looking to find someone who doesn't want to work—so that she would always be available to take care of his needs. He's insecure, a perfectionist who's never satisfied, plus . . . he has serious control issues."

"I want to get married—not adopted," Drew stated dryly. "What about halfway down the bar?"

"Big mother issues. Can't commit . . . and has a fear of intimacy."

I looked around the packed bar and then psychically surveyed the tables in the dining area behind us. "So far, no Mr. Wonderful for any of us here tonight," I sighed, before adding optimistically, "but that doesn't mean someone won't come in while we're here."

Diane and Drew grimaced and reached for their drinks.

"I'm so tired of this," complained Drew. "I hate being lonely! Why does finding the perfect man have to be such a struggle? Why can't we just follow a known procedure—like arguing in front of a jury—"

"—or treating a disease?" offered Diane.

"—and then be guaranteed an outcome? At least when I argue in court, I know there's going to be some kind of *outcome* to the trial, and all my hard work is going to lead to something—even if I lose the case. But in my personal life, it seems that it doesn't matter how hard I try—"

"I keep telling you that you need to be a little flirty," Diane interrupted. "When a man approaches, don't come across like a suspicious district attorney grilling a suspect."

"It's just that I don't have time to waste! I know what I want—so I go after it. It's worked for me professionally."

"I think that men usually like to do the pursuing," I said.

"Kim's right," Diane confirmed. "In your personal life, you have to look more approachable and feminine. Can't you give a guy a sexy smile? Look . . . raise your shoulder like this . . . "

"You must be kidding!" chortled Drew. "I have to act like Barbie to attract a man? I don't understand. Don't men *want* a woman who is intelligent and independent?"

"Look at all the families in here," said Diane longingly.

"Why don't we get one man for sex," suggested Drew, "and keep *that* relationship casual—and then have a guy pal who could be a best friend?

Wouldn't that be much easier than trying to find it *all* in one man?"

"Great in theory but lousy in practice," I reminded her. "We've all tried that. As soon as we have sex with someone, our brain goes into lock-down, and we're sucked back into that whirlpool of denial. We begin to fantasize that the man who we *know* is nothing more than a learning experience has suddenly become a Mr. Wonderful. It happens every time. We're just not capable of having casual sex."

Both my girlfriends nodded morosely. We sat in silence for a moment.

"John keeps telling me that we need to keep focused on the qualities we want in a Mr. Wonderful," I said. "So I keep adding stuff to my Mr. Wonderful list."

"I've been working on my Mr. Wonderful list," declared Diane.

"Me, too," seconded Drew with a sigh.

"I was complaining about how much time it takes to list all the qualities I'm looking for in a partner," I shared with them. "But John keeps telling me that it's definitely worth the effort. He says that the list we prepare indicates where we are in regard to our wisdom, enlightenment, and maturity. Every time we add another quality we'd like in a man, it demonstrates that we have discovered the difference between a man who is a learning experience . . . and the man who is a Mr. Wonderful. Whenever I have a bad date, or encounter, I add more qualities to my list. So far, I have over sixteen pages."

"Sixteen pages?" gasped Drew. "Are you writing another *book?* Mine is only half a page."

"I just had a date with a guy who ridiculed my work as a psychic," I told my pals. "So when I got home, I pulled out my Mr. Wonderful notebook and added that I want a guy who appreciates and celebrates all things psychic. I decided that I want a guy who can channel."

My girlfriends broke into laughter.

"You want a man who can channel?" choked Drew. "You'll be lucky to get a man who will *talk!*"

"Why not make it easier for the universe to fix you up with someone?" questioned Diane. "Maybe we're all getting too picky?"

"John is always telling me that we're not picky *enough*—that we have to avoid settling for less than what we know we want in a relationship just to be with someone."

"I hear that!" laughed Diane.

"Maybe there is no such thing," said Drew pessimistically. "Maybe we're all just kidding ourselves. Maybe John doesn't know what the hell he's talking about. It could just be some fairy tale to think you could have a heart, mind, body, and soul relationship. I can't even find a guy who is stimulating enough to go out with for coffee."

"No—it *does* happen!" I told her. "I have clients who have found their Mr. Wonderful. And John keeps telling me that 'he's worth the wait!'"

"And how long has John been telling you that?" inquired Drew cynically.

"Well . . . it's been a little while."

"Haven't you been divorced ten *years?*" she asked pointedly. "Do you really believe that it's still going to happen? You've just turned forty and you want children. And he's *still* telling you to wait? You can't do anything more than you already have been about meeting Mr. Wonderful—but you sure as hell could start the baby process. Why not just ask a male friend to do you a favor? Or go to a sperm bank before it's too late? What about adoption? Hasn't your mother been sending you magazine clippings about agencies in China . . . and Russia?"

"I've thought about all that," I said. "First of all, if I don't care enough about a man to marry him, how can I decide to have a child with him? I feel lonely *now!* I can't imagine how alone I'd feel if I went through the whole pregnancy and labor and delivery by myself, then raised the child all alone. Plus, how does one go about asking a man for his sperm? 'Excuse me, I'm not really interested in a long-term relationship with you—but I sure would love a tablespoon of your sperm.' My God!"

"And what if, after the child was born, the biological father demanded custody?" asked Diane.

"I could draw up papers beforehand," quickly answered Drew, waving away the question.

"I've thought about a sperm bank," I shared with them. "A client of mine did that, and she's very happy. The last time I talked with her, she was still single and had two healthy sons—all from the same California sperm bank donor."

Diane put her hand on my arm. "If you get sperm from a reputable sperm bank, you could have your babies before it's too late," she gently urged. "There might already be a small challenge with your fertility."

"I know! But what do I tell my child when he or she is old enough to ask about their father? I could provide the daddy's height and weight and coloring . . . and that he was frozen vile number 16748 . . . but I wouldn't know anything beyond that! So many important things would be a mystery . . . like his personality, sensibilities, favorite color, the way his face looks when he smiles, his likes and dislikes, his family, and specifics about his health background. It's all so impersonal. And who knows how many women share the same donor? What if my children met and married someone who had been conceived from the same donor as they had? It would be like marrying and having children with a stepbrother or sister!

"I believe that good agencies guard against that," said Drew.

"So . . . what about adoption?" asked Diane. "I've been thinking about that myself."

"I *love* that idea," I told her. "But John is begging me to wait until the end of this year. I told him I would—after all, I've waited this long. Everything he has told me was going to happen really has . . . all but meeting my soul mate. And, I *love* the sound of him! John told me that he's tall, has a ruddy complexion, is mature and enlightened, funny, considerate, is divorced, will make a wonderful husband and father—"

"So how are you supposed to meet him?" Drew asked.

"He's going to come to my office for a channeling session. I've asked John to let me know when he's coming so that I'm fully prepared."

"Obviously, he's not going to be disturbed if you can read his mind," grinned Diane. "And then he could see you in action . . . and get to know a lot about you at the same time. Sounds romantic."

"But don't get me wrong," I told them. "I have nothing against sperm donors or adoption. I'd love to adopt a child whether I meet Mr. Wonderful or not. It's just that I've heard so much from all my guides about my destiny . . . that I'm excited about what the future holds in store. I'm going to muster the patience and faith to hold out for just a little longer."

"Always the *waiting*," complained Drew as she took a long sip of her Margarita.

"Drew . . . do you have 'a guy with brains' on your Mr. Wonderful list?" asked Diane suddenly. I knew she was channeling. "And what about enlightened . . . non-smoker . . . well read and well traveled . . . spontaneous . . . monogamous . . . wanting to get married and have kids . . . cultured . . . articulate . . . passionate about what he does for a living . . . just like you."

Drew stared at her as if she had just provided the missing link on the quest to find the Holy Grail.

"Do you want me to help you with your list?" Diane offered. "We've been friends for years—I know what you want."

"And you need to keep adding to your list every time you have a bad experience," I advised. "You'll be that much closer to meeting your soul mate. Remember—everything happens for a reason."

"So . . . is that why all the guys who come into my life are so limited—because the Mr. Wonderful list I've compiled is so limited?"

Diane and I looked at one another and took a sip of our drinks.

"But you don't realize how difficult it is for me!" Drew wailed. "The only men I meet through work are other attorneys—who I'm definitely *not* interested in. Plus . . . judges, who are always married, and the scumbag suspects. Not a great dating pool."

"At least if you meet someone through work, you *could* go out with them," stated Diane. "It's inappropriate for me to date a patient's father—although most of the patients I see are brought in by their mothers or nannies anyway. Drug reps come in, but they're mostly women, too."

"You two think you have it rough!" I said, rolling my eyes. "How would you like your profession to either scare men off . . . or make them *laugh?* When I *do* have a date, for some reason, the guy *always* asks, 'Can you read my mind?' and I can see his eyes filling with fear. When I tell them that *all* women are intuitive, the evening goes downhill from there."

"That's so amazing to me," Drew commented. "I always thought that if a woman was desirable, a man wouldn't care if she was an executioner."

"And why are they so concerned about you reading their mind?" posed Diane. "Are they afraid you'll discover that they want to have sex with you? Isn't that normal? What's the big problem?"

"Maybe some men are afraid that Kim will discover that that's *all* they want," responded Drew, "or that they're married . . . or looking for someone to support them . . . or commitment phobic . . . "

"Oh, I see," said Diane. "Kim needs a guy who doesn't *care* if she can get psychically inside of him . . . because he has nothing to hide from her."

I nodded in agreement and took a sip of my wine before continuing. "To make matters even worse, my mother keeps saying, 'What's going to become of you if you don't have a husband and children? I can't die and leave you all alone!' She simply cannot comprehend that with all the men in this city, I can't even find a suitable date. She doesn't think I'm trying hard enough. The last time we had dinner, she suggested that I lie and tell a man that I'm a therapist or counselor. Then, as soon as he has fallen in love with me, I could tell him the truth. Then . . . it would be too late!"

My friends chuckled.

"So after I told her I didn't want any more advice, she began to send magazine and newspaper clippings in the mail to help fill me in on why I'm still single at my age—and what I've been doing wrong. The latest was *The Ten Major Things That Turn a Man Off.*"

"Did you bring it?" Diane asked.

"It wouldn't hurt to examine what it says," nodded Drew.

"No, I didn't bring it! But I should have—you two would have *loved* it." I laughed. "If I remember correctly, the article suggested that a wife should always be perfectly made up, every hair in place, that we should make certain that the house is immaculate, keep the children quiet so the hubby is not disturbed, ask his permission before we spend any money, and cook a nutritious meal every night and have it on the table when he comes home from work—"

"I thought it was *his* responsibility to provide the nutritious meal," said Drew, "by bringing home carry-out?"

"When was the article written?" asked Diane. "1960?"

"The only thing that's 'immaculate' about my townhouse," smiled Drew, "is the oven. I use it for storage."

"You *never* cook?" I asked her.

"I make microwave popcorn."

"Do you guys realize that every time we get together, almost all we talk about are men and the dismal state of our personal lives?" said

Diane. "We're multi–dimensional, enlightened women. Let's talk about something else."

"So how was your day at work?" I asked her.

"Strep, the flu, pink eye, head lice, vomiting, and diarrhea. That was all before lunch."

"Pink eye? *Head lice?*" whined Drew. "I think I'm going to get my tubes tied."

"How do kids *get* all that icky stuff?" I asked.

"During their first couple of years in school, kids get sick all the time," casually shrugged Diane. "You'll see when you have munchkins."

"I don't think I could deal with that," said Drew, aghast, voicing what I was thinking.

"First thing this morning," shared the pediatrician, "I walked into an exam room and greeted my four–year–old patient and his mother. I asked him where he felt sick, and he proceeded to vomit his breakfast all over me. He then turned to his mother and said, 'I told you I didn't like French toast!'"

We all laughed.

"What did you *do?*" I asked.

"Changed into a new lab coat," said Diane. "No big deal. Happens all the time. A bad day for me means diagnosing something that could become serious."

"My rape case settled today," sighed Drew with obvious disappoint-ment. "I *really* wanted to get the son–of–a–bitch rapist on the stand—I just *know* I could have gotten a guilty verdict."

"The married one who was raping his employees on business trips?" I inquired.

"No—that settled last month. This was a guy who installed security systems. My client had just gotten a divorce and had bought a house. Because she lived alone, she wanted some extra protection. So she calls a well-known burglar alarm place, and they sent out this guy—one of their top installers—to advise her about what kind of system she needed. Turns out they didn't do a background check and he had a record for sexual assault. The dirt bag comes back a few days after her system was set up 'to see how she was doing,' and naturally she let him right in the front door. She knew him . . . he was in uniform . . . so she felt safe. He raped her repeatedly over the course of several hours. He also gave her a raging case of herpes that she'll have as long as she lives."

"What kind of twisted moron rapes someone who can so easily identify him?" questioned Diane.

"You've never heard of date rape?" Drew responded. "So . . . this sicko isn't going to get jail time because my client decided at the eleventh hour that she just didn't want to go to trial. I can't say that I'm surprised—I warned her that opposing council would have argued that the sex was consensual because she *did* willingly let the guy in. It's her word against his . . . even with his record."

"Couldn't you have talked her into it?" I asked.

"That's unethical. I work for the client; and in regard to settling a case, I have to do what she thinks is best. But at least I got the rotten bastard on the run—when I filed the lawsuit, we got good coverage in the newspaper, so I'm hoping other victims will still come forward. My client can't be the only one he's assaulted."

"I'd much rather deal with head lice and diarrhea," responded Diane cynically.

"Somebody has to stand up and make these bastards accountable," Drew declared, her mouth tight and eyes narrow. She motioned to the bartender for another round.

"And how was *your* day?" Diane asked me. "I know you never discuss what goes on in your sessions . . . I was just asking in general."

"My day was great, except for the disgusting insect I saw in my office—"

"Was this a client you've worked with before?" demanded Drew protectively. "Did he *threaten* you?"

"No!" I said laughing. "It was a bug . . . a spider!" And I relayed what had occurred late that afternoon after I had ushered a new client into my inner office.

"We're ready to begin," I said to the client, after I made sure our audio tape was working correctly.

"Okay," she nodded nervously. "First, I want to ask about my health. I have these scary symptoms, and the doctors don't know what it is. I've been having this pain . . . "

At that moment, something caught my attention from behind where the client was seated. It was the biggest spider I had ever seen, and it was slowly climbing the far wall of my office. It was dark brown, its thick legs were long and hairy, and its body alone was fully as big as a man's hand! It was a *beast*—bigger than a tarantula—and it was impossible to just sit there and ignore it. I certainly didn't have anything lethal enough to kill it with—but that was a moot point because I had no intention of going anywhere *near* it! It was clear that I needed help in confronting the hairy monster. Maybe it could be shooed outside rather than killed? Perhaps the CPA next door could come to the rescue. But then I remembered that he had been frightened by an infestation of ants in his suite the week before. The office building had a full-time security officer who was rumored to be ex-military, and he was a big, strong, strapping guy. I imagined that a spider wouldn't scare him. I hoped that the fuzzy beast would remain motionless so I could concentrate on my channeling. I tried, unsuccessfully, to maintain a neutral expression as I returned my focus to the client sitting in front of me.

"Uh oh . . . you see something *bad* . . . I can *tell!*" she said fearfully.

In my peripheral vision, I saw the spider starting to run across the wall. I gasped—eyes wide—and instinctively pushed away from my desk, ready to flee.

"Oh, my God!" the client cried. "I knew it was something *terrible!* What are the angels saying? You can tell me. What *is* it?"

The furry brute suddenly jumped off the wall and fell to the floor. He was slowly hopping right toward my desk! I sprang to my feet and squealed.

"*Tell me!*" begged the woman, now completely alarmed, her eyes filled with panic.

"I've never seen anything like this!" I cried, unable to take my eyes off the spider.

"Is my health *that bad?* What can I do—"

"*Look!*" I cried, pointing dramatically to the floor behind her. I prayed that my client didn't have a bad heart.

Surprised and startled, she swiveled in her chair to see where I was pointing. When my client saw the beast, she leaped to her feet as if a nuclear warhead had been lit underneath her, almost knocking over the chair in her haste. We both stood staring fearfully at the hairy intruder. He started to make menacing, hopping movements as he got closer . . . and closer . . . and closer. We both screamed and tried to scamper around him. The beast started to *run* toward us—and we screamed again in unison.

As if perfectly on cue, the burly, uniformed security officer burst through my inner door, weapon drawn, ready to confront whatever danger was lurking. For a second he looked confused. We both pointed toward the spider.

"Whooo—eee!" he exclaimed, whistling his appreciation as he holstered his gun. "That's gotta be the biggest dang spider I *ever* saw! He's even bigger'n the Camel spiders I seen in the desert durin' the Gulf War. Will ya look at them furry legs!" He whistled again before turning his attention back to us. "By chance—do ya'll have a jar handy? One of them real big 'uns? With a screw-on lid?"

"No . . . I don't have a jar," I answered, brow furrowed. What would I be doing with a big jar in my office? The only containers I had with lids were the few pieces of Tupperware that I hardly ever used, and they were stored in the back recesses of a kitchen cabinet in my condo. In my whole life, I had never even *seen* an oversized jar with a screw-on lid. And supposing I did have one that I could magically pull out of my credenza, how would the security officer squeeze the monstrous brute in there with those big long furry legs? Would the spider bite him? Was it poisonous? I shuddered at the thought.

"Too bad," the officer lamented, shaking his head. He looked down at the beast. "This 'un's so big, I'm tempted to call the wife and have her fire up the barbeque!" He grinned back at us, but we weren't amused by his witty repartee.

The beast began to skulk away, sensing that his days were numbered.

"Get it!" we squealed, jumping up and down, pushing the security officer from behind. "Don't let him get *away!* Hurry! *Hurry!*"

"Ya'll calm *down!* There's nothin' to worry 'bout. I got this handled." There was a decidedly unsure tone in his voice. "At least this ain't as bad as when that gator crawled into the yard . . . but I sure wish I had my fishin' gloves."

"What are you going to do?" I demanded. "Be careful—he might bite— I don't want you to get hurt. Could there be other ones in here, too? Do you have to kill him? Couldn't you somehow just carry him outside? Do you think that I need to spray? What about—"

"Like I said," the officer turned back to face me, his expression full of exasperation. "I got this situation under control. You two little gals better high-tail it 'fore it starts gettin' nasty." He shook his head, and under his breath, he sighed, "This ain't gonna be purty—"

"Hello, ladies."

My story had been interrupted by a very nice looking man who approached Diane, Drew, and me as we sat at the bar in Carrabbas. Diane and I smiled at him. Who *knew* . . . he might be a nice guy. Drew didn't bother to look up from her drink.

"Waiting for a table?" he asked charmingly.

Diane and I nodded.

"I'm Bruce," he said with a confident grin. "I'm here on business, and I'm dining alone. May I ask you lovely ladies to join me?"

Diane and I politely declined. Whenever the three of us met for dinner, we made it a rule *never* to accept the offer of a drink or dinner from a man. If we did, it immediately established an obligation to spend time with someone who might turn out to be unappealing. We introduced ourselves. I saw that he wasn't wearing a ring. And I intuited that he was single and available.

"So what do you do, Bruce?" inquired Drew, still not looking up from her drink. She sounded as if she were cross-examining someone on the witness stand.

"I'm an attorney."

"Well . . . isn't that interesting?" she exclaimed with obvious boredom. "So am I."

Tell your friend that she might give this man a little more encouragement, John said suddenly. *It's not every day that a woman meets her Mr. Wonderful.*

I gasped and nudged Drew a little harder than I should have, almost knocking her off the barstool.

She turned quizzically and finally looked up at the man standing beside us. When their eyes met, I knew—in that instant—that my best friend's life had changed forever.

Part Four

Miracles Start Happening

Chapter 23

Meeting Mr. Wonderful

"Honey, you have to get up," gently prodded my guardian angel Jean Harlow, nudging me out of a sound sleep.

Years before, when I had asked John for advice about a makeover, he had invited the actress—who was now in spirit—to participate, citing that female grooming was an area outside his expertise. We immediately became fast friends, and she spent many evenings in my tiny condo reassuring me that I wouldn't always be alone.

When Jean woke me, I was having a vivid dream in which I was flying—soaring among the clouds—and I didn't want to let go of the stirring images. I loved those recurring dreams because they were always a precursor for some major transition.

Opening one bleary eye, I saw that my bedroom was still dark. Winston snored loudly on the pillow next to mine. His back legs were twitching, and I guessed he was happily dreaming about a stalking adventure. I brought the small illuminated alarm clock in front of my face. I had another precious hour to sleep.

"I'll wait until the alarm goes off," I mumbled to Jean, nestling back into my pillow as I pulled the covers over my head.

"C'mon, sleepyhead . . . you have work to do!" she trilled. "Today's the day!"

She was obviously not going to be put off. I reluctantly pulled back the covers, groggily sat up, and reached for my glasses. I turned on the bedside lamp and recoiled from the bright light. Jean took a seat on the large wicker chair next to my bed.

Her face was so beautiful that it always reminded me of a flower in full bloom, and she had a halo of thick, platinum blonde hair. She wore a silver, clingy satin evening gown with matching high heels. A satin evening coat trimmed in silver fox lay across the arm of the chair. Her earrings were large clusters of diamonds, and a substantial diamond brooch clung to the left strap of her gown. On top of her paper-thin opera-length gloves were two wide diamond cuff bracelets. On one gloved finger she wore a 150-carat sapphire ring—a Christmas gift presented to her in the mid 1930's by her true love, William Powell. Jean told me that for several years they carried on a torrid love affair, but to her endless dismay, he had never asked her to marry him. She discovered that Powell had been gun shy about marrying another actress after his disastrous relationship with Carole Lombard. He certainly was devoted to her now that they were both in spirit, and they spent much of their time together. I often saw him hovering near Jean, usually resplendent in tails and a black silk top hat. They always looked quite the elegant couple. However, there was no sign of Powell that morning. Jean was there alone.

She personified 1930's movie star glamour, while I, sitting on the edge of my bed, my hair in a tangle, wearing my thick glasses, a T-shirt from KRBE Radio, and white crew socks, embodied something else entirely! I told Jean how lovely she looked, and she smiled, her eyes full of mischief.

"While you slept, Bill and I had a late dinner and we went dancing," she explained happily.

So they were just coming in at this hour! Along with John and Claire, Jean had become one of my favorite guardian angels. I felt as though we were sisters. As I got to know her, I learned that we had enjoyed many positive past lives on the earthly plane, which had created a true affinity between us. Ten years earlier, at the time of my divorce from

David, she had joined my team of angels, and it was her responsibility to facilitate my meeting Mr. Wonderful.

"So . . . what's the rush this morning?" I asked her in a sleepy stupor.

"Today's the day!" she repeated.

"For what?" I asked, suppressing a yawn.

"Mr. Wonderful is coming into your office. You asked me to tell you ahead of time so you could get dolled up."

"He's coming—*today*?" Suddenly I was wide awake. I had asked her to let me know ahead of time because I didn't want to be taken by surprise like my girlfriend, Drew, who had since gotten married, moved to Seattle, and was expecting her first child.

"If I had told you yesterday, or last week, you never would have gotten any sleep."

She was right. I would have been tossing and turning in a nervous frenzy.

"C'mon, kid!" she urged, all business. "There's no time to waste. You need to tweeze your eyebrows, wash and condition your hair, and do your make-up."

She paused for a moment, placing a well-manicured index finger to the delicate cleft in her chin, eyes narrowing in deep concentration. "I like the new green leather skirt you just bought with the matching heels . . . and the white silk blouse. You need to wear a skirt—let's show him your legs! So you'll need to shave . . . all the way up!"

I always did my hair and make-up, but shave my legs? This must be serious! As a single girl, I didn't shave unless it was absolutely necessary. The only man coming in that day was a new client, and his appointment was 4:15 in the afternoon.

"That's him," confirmed Jean, reading my thoughts. She grabbed me by the arm and raced me to the bathroom.

As I got ready for work, my heart was fluttering with nervous excitement. I had waited so long that it was hard to believe that Mr. Wonderful was really coming into my life.

The irony was that on a day-to-day basis, I continually assured—and reassured—my female clients that their romantic destiny would come to fruition if they mustered strength, faith, and courage to *wait* for the right person to come along, and chose to enjoy their less-than-satisfying lives in the meantime. While I waited for *my* elusive Mr. Wonderful to arrive on the scene, I had many of the same choices as the other single gals I knew. I could go out with my girlfriends; spend time with my family; work on accomplishing personal or professional goals; or I could date just for casual fun.

As the days turned into weeks, and the weeks turned into months, I figured that it might ease the boredom and loneliness I was feeling if I dated, even though my angels warned me that any relationship that appeared superficially promising at first was sure to quickly stall and deteriorate.

But I wanted to be part of a couple—right *then*. I lived in a city of over four million people, and I reasoned that there just had to be someone out there for me. I asked friends to fix me up. I attended single's events with my girlfriends. What's more, I began to consider all the men I already knew who appeared available.

My next–door neighbor was a college professor who taught economics, and one day I saw him at the mailbox. I had never noticed how cute he was in a cerebral, teddy–bear sort of way. It was true that he had never asked me out, nor even looked in my direction, but maybe he was shy. Moreover, as a tenured economics professor, I figured he knew how to handle money, which was a real plus for me. He looked very surprised when I asked him for a date, and he accepted on the spot. We started to go out, and almost immediately, I saw a number of red flags— but I talked myself into falling head over heels for him anyway.

He was in his forties and had never had a serious relationship, but I decided that he simply hadn't met the right girl yet. Every time we went out, he flatly refused to show any sort of public affection, and I heard him constantly echo his disdain for couples who got married, had children, co–mingled their funds, and took on the debt of buying a home, which was exactly everything that I was dreaming about. It appeared that he was falling in love with me, so I assumed that his plans and goals might start to mirror my own and that his harsh philosophies and judgmental beliefs might soften into something more poetic and sentimental. I thought that being with him was better than being alone, but I found myself leaping back into a dysfunctional quagmire like the one I had shared with my ex–husband. The moment our relationship started to expand into emotional intimacy, the professor would inexplicably, and abruptly, run away. I would feel hurt, confused, distracted, and miserable when I wouldn't hear from him. As I kept checking for his messages, and found none, I couldn't imagine what I had done to make him turn tail and run. After a few days or a week had slowly passed, he would suddenly call and appear to be warmer and more loving than before, and I would allow him to race back into my life.

After this back-and-force lunacy went on for about six months, I couldn't take any more melodrama. I discovered that a man could have an unattached single status and yet remain completely unavailable for a relationship if he was emotionally constipated because of commitment issues. I had chosen to share my companionship and affection with a man who could never appreciate it nor was interested or inspired to give back in kind. I had learned more than I ever wanted to know about a man who couldn't commit.

Following that fiasco, I continued to ignore the advice of my angels, and I joined an upscale dating service to widen the prospective search for a suitable mate. Suddenly, to my delight, I received a flurry of phone calls from all sorts of men asking me out. When I met them in person, however, there were always comical consequences because, unfortunately, they never looked like their pictures, nor did they even remotely resemble the physical information they had provided for their written profiles that included their age, height, and weight.

At about the same time, one of my clients fixed me up on a blind date with a successful entrepreneur who asked me to dinner and then pointedly inquired about whether my breasts were "real" before the salad had even arrived. Then there was the divorced man who said he wanted a relationship but who would jump up and leave my presence every time he'd receive one of the incessant cell phone calls from his fourteen-year-old daughter who was upset that he was out with me. There was the distinguished OB/GYN who spent the entire evening discussing the sexually transmitted diseases his patients had contracted, and who became angry when I rejected his advances once we got back to my place. Then there was the date I threw out of my condo fifteen minutes after he'd arrived because he brusquely kicked my cat, Winston, after he rubbed against his expensive trousers. On another occasion, I went out with a Texas good-old-boy who disclosed he loved hunting and expected me to help clean his bloody animal carcasses so we could barbeque. Another whirlwind of romantic mishaps followed: the date who pretended he didn't know me when I slipped and fell on the pavement outside a busy restaurant; the attorney who met me for a swanky dinner downtown wearing a loud Hawaiian shirt, wrinkled baggy shorts, and frayed sandals, and who spent the entire evening bitterly complaining about his ex-wife; the outside salesman who conveniently "forgot" his wallet both times we went out, forcing me to pay for the dates; the professional psychic who swore my angels were telling him that we should sleep together; the guy who kept calling me by the name of his ex-girlfriend; the man who needed his controlling mother's approval before he could make any decisions about his personal life; and—best of all—the born-again Christian who begged me not to disclose my profession when he took me to a party attended by a large group of Baptist preachers and who earnestly suggested that I tell everyone I worked as an exotic dancer instead.

After participating in all of that romantic dysfunction, I felt emotionally and spiritually wrung out. Learning the hard way, as always, I came to the depressing conclusion that dating a Mr. Right Now was not in my best interests—no matter how lonely I became. My angels had tried to warn me, but I hadn't chosen to listen. In fact, it seemed that the more I dated, the further I felt from ever connecting with someone heart, mind, body, and soul.

Only when I surrendered to the perfect timing of the universe was I able to start developing the strength and courage not to settle for less than what I wanted—and what I deserved. So I mustered the determination to be alone again, and I waited . . . and waited . . . and waited for my Mr. Wonderful to come along. And in the meantime, I worked steadily on my issues, realizing that I had to *earn* the opportunity of being considered a Ms. Wonderful.

As the years crept slowly by and nothing happened, I began to doubt that I would ever meet my special soul mate. Jean and John kept reassuring me that I would meet him, but as my thirties unfolded—year after year—and then came to a close with no romantic prospects on the horizon, I was having a major challenge sustaining the faith that a soul mate would ever enter my life, no matter how many times the angels confirmed the information.

It was easy for me to commiserate with friends and clients when they, too, expressed disbelief that a relationship would transpire for them. The only thing that really kept me hopeful was when I had the opportunity to channel for a gal who *had* met a Mr. Wonderful. I reasoned that if a client had actually met a Mr. Wonderful then perhaps I could, too; and suddenly, my faith would re-ignite for a little while.

My focus returned to the present. I was sitting on the floor of my living room nervously doing my make-up, halfway listening to a morning news show on TV. My hair was already in hot rollers; I had never been coordinated enough to use a curling iron without sustaining third-degree burns.

I wondered what was going to happen when I met my Mr. Wonderful later that afternoon. Evidently my psychic ability wasn't going to spook him because he had scheduled an appointment for a channeling session. Would this really be the day? Would it happen as I fantasized? Would it be like Drew and her sweetie at Carrabbas? Would my soul mate approach, look into my eyes, take my hand, tell me I was beautiful and that I was the girl he had been dreaming about? And then . . . everything around us would disappear as we stared into each other's soul . . .

"Honey, don't forget that you have to act normal," said Jean, interrupting my romantic fantasy.

"What do you mean?" I asked her, mascara wand suspended as I looked back at her on the couch. "Don't I always act normal?"

"You have to behave as if he's just a regular client and that you know nothing about the future," she advised. "Let him think he's the one orchestrating everything. Allow him to believe that the idea of a romance is his idea."

"But if he's so enlightened, won't he recognize me as his Ms. Wonderful right away?"

"He'll find you attractive, but he needs some channeled information about another woman."

"Another *woman?*" I asked worriedly. "He's single, isn't he? And ready for a relationship?"

"Oh, yes, he's single . . . and ready for a relationship. There's no problem there."

I nodded and finished getting ready. As if I was cramming for a final exam, I mentally reviewed the Mr. Wonderful list I had developed over the years.

Once I finally got to work, it was the longest day I'd ever had. I tried to concentrate on each client and all of the channeled information, but I was distracted and jumpy. To make matters worse, my body temperature always rose when I channeled, and I was incredibly uncomfortable working in the tight leather skirt and control top Donna Karan pantyhose. Sure enough, while I was finishing my 3:00 p.m. session, I heard the outer door open and then quickly close. My Mr. Wonderful had arrived.

I was consumed with goose bumps. The female client for whom I had been channeling thanked me for the information, and I accompanied her to my inner door, opened it, and we walked out into the reception area. She hugged me, gave me more thanks, and we said goodbye. Heart pounding, I turned my attention toward the man sitting on the couch. I was so surprised—I was dumbfounded.

A very distinguished, well-groomed man of about fifty stood to greet me. He was about 6′2″, had gray hair, hazel eyes, a close-cropped gray beard, and a ruddy complexion. I smiled and offered my hand, and he took it without hesitation. As we touched, there were none of the thunderbolts that I had heard so much about when two soul mates reunite. This man appeared to be about fifteen years older than the men I had been dating who were all in their mid-thirties. I was forty—looked younger—and I still wanted to have children! Many of my clients who were married to men over fifty regaled me with stories about how they fell asleep on the couch by nine at night—I didn't want that! Besides, the men I had been dating were outgoing, communicative, and confident; this man seemed very soft spoken and reserved. I was more than a little confused.

I led the way into my office and offered him one of the big leather chairs that flanked my desk. I tried to hide my disappointment. This man did not seem to fit the physical or emotional description on my list at all.

As a preliminary to the session, I asked his name and age.

"Britt," he said softly.

I had never heard that name before. I liked it.

"I'm fifty-one."

I had been right about his age. Had Jean goofed up somehow? I *knew* that she was familiar with my Mr. Wonderful list.

"I was attending a single's event a few weeks ago, and a woman gave me your card," he shared in a quiet, resonant voice. "She said that you channeled for her a few times and that you were very good. She kept talking about you that evening, so I held on to your number."

He had a very heavy accent that I couldn't place, so I asked where he was from originally.

"I was born and raised in rural Mississippi, and I've also spent many years in Nawlins."

"I'm sorry? Where?"

"New Orleans," he more clearly enunciated.

He spoke so slowly and softly with his Southern gentleman–come-to-call accent that I actually was having a very hard time understanding what he was saying.

Can we get on with the session, please? demanded an irritated female spirit. She was obviously waiting to share some kind of message with the man sitting across from me.

I checked the audio tape and asked the new client if he had any questions about the process of channeling.

"No . . . I've done this before," he replied.

I began to access all sorts of information about his health, career, and members of his family. He nodded, comfortable with all the intuitive insights and predictions. This man fully understood the channeling process.

Following all of that, I asked what else he wanted to achieve in the session.

"I want to speak with my wife and make certain she's okay."

His *wife?*

"She passed away in February," the man explained. "And I need to know if she's all right."

Oh, my God. He was a widower! And his wife had just passed away in *February*? This was May 29. No man would be ready for another relationship so soon. He would still be naturally mourning her loss—had Jean gone completely crazy? But he went to a single's event, so perhaps . . .

Could we begin? the female spirit repeated peevishly. *I have things to do!*

Uh, oh, I wondered . . . could this be . . . the wife? She sounded extremely perturbed. The female spirit took shape in my mind's eye. She confirmed that she was indeed his deceased wife and that she has recently died of breast cancer. She was an attractive, slender brunette in her early fifties. Although she was scowling, it was easy to imagine that she was very pretty when she smiled. She began to provide no-nonsense information to the man sitting across from me.

"Your wife is a very lovely lady," I acknowledged. "She tells me that she is just fine. She wants you to give her clothes, jewelry, pictures, oriental screens, and furniture to family members who want them—or you're to sell them and keep the money. She doesn't really care. Your life is about to change, and she's eager for that to happen so she can move on and begin to enjoy her new life in heaven."

I stopped for a moment and regarded my new client. He sat expressionless and stone still. I continued.

"She feels that you are dragging your feet and the time has come to move forward. You are going to meet a soul mate, get remarried, and have children. And you're going to sell your house."

I stopped again. This was a lot of information for him to process. I was wondering how the wife could think that he was "dragging his feet" when she had passed away only a few months before. My new client stared back at me without saying a word.

"She says to stop feeling guilty about what you did—and *didn't* do— when you were married to her. It was okay that you continued to travel for business after she got sick . . . you had a good job and it was the only means of support the two of you had. She says that now, you need to think about the future—not the past. You two were never destined to be Romeo and Juliet . . . you were supposed to be teachers for one another. You were a good husband, and she wishes that she had appreciated you more. Also . . . you've gained some weight since her passing that you need to lose."

I glanced at the Southern gentleman, and he looked in pretty good shape to me. It was certainly none of my business, but her remark sounded awfully critical.

My, aren't we little Miss Susie Sunshine? she chided.

Why are you so angry? I inquired telepathically.

He keeps talking to me . . . and I want to move on! It's my turn to do exactly what I want for a change! And I have to hang around until he gets situated with his new romance. It's the last part of my spiritual contract with him—and I want it over with!

"How long were you married?" I asked the man sitting in front of me.

"Seven yeeaahs," he replied.

I couldn't understand what he had said. I asked him to repeat it. Still, I couldn't understand. So I asked him to spell it out.

"Seven y-e-a-r-s."

"Oh. *Years!*" I repeated in my rapid–fire Midwestern cadence. It sounded as if we were speaking two different languages.

"Can you tell me about mah romantic fucha?" he asked softly.

"Pardon? You're *what?*" This session was not going well.

"Romantic f-u-t-u-r-e," he obligingly spelled.

"Of course!" I replied, embarrassed. Suddenly, in my mind's eye, I saw the client and a woman working in a garden that was in the back of a nice two–story home. They were laughing and obviously enjoying their time together. I could only see the woman from the back. "Curly blonde hair, about 5'7", slender figure," I described to him. And then, in my mind's eye, the woman turned, and I could see her from the front. *It was me! The woman was me! I was there with him!* This had never happened in a session before! My eyes widened, my heart started to pound, my mouth dried up, my throat closed off, and I started to choke. My hand shook as I clumsily reached for my Styrofoam cup of water that sat on the edge of my desk. I could feel my face getting blood red. Hives started to bloom.

My sudden discomfort must have been obvious to him, but he remained completely silent, watching me with an inscrutable, neutral expression. What was I going to *do?* How could I possibly tell this man— a complete stranger—that the woman I saw was *me?* Wouldn't that appear self-serving? Wouldn't that put him on the spot? How was he supposed to react to that tidbit of psychic information? Plus, I wasn't feeling attracted to him in any way. I wasn't feeling any chemistry with him whatsoever. And it was obvious that I wasn't even registering on his romantic radar screen, so I had gone to all the trouble of getting dolled up for nothing. I'd shaved my legs, worn high heels, that miserable skirt, the control-top pantyhose, and had gotten all excited to finally meet my Mr. Wonderful, and we had spent our first interaction channeling his *deceased wife?* This was not the romantic vision I had in mind.

"So, you're telling me that I'm going to remarry and have a happy relationship?" he summarized quietly. Or at least that's what I thought he said. His manner, in complete disparity to mine, was as calm and peaceful as a placid lake on a warm, cloudless summer afternoon.

"Yes," I answered, giving him a few manic nods. For the first time in my life, I prayed that a man couldn't read my mind. I squirmed in my chair and regarded him worriedly, afraid that he might decide to pursue a more penetrating line of questions regarding his "fucha" personal life. But he didn't. Nor did his wife have anything more to share. Nervously scratching one of the larger hives, I asked if he wanted any other information. He shook his head.

"I appreciate the time you've given me," he said graciously, after what seemed like a very long silence. "You've just confirmed my own sense of things. Thank you."

Without another word, he stood, paid for his session, and left my office. My brow furrowed as I watched him walk down the hallway to the bank of elevators that led to the parking garage.

What a letdown! I'd never had a client respond to channeled information in such silence and without any semblance of emotion. I had once channeled for a CIA operative who was more open.

The client's deceased wife had been very outspoken. Perhaps she hurt his feelings? Should I have softened what she said about his weight—or simply not repeated it at all? But censoring information would have gone against everything I believed I was supposed to do as a channel, which was to share everything I heard verbatim. The only thing I hadn't shared was the glimpse of me in that garden. I wondered what he thought about the sudden shift in my manner. He didn't confirm—or deny—what his wife had shared. Did *any* of the information resonate inside of him?

I suddenly realized that my feet were killing me. I had been so emotionally revved up all day that I felt exhausted and *terribly* dejected. I kicked off the high heels and carried them back into my inner office. I was so let down! Jean had gotten me all worked up, and I had been expecting to be swept off my feet by my true love. Brett—or whatever his name was—had hardly spoken! And half of what he did say, I couldn't understand. We hadn't connected on any level.

"You did great, honey!" said Jean, materializing near my desk. She was flushed with excitement. John appeared next to her, smiling broadly. Then Claire joined them.

"It's so good to see you!" I said to the teenager, welcoming her. "I've missed you!"

"Since my Mom has been working on her channeling, I've been sort of hanging out with her."

"I'm *so* glad! How is your Mom?"

"She's fine," answered the teenage spirit. "Wait 'til she hears about this! I can tell her, can't I?"

"Well, sweetie, I don't think there's really anything—"

"Can I be maid of honor—unless you've already asked Jean?" she asked, giggling.

"That was the worst session I've ever conducted," I complained.

"No, it wasn't," John piped in. "You didn't say, 'repeat after me.'"

"There is *no way* that man is my soul mate!" I wailed, my eyes filling up with tears. "And I've waited all these years."

"Don't cry, honey," consoled Jean.

"Yeah . . . my Mom didn't like my Dad at first, either," said Claire.

"He didn't appeal to me!" I sniffed. "I'm a psychic . . . wouldn't I recognize my own soul mate?"

My phone rang.

"You need to take that," advised John.

Frowning at him, I swung my chair around and reluctantly grabbed the receiver.

"Good afternoon, Kim O'Neill's office," I answered glumly.

"Holy Mother of God!" cried my mother the moment she heard my voice.

"Mom? What *is* it?"

"Did he leave already?"

"*Who?*"

"The widower!"

She caught me completely by surprise. I never discussed my clients with her.

"Honey?" she pressed.

"I'm here."

"Your angels have been talking to me all afternoon about a new client who was going to come in," she shared breathlessly. "He's a Mr. Wonderful for you!" Then she burst into tears. "You're finally going to have your *babies!* I *told* you that you'd meet someone, didn't I? Let's go celebrate!"

Apparently, I had just launched into a new chapter of my life, and everybody seemed to feel all the joyous excitement and anticipation . . . but me.

Chapter 24

Channeling My Future Child

Punctual to a fault, I arrived at my OB/GYN's office on time for my annual October appointment, signed in at the reception desk, and then took my seat in the crowded waiting room.

Unlike me, all the other patients were in various stages of pregnancy. I had forgotten to bring a book, so I was left to entertain myself with mentally redecorating the doctor's office, rifling through old magazines, using my cell phone to check for messages I couldn't return in the quiet reception area, wishing I was ten pounds thinner so I wouldn't be embarrassed when the nurse weighed me, and committing to a new workout program that I would begin the next day at 5:00 a.m.

One by one, the pregnant patients were called, and I'd watch them hoist themselves out of their chairs and waddle inside the large brown door that stood sentry to the labyrinth of exam rooms. Their appointments seemed to take forever, and I couldn't fathom what they did back there that took so long.

Spending all of that time in the company of pregnant women made me feel like the only girl not invited to a party that I—just recently— really, really wanted to attend. I looked down at the wedding ring on

my left hand and smiled, still not believing everything that had transpired in the last four months.

Recently, in mid–June, I had been scheduled to appear at the
Bookstop, a unique two–story book emporium that had been converted
from its former life as a movie palace. When I arrived, there were a
number of chairs set up, and people had already started to assemble. I
was surprised to see the man that my Mom and my guardian angels
referred to as "the Widower," who had visited my office several weeks
before for a channeling session regarding his deceased wife. He was
there alone, seated at the back of the room. For some reason, I began to
feel butterflies.

Soon, when all the chairs were filled, the Bookstop's events coordi-
nator asked me to begin the lecture. I spoke to the group about communicating with angels and then took my place behind the skirted
table to sign books. I saw the Widower get in line; however, the line was
so long that I doubted he'd stay. After all, it was a Saturday night and I
guessed that he probably had much more important things to do.

One by one, I greeted the people who had come to see me, and I
signed my book for them. The line slowly snaked forward, and the Widower got closer . . . and closer. I could feel him intently watching me.
Oddly, the closer he got, the more intense my butterfly sensation became.

Finally, after about forty minutes, I looked up, and there he was.
Instead of moving to stand in front of me at the table like everyone else,
however, he approached me from the side so that the table wasn't between us. To my utter astonishment, in front of all those people, he got
down on his knees! Then . . . he leaned so close I could feel his breath on
my ear. "You are *so* beautiful," he whispered.

At that very moment, my heart and soul exploded with feelings yet
unknown to me, and my angels were shouting, "It's him! It's Mr. Wonderful! It's him!"

"You are *such* a beautiful woman," he repeated with a voice full of
emotion, searching my eyes as if he could see right into my soul. He was
still on his knees, obviously not caring what other people thought.

At that moment, everyone around us seemed to vanish. I stared into
his eyes, and suddenly I *knew*—without any doubt—that he was the man

for me. Like a fireworks explosion, I could feel our souls connecting, and it felt as though they were *reuniting*. This was the moment I had been waiting for all my life. Instinctively, I grabbed his arm; I wasn't going to let him get away! If he would have asked me, I would have left with him right at that moment. We hadn't even had our first date, but I was that *certain*.

"We need to do something about this," he said with conviction, his hazel eyes passionate and sincere.

"Okay," I nodded, wide-eyed.

"You . . . are my fucha."

"I'm your *what?*"

"My f-u-t-u-r-e," he responded, putting his large warm hand over mine.

Right then and there, I knew we'd always be together. I just hoped that he was a good speller.

"Kim?" the OB/GYN nurse called, jarring me out of my romantic day-dream. I jumped up from my seat as though I'd been shot out of a cannon. The friendly, overworked nurse gestured for me to follow her into one of the exam rooms; she weighed me, took my blood pressure, and, as she departed, asked me to disrobe and provide her with a urine sample.

After I did what she asked, I sat waiting on the exam table dressed in a thin cotton gown. I started to shiver, and I wondered why the office was so cold when they knew patients were going to be naked. I kept looking impatiently at my watch, as if that gesture had the power of magically summoning my gynecologist. I visited his office only once a year, but I was truly aggravated that I had to take a whole afternoon off from my busy channeling practice to fight all the Houston traffic and then cool my heels indefinitely for what amounted to a fifteen minute appointment.

After my angels had led me to Dr. Schnider, I learned that he had a well-earned reputation as one of the best physicians in the city. Another thirty minutes crawled by before I heard a knock on the door. Dr. Schnider greeted me with a warm smile, as always, and then apologized for keeping me waiting—explaining that he had delivered a baby that morning and so was running behind schedule. As he reviewed my chart, he asked how I was feeling, and I told him that I had never felt better. Then it was time for the internal.

"Move down . . . a little more . . . a little more . . . " he requested from his seated vantage point at the end of the exam table. I clumsily maneuvered my body toward him on the table covered with the white crinkly paper. I placed my feet into the stirrups at either side of his head. I was suddenly curious about whether he ever noticed a woman's feet and a nice pedicure.

"Okay, that's fine," he indicated, once I had gotten into position. In less than a few minutes, it was all over. I sat up on the exam table as Dr. Schnider was getting ready to leave the exam room. I asked him to wait because I had some big news that I wanted to share. I told him that since my last visit, I had finally met my Mr. Wonderful and had gotten married. The doctor smiled broadly and offered hearty congratulations. Then I told him that my new husband and I were going to start a family. My dreams were all coming true, I giggled.

In a rather somber tone, Dr. Schnider asked me to meet him in his office once I dressed. With a quick nod, he left the room. His whole demeanor had changed. Had I said something to offend him, I wondered? Perhaps he wasn't going to be delivering babies anymore? Maybe for some reason he no longer wanted me as a patient. But that was absurd, I told myself; he had been as personable as ever during the exam.

I dressed and walked into the hallway, where the nurse was waiting for me. She said the doctor had to take an emergency call, so he would be a few minutes. She ushered me into a tiny waiting room directly outside his private office. Photographs of the babies and children Dr. Schnider had delivered lined all of the walls. In some, he was still in his scrubs, cheerfully holding infants that had just been born. I was immediately entranced by that wall of babies. My children would have their picture on that wall, too, I decided happily. I fantasized about what my children would be like in temperament and appearance, excited about the "fucha" of my personal life and all of its endless possibilities.

Lost in this train of blissful thought, I was startled when the nurse touched my arm to get my attention. She led me to the doctor's private office and gestured for me to take a seat. He would be there momentarily, she said, leaving me alone in the room. Why was I there? Tapping my foot with impatience, I began to look around. Some large photos on his credenza were of smiling teenagers, and I guessed that they were his children. I wasn't surprised to see how good looking all of them were.

My doctor rushed into the office, this time with more apologies about keeping me waiting. Dr. Schnider disclosed that one of his other patients was laboring in the Women's Hospital across the street and he was preparing to help her deliver that evening. He explained that he had been rushing back and forth between the hospital and his office all morning. For the first time, I stopped thinking only of myself and noticed how tired he looked. If he was going to deliver a baby later that night, he still had hours and hours of work ahead of him. Although he was probably exhausted, he seemed to be handling the situation with grace and dignity. I suddenly felt very guilty about my frustration at having to wait so long. If I was the one in labor, I would want him to focus entirely on me; and all of his other patients who had routine exams scheduled would just have to cool their heels! Dr. Schnider was literally running back and forth trying to accommodate everyone. And, still, he had a smile for me!

"I want to share something with you," he said softly, opening a drawer of his credenza. He pulled out what appeared to be several graphs and placed them on the desk between us. They were charts depicting a woman's fertility levels at age twenty. The doctor intended to discuss my biological clock.

The chart pointed out that at the ripe old age of thirty a woman's fertility starts to sink like a lead balloon. I was over forty. I looked at the chances of fertility for someone my age, and the line of fertility plummeted to ground zero. My heart sank. But how could that be, I wondered? I had never tried to get pregnant before, but I just assumed that I still had plenty of eggs left. Then the doctor pointed to another chart. It denoted the risk of physical deformities in pregnancies after the age of thirty-five. Dr. Schnider gently told me that he was concerned about my being able to have a baby because I had waited so long. If I did get pregnant, I might not be able to carry the child full-term without miscarrying. What's more, if I could carry the fetus, the chances of birth defects were high.

I had never considered any of these realities. The doctor reassured me that, if necessary, there were fertility options open to me, but my mind was spinning, and I was no longer listening to him.

In the past, my priority had been *preventing* pregnancy because I hadn't met Mr. Wonderful. Now that he had finally come into my life, it appeared as though my dreams of a family were cruelly over before they could even take shape. Ironically, that very morning I had read a story on the Internet about how difficult it could be for older couples to be considered viable candidates for adoption. And Britt was ten years older than I was. Then I thought of a client I had seen recently who had expressed shock over my recent marriage and subsequent plans to start a family, citing that he didn't believe those "earthly" things were meant for me. Could he have been right?

An immense wave of sadness and loss washed over me. A big lump began to form in my throat as my eyes welled up with tears. I dug in my purse for a handful of tissues. I couldn't get out of there fast enough! I told Dr. Schnider that I needed to think, and without another word, I grabbed my purse and fled, past the nurse's desk and into the reception area, past all the pregnant patients waiting for their prenatal appointments, and out into the hallway.

I couldn't make it to the public bathroom down the corridor. I burst into a flood of tears, standing right there in the middle of the hallway. I had been completely unprepared for the dreadful sense of loss and the "but why me?" disbelief that I wasn't going to have the opportunity to have a child. I had always taken it for granted as my female prerogative: that someday, whenever I was ready, I would get pregnant and have a healthy baby. It truly never occurred to me that my opportunity could expire prematurely before menopause. What was I going to do? Should I get a second opinion? Would I have to endure years of painful, expensive fertility treatments? Where would we get the money? What if they didn't work?

Still standing in the hallway, now propped up against the wall, I started to sob even harder. Maybe I shouldn't have waited until I met Mr. Wonderful. Had I made a huge mistake? I thought of the men I had dated over the dismal years when I was single—and clearly, none of them had ever been my idea of a good candidate for the father of my children. My ex-husband, David, made no secret of the fact that he had as much interest in having a child with me as he did climbing Mt. Everest without a canister of oxygen. Now that I did have a heart, mind, body, and soul relationship, my age was the saboteur.

The tears were still streaming when I realized that I had run out of tissues. I was soundly bumped from behind by a little boy who was quickly and quietly chastised by his mother, and I realized that I needed to get out of the busy hallway.

I scurried to the ladies room, found an empty stall, squeezed inside, and sat on the toilet with my purse in my lap. I grabbed some toilet tissue and loudly blew my nose. I morosely thought of my new husband. I was going to dash all of Britt's dreams about having a child with me. Maybe he should find a younger woman. Why hadn't he come into my life sooner? Why . . .

Stop! Kim! You need to listen! telepathically shouted John, my angel. *You will have a child!*

"How is that possible?" I wailed out loud, not caring who could hear me. "Dr. Schnider said—"

There are other factors involved, the angel insisted. *Your destiny was to have your children later in life. We've talked about that.*

"But Dr. Schnider is a fertility expert, and maybe—"

Haven't we told you that first, you were destined to meet your Mr. Wonderful . . . and then you were going to start your family?

"Yes," I sniffed.

And before you met Britt, how many times did you tell us that you didn't really believe you would ever meet a soul mate?

"A lot," I conceded.

And the soul mate came, and you are happily married. Didn't that happen as we told you it would?

"Yes, that's true," I whined. "But now—"

Although what you thought was impossible has already come to pass, you now doubt that the next part of your destiny will materialize. How can someone who channels as a life's work have such an issue with faith?

"I don't know," I cried, shaking my head. "I'm so depressed."

Why don't I introduce the new spirit hovering around you? offered John.

"All right," I replied, without enthusiasm, feeling very sorry for myself. "I suppose I need all the angelic help I can get right now."

This spirit is planning on getting help from you.

"Huh? How could I help a spirit?"

Hi, Mom! said a childlike, disembodied voice.

"Who is *that?*" I asked.

I can't wait to be your son! answered the voice.

"John . . . who is that speaking to me?"

Your future offspring.

"You mean, my *baby?*"

Hi, Mom, I'm right here!

"Oh, my God . . . then I can really have children?"

Isn't that what we've always told you? chided John.

"You're going to be a little boy?" I asked the spirit, now sobbing again.

Yes—your little boy! said the childlike voice. *I'm coming first!*

"Does that mean I'm going to have a second child?"

Jean is coming next . . . but I get to come first!

"Jean, my guardian angel, is coming to me as a daughter?" I asked. "Really? I'm going to have a son . . . and a daughter? My little girl is going to be *Jean?* She never told me! I can't believe it!"

All kinds of rapturous things are continually happening behind the scenes that human beings are unaware of, John reminded me.

"This is the best news I've ever had! Will Britt and I have any problems getting pregnant?"

None at all, John confirmed. *But you have to be patient. Remember, each soul decides when he or she will be born. That is not your decision. However, you must do your part. With Britt as a husband, that is not going to be an issue. In fact, he's just made reservations at your favorite restaurant so you could have a romantic evening . . . and embark on the baby-making.*

"Can I talk to my baby any time I want?"

Yes, said John. *All souls hover around their chosen birth mother to begin the bonding process before birth.*

"The baby chose me as a mom?" I asked, incredulous. "Why did he pick *me?*"

Because you'll love me and support me and help me get into my life's work, said my unborn child. *And because I need your help with a big issue . . . patience. I'm not as patient as you are!*

My eyes widened. I heard John chuckle.

May God help you both, remarked John, clearly amused.

"I need to call Britt right away!" I said, my hands shaking as I fumbled inside my purse for the cell phone. He answered on the second ring.

"Sweetie!" I cried. "It's me! Guess *what?*"

"What?" answered Britt. "Are you crying?"

"Don't worry," I sniffed. "Everything is going to be okay."

"What did the doctor say?"

"He said, in so many words, that our chances of having a baby are slim to none."

Silence.

"Guess who's here with me?"

"Are you still in the doctor's office?" he inquired worriedly.

"No, I'm in the toilet."

Silence.

"John is here. And I just talked to our *baby!* He's going to be a boy! And he told me that I'm going to help him develop patience. Isn't that *funny?*"

Silence.

"And, sweetie, thank you for making those dinner reservations. But maybe we shouldn't take the time . . . why don't I get carry-out on my way home?"

"Those reservations were supposed to be a surprise," sighed Britt. "I'm going to have a little talk with John. If I had a dolla for—"

"A what?" I asked.

"A d-o-l—"

"Never mind, sweetie . . . you can spell it for me when I get home. I'll be there as soon as I can. We've got important work to do! I love you."

With that, I closed my cell phone, got up, and strode out of the bathroom, with John and the little spirit in close pursuit. I was in a hurry. Britt and I were going to make a baby!

Chapter 25

Psychic Pregnancy

"It must be ready by now . . . it's been over fifteen minutes," I said nervously to Britt as we lay in bed one Sunday morning. I was filled with anxiety about the results of our most recent home pregnancy test.

We had spent a small fortune over the previous six months performing tests at regular intervals. Each negative result made me cry, and I'd sink into an overwhelming daylong fog of depression. I *longed* to have a baby, and although Dr. Schnider was a fertility specialist, Britt and I stubbornly continued to try and get pregnant on our own. Plus, all of my angels—and our future child—kept telling us that we would conceive the old-fashioned way. As each day ticked by, I was getting older, so I fully realized that we were taking a huge risk.

"I can't wait any longer," I announced, flinging back the covers and jumping out of bed. I scurried into the bathroom.

"Sweet'nin, we're going to get pregnant," Britt reassured, as he always did. "If it's not today, then—"

"I'm afraid to look," I called to my husband.

"Why don't you ask John or the baby when it's going to happen?"

he asked from the bedroom.

"Because—I want to be surprised!"

"Well, since you have the psychic ability, it seems to me that you could make your life a lot less stressful if—"

From the bathroom, I let out a bloodcurdling scream. Britt came running.

"We're *pregnant!* We did it!" I cried, thrusting the pregnancy test stick at him.

Britt took a look and then grinned.

See, Mom, I told you I was coming! From now on, until I'm born, I'll be around you all the time. And Mom—I'm going to have a personality just like yours. We're going to be like twins!

"The baby is here!" I joyously told Britt through my tears. "And he tells me that his personality is going to be just like mine!"

"He must be a brave little fella," chuckled my husband.

One would argue, Britt, that you're the brave one, teased John, making one of his unexpected appearances.

I repeated what he said, and Britt laughed.

It was the happiest day of my life. A little soul had chosen *me* as his mother. The reality hit home as I acknowledged that I had no parenting experience whatsoever; I had never even held a child. It occurred to me that having babies was going to be the ultimate lifelong adventure.

"Do you think I'm going to be able to do it?" I asked Britt. All at once, I was worried.

"Do what?"

"All of it: the pregnancy . . . the labor and delivery . . . being a Mom?"

You can't be confident about something you haven't done yet, my angel John reminded me. *You're a good mother to Winston.*

"Let's take it one day at a time," wisely suggested Britt.

"What if the test was *wrong?*" I asked, suddenly consumed with negativity. "You know, sometimes you can get a false positive—"

Anal moment . . . anal moment . . . warned my guardian angel. *Can't you just enjoy what's happening? Your dreams are coming true.*

As usual, John was right. I decided then and there to try to keep my emotions balanced and centered during the pregnancy and enjoy every single moment of the miracle that was taking place inside of me. After all, it was a special privilege to have the opportunity to create a brand new life. And I had waited such a long time—and had navigated such a difficult path—in order to be in this place at this moment.

It occurred to me that I had a choice. I could consider all the different stages of pregnancy a hardship I had to endure or the most incredibly magnificent, magical period of my life that I would never have back again. It was only going to last nine months; and, what's more, it might turn out to be my only pregnancy. So I decided to make the most of it—starting right at that moment.

It wasn't until I was four months pregnant that I finally started to show, so I went on a much anticipated shopping trip for maternity clothes. I was so thrilled!

To my relief, the clothes were *much* cuter than I was expecting. What's more, the store had a big pillow-like garment in the fitting room that I could strap onto the front of me so I could see how the clothes were going to look when I was in my last trimester. After strapping on the garment, I turned to the side, and I simply couldn't imagine my tummy stretching that far. And I couldn't imagine what labor and delivery were going to be like. I kept pondering how such a big baby was ultimately going to move through what was now such a small passageway.

I left the fitting room and approached the crowded sales counter with my pants, tops, and underwear.

"Excuse me," said a woman, reaching for my arm. She looked at my little bump, and then her eyes moved to my face.

"I'm pregnant!" I announced happily. I could see that she, too, was expecting.

"How are you planning to nourish your baby?" she asked in a no-nonsense tone.

I had no earthly clue what she meant.

"You *are* going to breast-feed, aren't you?" she demanded.

"I'm considering formula."

"You *must* breast-feed," she dictated, her hand now grasping my arm. "Or your baby won't have all the nutrients she needs. You want to give your baby every advantage, *don't* you? The latest research has found that only breast-fed children reach their full potential. In fact, only breast-fed children have a good immune system." She moved closer and whispered, "I believe that the prison system wouldn't be as crowded if those poor young men had been breast-fed as babies."

"Ma'am, I'm ready for you," said the gal behind the sales counter, rescuing me.

"I breast-feed all my children until they're four," proudly announced the woman, thrusting several brochures about breast feeding at me. I took them to be polite, and then I turned back toward the sales counter.

"Don't make a selfish mistake that will ruin your baby's life!" she called over her shoulder as she left the store with her packages. "Your child's whole future is at stake!"

I stood at the counter, now consumed with worry. *Was I being selfish to feed my baby from a bottle? My mother didn't breast-feed. Could I really be hurting my baby's future? Perhaps I should have told the woman that my choices were none of her business.*

Next, I drove to a baby superstore to look at their cribs. A female customer approached me and asked how far along I was with my pregnancy.

"Four months!" I exclaimed with a huge smile.

"Don't think you're out of the woods," she said morosely. "I miscarried at four months. Everything seemed fine . . . and then, it just happened. You should have seen all the blood. You could miscarry, too." Without another word, she turned and walked away.

I stood wide eyed, protectively holding my tummy. *Could I really miscarry? Could I lose this pregnancy now that I'm so far along? Why would she tell me that? Maybe I should wait before I get anything for the baby. What if I miscarry now . . . after I've wrapped all of my hopes and dreams into this child I'm carrying? How would I feel having all of his darling clothes and toys at home in the nursery . . . and then suffer a miscarriage? Maybe I'd better wait to shop for him just in case . . .*

The thought of losing the baby I had come to love so dearly brought a hormonal fountain of tears, and I had to leave the store. I sat crying in my Honda for several minutes. Wiping my tears, I looked at my watch and discovered that it was already after lunch. And as always, I was famished.

Mom! You're going to be fine. Don't listen to her! Let's go get some lunch.

My unborn baby was there, as always, supportive and encouraging. Hearing his voice inside my head allowed me to refocus and trust once again that everything was okay with the pregnancy. From the moment we started to communicate, my unborn child had remained steadfast and positive, and it was largely through his efforts that I had stayed my course and was able to maintain—most of the time—a positive and optimistic attitude. I really, really wanted to enjoy every moment of this time that I would never have back again.

I reached for a green-grass nutrition bar from the depths of my huge purse.

Mom, can we get some real food?

I laughed. He was right—we needed some serious recharging. I decided to cheat on my prenatal healthy eating plan. I headed to a small deli that I loved and ordered a chopped liver sandwich with sharp Vermont cheddar, a huge kosher pickle, potato chips, a frosty root beer, and a hefty slice of their homemade cheesecake. As I waited impatiently for the guy behind the counter to make my lunch, I acknowledged the gal standing next to me who was also waiting for her food. She was glancing at my stomach.

"I'm pregnant," I told her.

"Yes, I can see that," she said. "Isn't it *miserable?*"

"What?"

"Being pregnant," she said sarcastically. "The fatigue, the bloating, the gas, the morning sickness, the acne, the weight gain, the hormones—"

"I love it," I interrupted. "This is the best time in my life. I'm making a baby, and at the same time, I'm still doing everything I did before . . . except all the working out. My hair is thick! I don't have to think about a flat tummy, my boobs are really cute, and people always allow me to get in front of them when there's a line . . . anywhere! And now that I know where the bathrooms are in all of the places I go, I feel like I have the world by the balls!"

"Just wait," she responded, rolling her eyes at my naiveté. "I have three. Labor hurts more than anything you could imagine. You'll see. Once hard labor begins, you won't believe it. You're going to wish you were dead."

"I'm going to get an epidural."

"Don't kid yourself—they don't always work. And guess what? If your OB/GYN isn't there in time, you can't have one. Plus, if there are too many women giving birth at the same time, the anesthesiologist won't be able to service everybody."

"I don't remember my doctor telling me that," I responded, my eyes widening.

"They never do," she said.

"Oh, my doctor is fabulous—"

"My sister wanted an epidural, and the anesthesiologist wasn't experienced enough and damaged her spine. She's never recovered."

My eyes widened even more, and now my stomach felt queasy.

"My cousin in Memphis died in childbirth last year," the woman continued.

"You're *kidding?*" I asked. "In this day and time?"

"It happens more often than you'd believe. Janet was thirty–one. How old are you . . . mid–thirties?"

"I'm forty–four."

"You're *pregnant* at 44?"

"My Mr. Wonderful didn't come along until I was 40," I explained.

"You know, you're going to be the oldest mom when your kid goes to school," she said. "He's going to be embarrassed."

I just stood mute.

"Well, good luck," she said, shaking her head. "You're going to need it."

My sandwich was ready, but I had lost my appetite. I paid for my lunch, returned to my car with the big deli bag, and threw it on the passenger seat. I planked down behind the wheel and began to cry again.

Was labor going to be that bad? Should I forget about the epidural? What if my spine was injured? How would I handle a natural childbirth? Was I too old? Could I die and leave my husband and baby alone? Britt had been a widower when we met. He had already lost a wife. Was I kidding myself? Could my body really do it? Would I embarrass my son? Why didn't I tell that woman to mind her own business? I was getting angry with myself. Next time a stranger gave me unsolicited advice, I was going to be assertive.

Consumed with fear and depression, I pulled the slab of cheesecake out of the deli bag along with the plastic fork and inhaled it like a starving refuge. I was still hungry, so I grabbed the chopped liver sandwich and munched as the tears rolled down my cheeks.

That night I had a dream. I was standing on a street corner with my dead baby in my arms. His tiny newborn body was beginning to shrivel, and his hollow, haunted eyes stared sightlessly up at me. It was frigidly cold, and we were buffeted by penetrating winds and driving snow. I was bundled up in protection against the extreme weather, but my baby was wrapped only in a small, threadbare blanket. I had given birth to a healthy baby boy, and I had killed him through my deliberate neglect. My precious baby died because I forgot to feed him. It was all my fault. As I looked down at the corpse of my infant, my grief was so intense that it woke me out of a sound sleep.

"Oh, my God!" I wailed in the darkness. Instinctively, I reached for my pregnant tummy. The baby was still there.

"Another pregnancy dream?" muttered Britt, who lay beside me.

"These are worse than my psychic nightmares," I said, reaching for a tissue. "I dreamt again that our baby was dead."

"Everything's going to be okay," he said, burying his head deeper into the pillow.

There was no way I could go back to sleep. After I went to the bathroom, I padded back to the dark bedroom and reached for the stack of pregnancy and childcare books that I had piled on the nightstand. I grabbed one and quietly stumbled to the living room. I turned on the lamp, settled on the couch, and opened the book.

I'm right here, Mommy! my unborn son comforted. *You're not going to forget to feed me. I'm going to be just fine.*

"Why do I keep having these terrible nightmares?" I asked him forlornly.

I know what would make you feel better, suggested the baby. *Why don't we eat the rest of that chocolate cake you brought home from the restaurant tonight?*

The doggie bag! What a great idea. Although he hadn't yet been born, the baby and I were completely simpatico. I put the book down and went into the kitchen. Standing by the sink, I polished off the cake and then made some hot tea. A short time later, I felt soft rhythmic movements coming from my tummy. The baby had the hiccups as he did every time I ate anything. I placed my hands on top of my tummy directly over the area where he was moving. I loved feeling him. Although I could have psychically found out when he was coming, I chose for the delivery date to be a surprise. I happily wondered when he would be born and what he would look like. A peaceful contentment washed over me, and I wished those days could last forever.

I settled cozily on the couch to resume reading. The book had been written by a woman who believed that, in recent years, parents had become far too permissive and lenient. I read that every time she and her two little boys were going into a public place, she warned them about screaming and yelling. I frowned in confusion. Why would she have to warn her children about screaming and yelling, I wondered. Why would a child raise his voice like that? What would possess a child to misbehave in public—or God forbid—throw a tantrum?

I had a special fantasy about how life would be after the baby came. Our child was going to be quiet and well behaved and he would possess beautiful table manners, even as a toddler. There would be no screaming or tantrums in public or anywhere *else* for that matter. I wasn't going to allow it. After I gave birth, I would return to my healthy eating habits and insist that there be no junk food in the house or trips to McDonalds, as when I was a kid. Once the baby came, my special dream was for us to have a quiet home–cooked dinner with nice napkins, flowers, and candlelight. It would be a time when we would emotionally reconnoiter and bask in each other's quiet company. I also decided that I wasn't going to have toys and books scattered all over the house. My son would keep all of his things in his room, neatly organized and put away after every playtime. I would see to it.

I suddenly heard raucous, boyish laughter. *It's a good thing I'm coming! Don't worry, Mom . . . it won't take me long to break you in.*

Now I was really frowning. What was so funny, I wondered?

Chapter 26

Labor Day

Another hard contraction was gripping me. I had been in labor for only two hours, but the pressure and discomfort already felt very intense. Thanks to Britt's clever driving, we had negotiated the snarl of lunchtime traffic in the congested Galleria area and had arrived at the Woman's Hospital in record time.

"Britt—pull up—to the entrance—and let me off!" I barked between pants, like a general commanding his troops. "Park the van—and meet me—inside."

"But—"

"Don't argue—with me! Just—DO IT!"

The contraction started to weaken, and I felt immense relief. There was no discomfort at all in between the contractions, but I knew the next one would be building soon. I flung the door open, grabbed my purse, and hoisted my hugely pregnant body outside. Leaving the door to our minivan ajar, I waddled into the hospital as quickly as I could. I heard Britt screech away as I made my way to the elevator. I stepped inside just before the doors closed. Naturally, because I was in a hurry, the elevator stopped slowly on every floor. Finally, the car bounced to a halt on Labor & Delivery. I waddled out and hurried toward the nurse's station at the far end of the long hallway.

"Kim O'Neill?" shouted two nurses, who began to run toward me. I guessed that Dr. Schnider must have alerted them that I was coming.

"Can I get my epidural *now*?" I begged, frightened about what I was going to experience when the contractions strengthened as my labor progressed. I was very surprised that the mounting discomfort was already weakening my resolve to remain positive and cheerful.

The nurses grabbed me on both sides, and in no time at all, I had emptied my bladder, undressed, pulled on a hospital gown, and was helped into the bed where I would eventually give birth. Then one of the nurses examined me and declared that I was indeed in labor but that it was going to be quite some time before I had the baby. She hooked me up to a fetal monitoring machine.

"Will I be in here all by myself?" I asked, looking around the big hospital room.

"Yes," she replied. "This is generally a slow time of the year for births, so all of our patients have private rooms right now."

"How soon can I get my epidural?" I pressed. "Can you call Dr. Schnider right now, and—"

"No, honey," said the nurse. "He can't okay it unless he's here at the hospital."

"But what if he gets stuck in bad traffic, or—"

"Don't worry," she replied gently. "He's got plenty of time to get here. You've just started to labor."

"But I've had hypnosis to shorten the labor!" I argued. "It helped me with public speaking!"

"This is your first baby, honey," patiently responded the nurse. "You'll be laboring for a long time. You haven't even started to dilate."

"How can that *be*?" I whined, as another contraction started to build. "I'm already really uncomfortable—"

"We've contacted Dr. Schnider to let him know how you're doing," she said to assure me. "He'll be here later."

"*Later*?" I huffed and puffed. "But I'm in hard labor *now*!"

The nurse kindly stayed with me as the contraction steadily rose to its peak and then slowly began to weaken. I let out a huge sigh of relief when it was over. The nurse started to leave.

"When are you *coming?*" I asked the baby out loud.

"Oh, I'll be back soon to check on you," replied the nurse, thinking that I was speaking to her.

Mom, this is it! I'm going to be born in just a few hours. We're doing great!

Britt rushed in with my overnight bag and threw it in the corner. "I got here as soon as I could," he said. "There was no parking."

"That's why I asked you to drop me off at the door," I answered wryly.

"I should know never to argue with a psychic," he smiled, grasping my hand. "So . . . what do the nurses say?"

"They think that my labor is going to last a long time," I said, very disheartened. "But the baby tells me that he's going to be here quickly, so I must be in hard labor now."

"Do you want to change into one of the nightgowns you brought in your bag?"

"No, I'd better stay in this," I said, gesturing to the blue hospital gown.

Another nurse came in.

"Are you the Daddy?" she asked Britt warmly.

"I am," he replied, politely nodding to her. "Thank you for taking care of my wife."

"Where you from?" she inquired.

"I was raised in southwest Mississippi and then spent a number of years in Nawlins."

"Well, doesn't that beat all?" she replied with a hearty laugh. "I'm from McComb, Mississippi."

They began to discuss a restaurant they both enjoyed called the Dinner Bell and how Southern cooks really knew how to make stewed squash, fried okra, fried eggplant, butter beans, biscuits smothered in gravy, and fork–tender meats.

"Has this man had anything to eat today?" the nurse asked me.

"No, he hasn't," I answered, feeling guilty.

"Then why don't you go down to the cafeteria for some lunch?" she recommended to Britt. "She's going to be hours yet, and you're going to need your strength."

I was amused that she thought Britt was going to need *his* strength. Giving birth was strictly a two–person job, and those two people were the baby and me. While Mr. Wonderful played a key role in the conception, he was now relegated to the position of a supportive—yet help-less—bystander.

Another contraction began, and I squeezed Britt's hand.

"Remember not to tighten up," he helpfully suggested. "That's going to make it more intense."

"*More* intense?" I groaned.

He went to the end of the bed and began to rub my feet, which he knew I loved.

"Don't do that!" I snarled at him. "It's irritating me!"

Britt recoiled from my foot as if it were radioactive.

"This—is harder—than I thought—it would be." I whimpered.

"Look at the monitor, Sweet'nin," my husband instructed. "You'll be able to see how the contraction is building . . . peaking . . . and then coming to a close. Isn't that amazing? That could help you."

"I don't need the frigging machine to tell me . . . I can *feel* it!"

The nurse peeked under my gown and shook her head. I wasn't dilating.

"He told me—the birth—is going to be—in just—a few hours," I told her.

"*Who* told you?" she asked, confused.

"The *baby!*"

She just stared back at me. Then she turned to Britt. "Why don't you go downstairs for a bite to eat and come back later?"

The contraction slowly wound down. I sighed with relief.

"Go ahead, sweetheart," I urged him. "I'm fine." I didn't feel fine at all, but I knew he had to eat. Was the baby wrong about the timing, I wondered? Wouldn't the obstetric nurses know best? However, if I was indeed just starting labor, as the nurses believed, then were the contractions going to get far *worse?* How would I manage *that?*

"Okay, Sweet'nin, I'll be right back," he said reluctantly. "Can I get you anything?"

I shook my head and mustered an anemic smile as he and the nurse left the room together. Now that I was between contractions, I once again felt very comfortable. I reached for my cell phone and called my Mom. She had divorced my dad and was living in peaceful bliss by herself in a cozy apartment. After the divorce, she had become an interior designer. I remembered that she had an appointment with a new client that morning.

"Hello?" she trilled.

"Am I bothering you?" I asked. "Are you with the client?"

"I always have time to talk to you."

" Guess where we are?"

"Where?"

"The hospital!"

"Jesus! Mother of God!" shrieked my mother.

I winced and moved the phone away from my ear.

"Do you still want me there when you deliver?" she asked breathlessly.

"Of course," I told her. "But I don't think you have to rush. The nurse told me that I'm in labor but I'm not dilating—"

"That doesn't mean anything! What did the baby tell you?"

"He's going to be born this afternoon. But take your time . . . I don't want you in an accident."

She abruptly hung up.

I looked around the room, wanting to imprint the memory of this day so I could carry it the rest of my life. I was very grateful to have the large room all to myself. It was decorated in soft pastels. This was definitely not a clinical, generic hospital atmosphere; great care had obviously been taken to create a warm, softly lit, bedroom–like environment. It was very cozy. From the picture window to my left, I had a nice view of the Medical Center. The only machine in the room was the fetal monitor.

Another nurse came into the room and approached the end of my bed. She was holding a razor.

"I shaved my legs this morning," I told her.

"It's not your legs that I'm going to shave," she said. She lifted my gown and got right down to business. In no more than two minutes, she had finished. No nicks, no cuts, and no pulling or yanking. It was amazing! I had never been able to shave any part of my body without at least one casualty.

"Why do I need to be shaved?" I asked.

"So the doctor can see what he's doing," she replied. "Plus, hair can carry bacteria."

Wishing me well, she beat a hasty retreat. I looked at the wall clock. It was close to four. Another contraction began, and it rapidly intensified. I grabbed the sides of the bed with white knuckles.

A nurse came in to check me. She pursed her lips and shook her head.

"I have—to be—dilating," I panted. "These—are hard—contractions!"

"You're only at two," she said calmly. "You're not even getting close to—"

"*Please* ask Dr. Schnider for the epidural!" I wailed.

"I'll call him again," she said. Her tone sounded noncommittal.

About fifteen minutes later, a tall, distinguished doctor strode into my room. He announced that he was there to give me the shot.

"Thank God! I've never been so happy to see anyone in my life!"

Although I had heard many melodramatic stories about epidurals while I was pregnant, I would have agreed for him to shoot me in both eyeballs if that would have given me some relief.

A nurse helped me sit up on the side of the bed. She stood directly in front of me and firmly grabbed my upper arms and held me to ensure I would remain motionless during the procedure. The doctor moved behind me. Another contraction started.

"You're going to feel a stick," warned the doctor.

I felt something bearing down on my back, but because I was having a hard contraction, I really didn't feel the big needle going into my spine. Suddenly . . . miraculously . . . the contraction weakened so dramatically that it just felt like a minor pressure. I couldn't believe it. It was rapturous!

"Thank you! Thank you! You're incredible!" I gushed to the anesthesiologist. He smiled, and I guessed that he had heard that reaction many times before. "I'm going to name my son after you," I babbled in near delirium at being almost pain free. "What is your first name?"

"Leonard," he responded.

"Oh . . . well . . . that's a very nice name," I said quietly.

The doctor smiled, turned to the nurse, spoke to her, and then left the room.

I felt like a new woman! Suddenly, I wasn't scared anymore. Now the birth was going to be fun. From that moment, I knew I would be able to fully enjoy my labor.

Britt returned and looked extremely surprised to see me sitting up in bed with a huge smile on my face.

"Hi, Sweetie!" I called brightly. "I feel *fantastic!* I'm sorry I was a little nasty before. Want to order a pizza? Do you think Star would deliver to the Medical Center?"

He furrowed his brow in surprise.

"She just had an epidural," explained the nurse.

"Oh!" he said. "Great! How do you feel?"

"Do you want to name the baby Leonard?"

Britt frowned in confusion.

"Honey! I'm here!" loudly exclaimed my Mom, hurrying into the room. She came to the bedside and gave me a big hug. "My baby is having a baby! I can't believe it! I'm so excited to be here!"

"Hi, Mom," I said with a radiant smile. "We're having so much fun."

With an astonished, disbelieving expression, my Mom turned to the nurse and asked, "She's in labor, isn't she?"

"Epidural," the nurse simply answered.

"Thank God! I never had one of those."

The nurse lifted my hospital gown to examine me again, and this time her eyes popped. "I'll call the doctor." And with that she scurried from the room. A contraction started, but all I felt was a moderate pressure.

"Look," said Britt, studying the fetal monitor. "You're having a big one."

"Am I?"

Mom, I'm going to be here soon! Everything is okay. I can't wait for you to hold me. I want my name to be Flynn . . . not Leonard.

"The baby wants to be called Flynn," I repeated aloud. "I love that name!"

"So do I," said Britt.

We're here, too! said a chorus of familiar voices. *You're going to be a mom!*

"John, Jean, and Claire are here!" I joyfully announced to Britt and my Mom. A nurse wheeled in a cart and positioned it to my right. That's where they would weigh and check the newborn, she told us. A tiny blue cap lay waiting for our infant son.

Dr. Schnider hurried in wearing scrubs, acknowledged Britt and my Mom, and smiled at me. Without further ado, he sat down on the stool that had been placed at the end of my bed. After examining me, he said, "Won't be long now."

"That's what *he* said!" I exclaimed happily.

"*Who* said?" asked the doctor.

"The baby!"

A team of nurses rushed into the room. I knew the baby was coming because, all at once, the room was filled with an excitement and anticipation that was palpable.

The next time I speak with you, Mom, I'll be in your arms. I'm coming—right now!

Just then another contraction gripped me. I began to feel a lot more pressure. Even with the epidural, I was getting really uncomfortable again. I felt the need to push.

"Don't push yet," said Dr. Schnider. Then he addressed Britt and my Mom: "Would you like to join me down here to see the birth?"

"I think I'll stay here to comfort Kim," Britt replied queasily, standing at the bedside tightly clutching my left hand. My Mom, however, immediately went to stand behind the doctor so she could see everything that was happening. At that moment, I felt a hard, concentrated pressure. The doctor told me to push and count down from ten.

"Now!" he prompted.

"Ten . . . nine . . . eight . . . seven . . . six . . . five . . . four . . . three . . . two . . . one!" I gasped.

"Now stop," he instructed. "And rest for a moment."

The pressure was incredibly intense.

"Push!"

I pushed with all my might.

"Stop."

I tried to catch my breath. This was hard work.

"Push!"

I pushed one more time. The baby literally flew out of my body and into Dr. Schnider's waiting arms. My first labor had lasted a little over five and a half hours.

"It's a boy!" the doctor exclaimed.

Britt and I were crying at the miracle that we had helped create.

"I have a grandson," sobbed my Mom.

As the nurse took baby Flynn from the doctor, I saw that he had dark hair. I watched intently as the nurses weighed him, took his footprints, and performed some tests to make certain everything was as it should be.

"Ten toes, ten fingers," the nurse called out. "Eight pounds, three ounces. And he's 21 inches long." The nurses wrapped him in a tiny blanket and placed the blue cap on his head. Then she handed him to me. In complete wonderment, I cradled Flynn in my arms. He looked up at me with his dark blue eyes. Suddenly, we were the only two people in the room. The rush of absolute love that passed between us confirmed that our souls would always be connected in the most special way. In what seemed like the blink of an eye, I knew my life had changed forever. I wondered how I had ever done without him?

At that moment, I was startled by a loud, familiar telepathic voice inside my head.

I'm coming next!

It was Jean, the guardian angel who had been my best friend for so many years and who had helped bring Britt into my life.

Next year! she promised. *I'm going to be your daughter. I can't wait!*

"Dr. Schnider?" I called happily. "Guess *what?* We're going to be back next year—when our little girl is born."

"How do you *know* that?" he asked with a puzzled expression.

"Because—she just *told* me."

Chapter 27

The Haunted Townhouse

"It's available immediately," eagerly said Mr. Marsdon, the owner of the townhouse. "I'm willing to negotiate the rent. And I'll waive the security deposit. How soon do you want to move in?"

The spacious three-bedroom brick townhouse had new carpeting, extensive crown molding in every room, custom shutters throughout, lots of windows, a full-size washer and dryer, new kitchen appliances, and covered parking, and it was only ten minutes from my new office. Plus, it was located in the heart of a quiet, wooded community filled with multi–million–dollar estates.

"We've been looking for something that would accommodate our growing family," I heard my husband, Britt, tell him, as the two men stood in the kitchen. I continued to explore the unit with year–old Flynn on my hip. I was hugely pregnant with our second child, and we were in desperate need of a bigger home. We had already been searching for months, but every rental unit we saw was either dismally rundown or exorbitantly expensive. As I walked from room to room visualizing where I would place our furniture, I was trying not to get too excited.

I heard Britt casually inquire, "How long did you say this unit has been empty?" I had been married to him long enough to know that he was on a fishing expedition. I, too, couldn't imagine why the owner was motivated to negotiate in a real estate market so hot that even the poorly maintained rentals were snapped up faster than items marked last-clearance after Christmas.

"Well, I bought this place after it was first built," shared Marsdon, scratching his head. "I've always been able to *attract* nice tenants, but everybody always moves out . . . usually after only a month or two."

Britt remained silent.

"I own a number of rental properties," he continued. "But for some reason, this is my problem child."

"Why do you think that is?" asked my husband.

"I have no clue," Marsdon responded, earnestly shaking his head. "As you can see, my wife and I have really fixed it up nice."

Mr. Marsdon certainly couldn't be faulted for his honesty. I waddled back into the kitchen with Flynn, who was now starting to get cranky. Britt searched my eyes, silently asking for psychic input.

Everything seemed fine to me. The townhouse felt as if it had great energy. It was three times larger than the condo we were currently renting. It had been freshly painted and felt new. The neighborhood was quiet. I was due to give birth in two months. I had a whiny baby in my arms, and I was starving. We hadn't seen anything remotely as nice for even twice the money. I looked back at Britt as if to say, *we'd better snap this up . . . now!*

Our negotiations with Marsdon went without a hitch, and we were relieved and excited to take possession of the sumptuous townhouse the following weekend. It was after eight that night when the movers finally finished and we were able to reassemble the baby's crib. Once Flynn was asleep, I sent Britt to the store. I made our bed, undressed, and then realized that I had no idea which wardrobe box held my robe and pajamas. Too exhausted to care, I threw myself on top of the bed. I closed my eyes. It was so blissfully quiet that I could hear the wind rustling through the large pine trees that surrounded the property. I thought that I heard doves cooing. I felt truly fortunate that we had found such a beautiful place.

All at once, I heard the unmistakable sound of heavy footfalls at the bottom of the stairs. *It wasn't Britt.* Somebody had broken in!

Dressed only in my panties and white crew socks, I flew off the bed and waddled toward the nursery like a naked madwoman. Being so pregnant, it was difficult for me to maneuver swiftly. With one hand supporting my ponderous breasts and the other propping up my huge belly, I fled toward Flynn's room.

The staircase that separated me from the nursery loomed ominously to my left. I could hear the footsteps almost at the top. I knew the intruder could easily grab me as I tried to clumsily dart past, but I had no other option. *What if the intruder had broken in to kidnap my baby?* In full flight, I decided that if the assailant tried to take Flynn from me, I would turn into the Terminator.

At that very moment, the footfalls abruptly stopped. The resulting silence was even more dreadful and startling. I fully expected a knife-wielding intruder to jump out of the shadows.

As I peered around the corner, my heart was pounding and my breathing was labored from panic and exertion. To my utter astonishment, the steep, dark staircase was completely empty. I padded to Flynn's room and found him sleeping peacefully. With the exception of his soft snoring, the townhouse was completely silent again. It was deathly quiet.

My heart was still beating furiously as I cautiously tiptoed back to the stairway. There was no one there. I stood staring down at the first floor landing for a few moments before returning to the master bedroom. The house remained silent. I hoisted my body back onto the bed and took a deep breath. Moving day was hard enough, but now this? *I'll figure it out tomorrow. Maybe it's my imagination. Britt will be home soon. I'm so tired . . .*

Just as I was closing my eyes, the loud, heavy footfalls started again at the bottom of the stairs. I was instantly alert, jump-started by a flood of adrenalin. The CLUMP . . . CLUMP . . . CLUMP continued slowly and steadily toward the second story. There was no time to make a phone call for help, I had nothing to use as a weapon, and I certainly couldn't hide—I had a baby to protect! I lowered my swollen feet to the floor and hurried back toward the nursery. I kept praying, *please, God, don't let anything happen to Flynn . . . and don't let me be killed. Please let me live to raise my babies!*

I quickly decided that if there was going to be a confrontation, I wanted to get it over with. My heart was beating so wildly that I was sure I was going to have a heart attack. The footfalls reached the top of the stairs just as I looked around the corner. There was no one there! I was stunned to find the staircase empty.

My pregnancy had created nonstop hormonal-driven churning emotions, and my immediate relief was eclipsed by an indignant rage that washed over me with a startling suddenness. Bristling with anger, I stood at the top of the stairs squinting steely-eyed toward the first floor. Was this someone's idea of a sick joke?

I looked down at the carpeted staircase. I was suddenly baffled. The incredibly loud, heavy CLUMP . . . CLUMP . . . CLUMP noise sounded like footsteps mounting bare *wooden* stairs. Then the not-so-obvious dawned on me. The frightening sounds had been made by a very noisy, tangible spirit! No wonder Mr. Marsdon couldn't keep the townhouse occupied. As a professional channel, I didn't feel threatened by spirits; as long as there was no threat to my family from a *human* intruder, I felt safe and secure. I had to wryly acknowledge the irony of the situation. It appeared that our hapless landlord had finally found the right tenants.

Several days passed without incident as we unpacked boxes and tried to organize our new home. There were no more heavy footfalls on the stairs, so Britt and I began to assume that it had been a onetime supernatural occurrence. We were soon to discover that our assumption had been very wrong.

A week later, I was in my typical rush getting dressed for work. I swung open the closet door in the master bedroom, and I was stunned by what I saw. The inside of my closet had been transformed into a scene right out of the American Old West. I saw a man hanging by his neck from a piece of rope that was attached to crudely built wooden gallows. The man was quite dead, and his body grotesquely swung and twisted, giving the impression that the gruesome execution had just taken place. His matted hair and scruffy beard made it impossible to guess his age.

I slammed the door shut. I knew it had been a psychic vision—but of *what*? And of *whom*? I waited for a few seconds before re-opening the door. The gallows and the dead man had disappeared. The only things that remained were the familiar jumble of clothes and shoes still waiting to be organized from the move. I couldn't help but imagine the reaction that previous tenants must have had if they, too, had witnessed the same macabre spectacle in the large, walk-in closet.

Throughout my workday, I was, of course, distracted by thoughts of the townhouse. What kind of place had we moved into? That evening, after we put Flynn to bed, I made some coffee, and Britt and I sat down at our kitchen table. I needed to channel about what had happened, and I also wanted to ask my guardian angel John about what we could expect from our resident spirits in the future. Britt could not hear him, so I repeated the angelic conversation as it transpired.

"Thanks for invitin' me to ride in, Little Missy," said my angel, in a very good imitation of John Wayne. He took the seat next to Britt.

"John!" I interrupted. "Why didn't you *tell me* about this place before we moved in?"

"There was no reason to," shrugged the angel. "You needed more spacious accommodations, you had a fixed budget, you desired a peaceful neighborhood, and you wanted to be close to the office. This dwelling fit the bill admirably—on all counts."

"But it is overrun with spirits!" I argued.

"So is most every other dwelling on the earthly plane," he said. "These spirits are simply more tangible than most. Poor Marsdon—he hasn't seen or heard them . . . but all of his tenants have."

"But these spirits are not like angels or deceased family members—they're uninvited."

"They were here first," John pointed out. "You're the ones who are uninvited."

"But we're human beings," I persisted. "We belong here!"

"Have you never heard the expression, 'squatter's rights'?" he asked.

"Why don't spirits just stay in heaven?"

"Why didn't you just choose to remain in your old condo?"

"We needed something bigger."

"The spirits were, apparently, needing something other than what they could find in heaven."

"But how could anything on the earthly plane compare to heaven?"

"When a physical body dies, the soul departs and makes the journey back to its home in heaven," replied John. "A soul, otherwise known as a spirit, can remain there, or it can choose to return to the earthly plane. Sometimes a spirit has a special connection with a certain place on earth.

"But the spirit in my closet was hung," I argued. "How 'special' was that?"

"I said that a spirit can have a *special connection* to an area. The soul may return to a place where it enjoyed great happiness . . . or revisit a place where it experienced trauma. Most people on the earthly plane have a number of spirits co-existing with them as spiritual boarders."

"But how come they don't know it?"

"Who says they don't know it?" smiled John. "How many times do people investigate a noise they can't identify . . . and then find no apparent cause?"

Britt and I exchanged glances, relating to what he had said. But I was still confused.

"Why would a spirit choose to revisit the earthly plane to reenact something so terrible . . . when it doesn't have to?" I asked.

"Why do human beings choose to reenact the same torturous issues over and over again by creating a succession of difficult relationships or unsatisfying jobs?"

"Sweet'nin," said Britt, gently touching my arm. "Why not open the floor to John?" It was my husband's way of politely saying, *stop arguing and listen so we can find out what's going on.*

I pursed my lips, took a sip of hazelnut coffee, and respectfully asked John to proceed.

"What I have to share will likely amaze you, because it took place on the very spot that you now call home," he began. "Everything you have seen and heard in your new home—and *will* see and hear—is a spiritual reenactment of what transpired in the past."

Britt and I nodded, eager to hear the true-life story.

"In the early 1840s, this parcel of land held a makeshift jail, housing individuals accused of crimes that ranged from stealing chickens to murder. Some of the prisoners were guilty, and some were innocent . . . but swiftly and surely, all met with the same fate. Each of the accused was forced to climb the stairs leading to the crudely built gallows—"

"I *told* you that I heard that CLUMP . . . CLUMP . . . CLUMP sound!" I gasped to Britt. "I was so scared! It sounded like someone climbing *wooden* stairs—"

"—that are no longer there," said Britt, finishing my thought.

"But *were* right here—where we live now," I said. "I thought I was going crazy."

"Excuse me, you two," said the angel. "May I continue?"

"Sorry, John," I said, duly chastised.

"As I was saying, each of the accused was forced to climb the stairs that led to the gallows. The small gallows that stood right next to the jail could only accommodate one hanging at a time. Although this particular part of the Old West wasn't yet very populated . . . there were always a handful of spectators who gathered to watch with morbid curiosity."

"I've read that people used to bring their children to watch executions," I said, shaking my head.

"The self-proclaimed local law authorities had the first and last word, and there was no recourse to the decisions they made. Lacking a system of checks and balances, the innocent were routinely hung along with the guilty, having no one to fight for their rights."

Then John asked us to look outside through the sliding glass door off the dining room. Britt and I swiveled in our chairs. The angel directed our attention to a gnarled old tree that stood just a few feet from our front door.

"Before the gallows was built, hangings were conducted from that very tree. However, this practice was soon discontinued due to the inconvenience of branches snapping before the accused could sufficiently strangle."

Britt and I stared wide-eyed.

"After the gallows was constructed, the hangings were carried out like clockwork and continued for several years until the local citizenry began to voice their objections to the increasing number of executions being conducted without benefit of a fair trial."

"All the mysterious sights and sounds now make sense," I said, truly saddened and shocked by what John had explained. The noises were actually a tangible reenactment of footsteps taken long ago by condemned prisoners climbing the stairs to the gallows where they met a premature, horrible death.

"The closet in your bedroom stands just where the gallows did," John added.

"While we live here, do I need to resign myself to the possibility of witnessing other hangings—whenever I need to change my clothes?"

"In so many words . . . yes," he answered.

"Can I turn off those images somehow?"

"In so many words . . . no."

I frowned. I had already known the answer before I posed the question. Years before, I had learned that my psychic ability did not allow me to discriminate. Picking up on the bad as well as the good was part of the territory.

"Remember that your spiritual boarders wish you no harm," John assured us. "You will enjoy living here."

"No wonder Marsdon gave us such a good deal," commented Britt.

"There is one more insightful tidbit of information that I need to relay about spirits in this building," said John.

"*More* information?" I asked, all at once overcome with a shivering sensation.

"There's something taking place in Flynn's room."

"In the baby's room?" I gasped, consumed with fear. "Is he *safe*?"

"No need to become overwrought," the angel said, patting my arm. "Are you curious to learn why your offspring becomes fussy in the middle of the night?"

"Ever since we moved in!" I quickly responded. "He's never done that before . . . so we figured that it was part of adjusting to a new environment."

"He has spiritual playmates," John informed us.

"Oh . . . you mean like our deceased family members?" I asked. "Britt's Dad comes to visit; and my grandfather and grandmother, and my Aunt BeBe—"

"*They* know better than to wake the baby."

"So . . . who *is* it?" I asked, now really shivering.

"Murder victims."

"*What?*"

"Flynn is the first little boy to occupy this townhouse since it was built," John pointed out. "There is a small group of boys—in spirit—who are most excited that he has moved in."

"You've got to be kidding."

"Not at all," replied John. "The boys—who were best friends—belonged to several close-knit pioneer families who lived on farms in this area. On a summer day in 1847, they were all wrongly accused of stealing. In spite of the fact that their families argued their innocence and begged for mercy, each was forced up the stairs to the gallows—one by one—where they were hung. And here they remain, by choice, cavorting in perpetual boyhood—much like the Lost Boys in Peter Pan's Never-Never Land."

"Flynn can't talk yet, so he couldn't tell us that anything was going on," I realized, upset. "What should we *do?*" I was immediately concerned that the roughhouse antics of a group of unruly young boys in spirit were scaring our baby.

"Communicate with the spirits and simply ask them to leave Flynn's room," John suggested. "Address them in a reasonable and respectful manner. They have no desire to cause any harm to you . . . or your baby."

I put my hand on my bulging tummy and thought of the little girl I was carrying, fretting about how she might be affected by the spiritual Grand Central Station atmosphere of the property.

"None of the resident spirits wishes to cause any harm," repeated John, reading my mind. "They wish to coexist peacefully."

Naturally, I decided not to waste any time following through with John's suggestion. After thanking him for the information, I lumbered up the steep flight of stairs to the second floor with my husband in tow. Britt and I quietly tiptoed into Flynn's room. We stared down at him in his crib and watched him as he slept soundly.

I looked around the room and saw nothing amiss. A menagerie of stuffed animals sat motionless on the floor, ready for play. Toys and games that colorfully filled Flynn's dresser shelves remained undisturbed. The nursery was peaceful and serene, and I was beginning to feel a little silly. Everything seemed so . . . normal. But I reminded myself that spiritual beings are not always present at every given moment—

and that certainly doesn't mean that they don't exist. From experience, I knew that John would never send me on a wild-goose chase, but my logical thought processes suddenly began to discount the incredible story he had shared. Although I had been witness to other supernatural occurrences, I had not seen—nor felt—any tangible evidence of the young spiritual pranksters in the nursery.

Britt was regarding me with a "So what gives?" expression, and I gestured toward the door. We began to tiptoe back out of the room. Then, as if on cue, the group of boys materialized, seemingly oblivious to our presence.

They were dressed in dirty, torn clothing reminiscent of the Old West, and they began to make a racket with their boisterous laughter and off-key singing. They moved around the room as if very comfortable there, rousing each other with teasing banter and playfully thrown punches. I wondered why we had never heard them on the baby monitor. I poked Britt excitedly, but I could tell from his blank expression that he couldn't see or hear them.

Several of the young spirits approached Flynn's crib and reached in as if to gently nudge him awake.

"C'mon!" one boy softly called to him. "Let's play!"

Flynn responded by turning away and howling with frustration. It was obvious that he could see and hear his unwelcome visitors, but he wanted to continue sleeping.

"Aw, c'mon!" said the boy spirit again, this time nudging Flynn a little harder. "Don't you wanna play?"

Flynn started to cry and kick, upset that his slumber had been disturbed. These were exactly the same sounds he had been making throughout the night since we first moved in. Now I had firsthand knowledge of what had been happening.

"Let him alone," said another one of the boys. "I told ya before—he's too little." He picked up one of Flynn's toy airplanes and asked his friends, "Whaddya 'spose *this* is?"

"Hey—you boys!" I said in a furious whisper, forgetting all about John's advice to be 'reasonable and respectful.' "You're scaring my baby! I want you to leave! And don't *ever* come back!"

The spirits were startled by my outburst, and they seemed shocked that I could see them so clearly. The boy immediately dropped the red toy airplane. In an instant, they were gone. My outburst and the sudden shift of electrical energy in the room caused Flynn to kick and fuss for a few moments before he went back to sleep.

I didn't want to disturb Flynn any further, so I pulled Britt out of the room. Once we were in the hallway, I excitedly shared what had happened. Then I asked him if he thought we needed to move Flynn into our room in case the Lost Boys came back. Britt smiled, yawned, took me by the arm, and led me toward our bedroom, all the while assuring me that everything would be okay. For the first time since we moved in, Flynn rested peacefully for the remainder of the night, which meant that we could, too.

The next morning was a Saturday, and I was awakened close to seven by a series of swift, strong kicks inside of me. Our daughter, whom we would name Megan, wasn't due for another month, but she was certainly making her presence known. I reluctantly opened my eyes. Although still in bed, Britt was already awake. The sun was softly filtering through the closed blinds, birds were gaily chirping, and we could hear Flynn happily talking and singing in his crib down the hall.

Not a morning person, I was only half-listening as Britt started to talk about going to our favorite place for breakfast and then detailing all the things he wanted to do in preparation for the new baby's arrival. I groggily remembered the supernatural experience from the night before. Had I just imagined it? I stumbled down the hall into Flynn's room. He grinned brightly when he saw me and held out his arms. As I gathered his little body into a tight hug, something out of place caught my eye. It was the bright red toy airplane that lay on the floor next to the bureau—exactly where one of the Lost Boys had dropped it.

Chapter 28

Inner Peace at Last

Although I was very grateful for all of my existing blessings, there was still one big important thing to manifest. My desire for it bubbled up unexpectedly a few months after my second child, Megan, was born; and when it came, the passion to attain it exploded inside of me like the eruption of Mount Vesuvius, and it was just as impossible to ignore.

For the first time in my life, I wanted to own a home with a yard where my children could play. I began to fantasize about a wooded property that would provide shade against the hot and humid Gulf Coast summer, with a tree in the back to which we could anchor a big tree house. I visualized planting a flower garden and growing vegetables that I could turn into homemade soup or a hearty stew.

Britt voiced concern about all the added expenses and responsibilities a house would entail. Being mindful of our budget figured prominently after our first child, Flynn, was born. It was at that time that Britt became a stay-at-home dad, while I maintained my channeling practice to support the family. Although we had to make some financial adjustments with our lifestyle, it worked perfectly for us.

Budgetary concerns notwithstanding, I argued that as long as we lived in the supernatural townhouse, we were paying off our landlord's mortgage. What's more, the townhouse had only a tiny patio, and soon the children were going to need a place where they could run and play outdoors. I also submitted that if we put our minds together in a positive, consistent manner, we could manifest anything we chose.

Always the practical one in our relationship, Britt believed that if we paid off our credit card debt, we could begin saving money for a substantial down payment. Naturally, I understood his logic, but I reasoned that the babies might be in college before we could get all of that accomplished. When he agreed to "cautiously give it some thought," I sprang into action by offering to do all the research into the real estate market.

Considering myself on a mission, I endlessly thought about what I wanted, fully convinced that I could bring it to life. I started the mission by searching the Sunday paper and the Internet for all of the available properties that would meet our criteria. With my Type-A tendencies, I figured that within a week or two we'd find the perfect house, with a fenced backyard, in a close-in neighborhood, with affordable taxes, and in a desirable school district. After all, I reasoned, we resided in the fourth-largest city in the country and there just *had* to be hundreds of homes to choose from.

Every weekend, like intrepid explorers, our minivan became real estate central. We set out with a cranky, impatient toddler and a four-month-old baby, armed with a fully stocked diaper bag, as well as numerous baby bottles, soy formula, water, juice, Cheerios, and jars of mashed fruits and vegetables. We'd leave early Saturday morning and spend the entire day on the road. Between feeding the babies, changing their diapers inside the van, and grabbing a quick lunch, we'd look at properties that continued to be far beyond our financial reach. My optimism turned into a desperate, futile longing. In the weeks that followed, I brought along dark chocolate and Tootsie Rolls that I could dig out during moments of despair as we drove . . . and drove . . . and drove.

When we first started to search, I was inspired by the buoyant anticipation that fuels only the truly optimistic—or the truly wealthy—or the truly insane—when trying to acquire real estate. I was very disheart-

ened to learn that, close to town, the best schools were often surr
by the most expensive homes. So we gradually expanded our searc

True to form, Britt remained emotionally unflappable even after
months of nonstop weekend forays. He simply could not understand
the urgency of my resolute determination to find a house and was utterly mystified by my sporadic tears of frustration and hopelessness. He
kept reminding me that we weren't out on the street and that our rented
townhouse was serving us nicely, especially since we had come to terms
with all of the spirits. He insisted that we would find the right house at
the right time, while repeatedly reminding me to "bloom where you are."

"But *how?*" I'd wail, week after week, month after month, as we'd
travel from neighborhood to neighborhood. "The babies need a yard!"

My husband calmly dealt with my bipolar-like mood swings. Every
Friday afternoon I was bubbling with enthusiasm. "We're going to find
our house this weekend! Let's go *now*. Look at all of these properties I
found on the Internet—they're perfect for us."

Each Sunday afternoon, however, after spending countless hours
searching miles of neighborhoods I didn't even know existed—and that
weren't right for us—with two babies screaming and crying intermit-
tently from their car seats, and a husband who didn't seem to care if we
ever found a home, I was ready to throw myself in front of a moving
freight train. Britt would lecture that I was being irrational, advising
that I find a way to remain completely neutral during our home search.
After all, he'd continually say, it's an adventure. Enjoy the journey. What
we're looking for is just a building—

"Just a *building?*" I'd always respond, in a snit over the fact that he
could be so unemotional about finding a nest for our children. Was he
nuts? What happened to Mr. Wonderful? How did I end up married to
him, anyway? Then, while he remained silent, I'd mutter to myself all
the way back to the townhouse.

A few months later, on a sweltering Sunday afternoon in June, after
we had exhausted our search for that weekend, I stared glumly from
the dirty windows of the minivan. It was becoming apparent to me that
we were never going to find a house.

"Why does this have to be so *hard?*" I asked Britt tearfully, grabbing a
bag of Tootsie Rolls.

...swer, John materialized in the seat behind me. ...othless grin, and Flynn laughed, waved, and said, ...y smiled at them before turning his attention to me. ...be hard at all," John answered simply. "You're cre-

...that?" I asked, perturbed.

"By giving the universe mixed messages."

"I am not!" I insisted. "Why haven't you given us any help? Why don't you just tell us where to look?"

"I *have*, but my words fall on deaf ears," John replied. Then, feigning tears: "I feel so alone . . . so unappreciated—"

"How can you joke when you know I'm upset?"

"I don't get in the way when you are making deliberate choices."

"What are you *talking* about?" I asked him. "You think I *want* to be upset?"

"I do," he nodded. "You've made that choice every Sunday for how many months?"

"Nothing is going right!" I complained. "And I've *tried* to be optimistic—but it doesn't seem to matter, regardless of how hard I try."

"Every Sunday afternoon, after the unproductive searching, you keep insisting that you will never find a house."

"So?" I responded. "I always start *out* by being positive. Doesn't that count for anything?"

"Yes, that's true," he conceded. "But when you don't get what you want in immediate time frames, you abruptly shift gears . . . and the universe listens to that."

"I don't understand."

"The universe remains completely neutral to the energy put forth. When your pendulum swings from one mindset to the other—"

"They cancel each other out?"

"Yes," he confirmed. "You must become aware of all of the negative thoughts you have, and all of the negative statements you make. Every thought and every single utterance is followed by the universe as direction from you."

"It *is*?"

"For example, every time you repeat 'we will *never* find a house,' the universe understands that you are asking for just that."

"How can I remain positive when nothing is happening?"

"There you go again!" said the angel.

I furrowed my brow in confusion.

"By saying 'nothing is happening,' you are creating just that."

"But I need to let off steam sometimes."

"No, you don't," John persisted. "When you 'let off steam,' you're actually having a spiritual tantrum, which creates more internal unhappiness and frustration. When you focus on negativity, you're breathing life into it . . . like adding fuel to the fire."

"When I start to get depressed, it would help if Britt was willing to talk about my feelings . . . instead of just remaining silent."

"You get upset with your husband because he refuses to get sucked into your quagmire of dysfunction. You are not going to bend him to your will. When you start to travel that road of negativity, he has to concentrate on tuning you out to remain positive. You do not make it easy for him. And when he remains neutral, which is very much to his credit, you call him names."

"I do not!"

"When he doesn't readily agree with your pessimistic assessments about the home search, you accuse him of being cold and unfeeling," said John.

It was true. I stole a glance at my husband, to whom I was repeating the angelic conversation. He was looking at the road, trying not to grin.

"You must express gratitude every day for everything you have . . . and will have," John advised.

"But how can I express gratitude for the house I can't find?"

John groaned and began to hit the front of his forehead with his palm. Flynn laughed and began to mimic him.

"Okay," I said. "I didn't realize that I was sabotaging everything. Help me shift my negative thought patterns. Tell me what to do."

"First," began the angel, "you must write down everything you want to create in your life."

"Okay," I agreed. "I'll do it tonight."

"Second, you must give thanks every day for everything you have and everything you want to manifest."

"I'm to give thanks for things I don't have yet . . . like I'm visualizing that I already *have* them?"

"Now you're getting the picture."

"Oh!" I exclaimed. "And then, no matter what happens, I should choose to remain positive? And if I do, I won't be unknowingly drawing any negative stuff to me?"

"I think you have the essence of what I'm trying to communicate."

"Are you telling me that if I remain positive and optimistic, and have faith that I can manifest all my dreams, then the whole process will happen faster?"

"When you aren't getting in the way," smiled John.

I sighed deeply.

"Ask John where we're going to find our house," suggested Britt softly.

"Spring," quickly announced the angel.

"*What?*" I responded. "But . . . Britt suggested that *months* ago. I thought he was joking."

The van remained uncharacteristically silent.

"Is that why I keep hearing the song *Younger than Springtime?* Is that why I keep seeing and hearing the word 'spring' everywhere? On bumper stickers, on the radio, in magazines—"

"I attempted to share this information with you when you first began the search," lamented the angel. "But you kept insisting that you *had* to find a property close to the city."

"Why didn't you just intuitively hit me over the head?"

"I did," he said. "I believed that if I asked Britt to pass the information to you, it would have confirmed its importance. You chose to ignore that, too."

"Months have gone by!" I gasped. "Is the house still—"

"No, it was recently sold," said John. "However, in the meantime, another property has become available. I advise you to secure it quickly . . . it will not remain on the market very long."

"But Spring is at least thirty miles from Houston . . . and way out in the country! Do they even have decent schools . . . or carry-out?"

In unison, both John and my husband gave me looks that would curdle cream. My hand flew in front of my mouth. I was sabotaging things again! For me, being positive and open to everything—and anything—was going to take practice.

When I wrote my list of goals, I realized that I had never thought about a realtor. So I put my new manifesting skills to work and focused on attracting the person who would understand our needs.

The following Saturday, I had just finished conducting a workshop when a gal approached and handed me a business card. I looked at the card and was consumed with shivers. *Beaty C. Lewis, Heritage Texas Properties.* I shook her hand and just *knew* that we had been good friends in previous incarnations on the earthly plane. She was the one who was meant to help us! I had used the positive thinking skills that John had recommended, and they were already starting to work. It was just the confirmation I needed. I asked her if she would be interested in assisting us to find a home in Spring, and she indicated that she would be delighted.

That Monday, I contacted her and described what we were looking for. She immediately faxed a number of MLS listings, and we planned to meet the following weekend. I shared with her that Britt and I had always believed that we'd immediately recognize the property that we were meant to have because we were angelically directed; and, considering the fact that we were conducting the search with a baby and an impatient toddler, neither one of us wanted to waste time exploring a house that we didn't feel was right for us. The realtor seemed fully comfortable with our sensibilities.

The very next Saturday, we drove almost an hour north of the city to the small community of Spring to visit a number of properties. When we met in front of the first house, I couldn't believe how much more we were going to get for our money compared to what was available in neighborhoods closer to Houston. We reminded Beaty that we were going to trust in our intuitive feelings to make the day as productive as possible. She nodded her understanding.

We approached house after house; and once we'd walk through the front door and I'd hear John say *not the one,* we would look no further. It would have been a waste of time. Beaty would nod and say, "Well, you're the psychic. If it doesn't feel right to you, then there's no reason to stay."

Although we didn't find the property that first day, I remained resolutely positive and optimistic, certain that we *would,* eventually. Beaty agreed to meet us the next day, on Sunday, so we could continue the search.

After we waved goodbye to Beaty, Flynn and Megan were unusually quiet and content, so John suggested that we explore on our own and investigate the listings that the realtor had scheduled for the following day. Using the MLS sheets as a map, we made our way to an older subdivision that had several homes for sale. Once again, I was astonished that these properties were in our price range.

Large, two-story brick homes were nestled among stately oak, pine, and magnolia trees. Multicolored flowers grew in profusion on the well-manicured, fenced lawns. As we slowly drove down each street, the residents who were in their yards gardening looked up from their work and smiled and waved at us. People jogging with their dogs smiled and waved. Small children were roller-skating and riding bicycles on the sidewalks.

The neighborhood had fantastic energy; and, ironically, there was angel paraphernalia everywhere. We saw a number of quaint wooden angels standing in gardens, angel dolls sitting on bedroom window ledges, angel address signs hanging inside patio doorways, angel sculptures on mailboxes, and quite a few bumper stickers that read "Caution! I brake for angels!"

When we pulled to a curb to change the babies, two children approached with cups of icy lemonade from their stand, offering them to us—for free—because it was so hot and they thought we might be thirsty. I wondered if we had somehow transitioned back to the last century through a portal on the busy freeway. For a moment, I envisioned George Bailey from *It's a Wonderful Life* running down the street during the holidays shouting, "Merry Christmas, Kim and Britt! Merry Christmas!"

We had just turned a corner onto the next street when Britt brought the minivan to a lurching halt, startling me. He gestured to a house on the corner. There was a for-sale sign in front. "This is it," he said simply.

The home had light-colored brick, big windows, lush gardens of blooming flowers, and a fenced yard filled with massive pine and oak trees. A man whom we believed to be the owner happened to be mowing the grass, and he stopped to wipe his brow. Then he saw us parked in front of his house and without hesitation smiled and waved. We tentatively waved back. He went back to his mowing. Britt and I sat silently staring at the house for some time, each lost in our own thoughts. We reluctantly drove away, eager to return the next day.

After a sleepless night, we met Beaty in front of the house just after noon on Sunday. She explained that the property had been on the market for only two weeks and it was even bigger than what we had hoped for. In spite of our credit card debt, the price was in our budget and so were the taxes. Plus, the public schools in the area were considered exemplary.

"Don't act too excited in front of the owner," cautioned Britt, as we approached the front door. He was already focusing on negotiating the best price.

I nodded solemnly. Buying a house was going to be the biggest purchase we had ever made together, and I didn't want to complicate the process by putting all of my emotional cards on the table before my husband had a chance to haggle.

We rang the bell, consumed with nervous anticipation. The owner, the same man whom we had seen the day before mowing the lawn, opened the front door with a warm welcome and gestured for us to cross the threshold.

I walked into the entry, and the house seemed to immediately embrace me. I heard John say *This is the one.*

"It's *our house!*" I exclaimed. "We finally found it!"

The owner looked stunned.

Britt shook his head and rolled his eyes, but I could tell that he was just as excited. With baby Megan in my arms, I quickly went from room to room. I found the big kitchen where I would cook . . . sometimes. There was a window box where I could grow herbs. I discovered a walk-in pantry. The kitchen had more drawer and cabinet space then we would ever need. I loved the beautiful wood floors.

What's more, I noted that the kitchen, eating area, and den were all one open area, which would allow us to keep a watchful eye on the babies. The den had a substantial fireplace with a wide mantel, and I imagined how it would look decorated with our Christmas stockings. Louvered doors off the kitchen led to the carpeted living room, which was going to make a great first-floor playroom for Flynn and Megan. The upstairs held all the bedrooms and two full baths.

Then the owner invited us to see the huge backyard. The French door off the utility room led to a spacious covered patio. Beyond the patio was a fenced, very private backyard in full bloom. I looked up at the majestic pine trees that towered above us.

We put the kids down on the grass. Flynn laughed, stretched out his arms, and ran in circles, pretending to be an airplane. Megan, who was just beginning to crawl, looked at the grass wide-eyed as if she had suddenly been transported to outer space. Although we had frequently taken the kids to a park close to the townhouse, what they were most accustomed to seeing in the city was concrete.

My eyes were filled with tears as I looked at Britt. He winked at me and then wisely asked to see some recent utility bills, which the owner had obligingly assembled to show us. They were surprisingly reasonable. It also didn't escape us that Flynn and Megan were obviously happy and oddly giggling with delight the entire time we were there.

We wasted no time in putting in a bid, and the owners accepted immediately. It was a miracle! The babies would have their own home—with their own grass—and their own trees. Everything had fallen into place once I got out of the way. John had certainly been right about the power of positive thinking.

We began the process of securing a mortgage and scheduling all of the inspections. During that time, the owner of the house e-mailed an open invitation for us to visit the property whenever we wished. I was thrilled, of course, by his generosity because I wanted to measure rooms, decide on paint colors, and allow Flynn and Megan another brief exposure to the backyard.

When we arrived back at the house, the owner greeted us warmly and led us into the kitchen. I was very surprised to see my book *How to Talk With Your Angels* sitting on the counter. He explained that he had found out about the book from visiting my website, and he was quite intrigued by my line of work. He shared that he was definitely going to share the book with his wife, who he believed would have a special interest in what I wrote about. I thanked him, and he excused himself so we could explore our new home.

About twenty minutes later, we were preparing to leave. I found the owner sitting on the patio and told him that it was obvious that our children already seemed very comfortable there and that we looked forward to building our future in a house that had such happy energy. I promised that we'd take good care of the property.

As he looked kindly at Flynn and Megan, I saw his eyes welling up. He began to reminisce about his three grown children, for whom he had a great affection. He led us back inside to show us several of their childhood pictures that were displayed in the den. I saw a photograph of two little girls and a boy who looked quite close in age, and all three were laughing for the camera. He then proudly shared more recent pictures of the children, now grown, along with photographs of his grandchildren.

It was then that he disclosed that one of his daughters had been killed by a drunk driver in a horrific accident on her way to work one morning. She was only 30 years old. Britt and I expressed heartfelt sympathy, and we thanked him for sharing the very personal—and painful—family history with us. He then offered what appeared to be a business card to Britt and me as we left, and we acknowledged him for being so generous with his time and hospitality. I shoved the card into the side pocket of my bulging purse.

Once the children were wrestled into their car seats, I climbed into the van, distracted by thoughts connected with everything we had to get done before the move.

"Take the card back out!" commanded John, startling me. I looked back to see that he had materialized in "his" seat, the one in the second row right next to Megan. "Look at it *now*."

"Okay, okay," I said peevishly, as I reached for my purse. I quickly discovered that it wasn't a business card at all. It was a white card with a silver guardian angel medallion affixed to it; and next to the medal was a photograph of a smiling, lovely, dark-haired girl. The card read:

Guardian Angel
Please accept this guardian angel
In memory of our beautiful daughter
Leanne
Who was killed by a drunk driver on 12/13/99
May it protect you always.

Leanne was the deceased daughter he told us about. I felt shivers, and it dawned on me that I had been given the card for a very important reason. Suddenly, the spirit of the young woman materialized next to Flynn! She smiled a hello. The children already seemed to know her, and she began to playfully tickle them. They broke into squeals of laughter. Now I knew why they were always happy and giggling when we were in the house. Leanne had been interacting with them! *Why was she interacting with us, I wondered?*

"Because I'm going to stay at the house," she answered, reading my thoughts. "I'll be living there with you." My eyes widened, and I looked at John. He regarded me with a knowing expression.

"You're not going to move on with your Mom and Dad?" I asked her.

"The house holds very happy childhood memories for me," explained the spirit. "I want to live in that peaceful, happy energy. And I'm so glad that Flynn and Megan are moving in. It will be like old times. Do you mind that I'm staying?"

"No!" I told her. "Living with you will be a very different experience than what we've encountered with the spiritual boarders we have now."

"But I was in the house first," she said, a mischievous gleam in her eye. "I will consider *you* the boarders!"

John, Britt, and I all laughed.

"I don't know how peaceful the house will be when *we* move in," I warned her. "We tend to be kind of noisy."

"Good," she said. "My house has been too quiet."

And with that, Leanne vanished. When she did, both the babies started to whine and fuss.

"You'll get to spend time with Leanne," I assured them. "As soon as we move into the house."

Then, in my own private space, I hoped that neither of my children would end up on a therapist's couch because their mother, the channel, encouraged them to build relationships with spirits. On the other hand, I thought, why *not* support their involvement with wonderful, enlightened beings—whether human *or* spirit?

The big day finally arrived the last weekend of August. Britt stayed behind at the townhouse to oversee the movers, while I took the children to the new house so they wouldn't be underfoot. While they played with their toys in the living room, I walked from room to room of the empty house, marveling that it was really ours.

When I reached the kitchen, I was surprised to find a bouquet of my favorite sunflowers in a vase on the counter. As I approached, I saw a card. It was addressed to me in a pretty, feminine script. With mounting curiosity, I tore open the envelope and found a personal note from the owner's wife, who had recently moved out of the house. With touching sentiment she wished us great happiness in the home that held so many wonderful memories for her. In the last sentence of the note, she shared that her daughter, Leanne, would remain a tangible presence in the house, and she hoped that we would enjoy her company. I was astonished—not only because she possessed the awareness of her daughter's lingering presence, but that she was intuitive enough to know that her daughter's spirit intended to remain in the house and that we would be comfortable with that fact!

In the busy days and weeks that followed, we settled comfortably into the new chapter of our lives as homeowners in the small community of Spring. When Britt and I worked together in the yard, I was consistently reminded of the first intuitive glimpse I had, years before, of my future with him and all of the blessings that were yet to come.

We welcomed Leanne into our family without hesitation, and she lovingly interacted with Flynn and Megan as if she were a spiritual big sister. We began to build our own family memories, mindful that we were but the caretakers of Leanne's enchanted home.

Particularly on the weekends, it was commonplace for Britt and me to be awakened by the sounds of Megan, still in her crib in the bedroom down the hall, cooing, giggling, and blowing kisses to Leanne as they played her favorite game of peek-a-boo. Moments later, we'd hear Flynn, from the crib in his room, saying, "Hi! . . . Hi! . . . Hi!" to Leanne, and then regaling her with animated baby talk about his trucks, books, and toy plane collection. It became routine to hear her unmistakable footfalls in the upstairs hallway, or softly treading upon the wood floors between the kitchen and the den. Overnight guests have commented that they've heard "walking" and a "presence," but they have felt no fear of the loving, generous, and benevolent spirit who had become so precious to us.

Since we finally had room to entertain, I decided to host a special holiday brunch three weeks before our first Christmas in the new house. I invited Britt's adult daughter, Jen, and her husband, Shelby, to join us. Jen and I had become close friends since her Dad and I married, and I truly admired her. She was a brilliant, enlightened, sensitive, and beautiful woman who worked as a corporate attorney for a large law firm. She lived several hours away in Austin, so her sporadic visits were always looked upon with great excitement.

In preparation for the big party, Britt and I put up all of our Christmas decorations. Brightly wrapped presents sat under the evergreen tree, holiday music filled the air, and stockings hung from the mantle over a roaring fire. The table was set with red linen napkins, glowing candles, and—for the grown-ups—my best china. A crystal vase held festive evergreen sprigs and red berries. Place cards sat in front of each setting. Because the children absolutely adored their big sister and were thrilled by her attention, I placed Jen between them.

Amid much fanfare, Jen and Shelby arrived, laden with Christmas presents for us, which were placed under the tree to open after breakfast.

I had spent hours planning the special meal. While the thick-cut bacon sizzled and the hazelnut coffee was brewing, I finished making my grandmother's recipe for Swedish pancakes and cooked them in a cast-iron skillet. At the same time, I was also making cheese omelets and toast from the bread that I had baked the day before. After I placed a big bowl of fresh fruit on the table, I opened a bottle of chilled champagne and made mimosas. For the babies, I fixed sippy cups of soy milk.

As I hurriedly prepared the children's plastic plates by painstakingly cutting their food into tiny pieces, I called the family to the table. Britt lifted the children into their highchairs, and everybody took their seats. I carried the steaming plates to the table and sat down. I looked around the table at Britt, Flynn, Megan, Jen, and Shelby.

"Merry Christmas!" I said in a joyful toast, lifting my glass.

All of the grown-ups lifted their glasses in turn.

"Kim, it's so wonderful of you to have invited us," said Jen. "We always love spending time with you and the munchkins."

"This is our first holiday party in the new house," I said. "Let's all enjoy a relaxing meal."

As if on cue, and with the swiftness of liquid mercury, Flynn threw his fork across the table at Shelby. He then grabbed his plate of hot food and—with a naughty grin—tossed it like a Frisbee in my direction. The fresh fruit, pancakes, sticky maple syrup, and greasy bacon became airborne missiles, splattering me and everything else in their path.

I gasped and stared wide-eyed as food dripped from my hair and the front of my blouse, as well as from the surrounding walls, the bay window, and the curtains. Flynn laughed and pointed at me with glee.

Before anybody could react, Megan picked up her plate and dumped her entire meal on top of her head. She casually discarded the plate, and it hit the wood floor with a terrific clatter. Megan looked down at it and waved, "Bye, bye!" Turning to her big sister to share her Christmas glee, Megan reached for the bits of syrupy pancakes that were dripping down the front of her bib and rubbed them onto the arm of Jen's cashmere sweater. "Here!" she told her, just before massaging the rest of the food into her wispy blonde hair and all over her face, giggling with amusement.

As Britt and I jumped up from the table to clean the mess, I heard the lilting sound of Leann's laughter. My husband grabbed my hand and grinned at me as if to say, *these are the good times*. He was right. I squeezed his hand and smiled back at him.

That night, after I got ready for bed, I found the card that Leanne's mother had left for me—months before—inexplicably laying in my path on the bedroom floor. Dropping to my knees, I opened the card and read it again. I wondered if she was asking me to look after her beloved daughter as one mother might to another? Or, perhaps, at that special time of year, she was acknowledging me for already having done so?

I smiled and held the card to my heart, imagining that I was gathering Flynn, Megan, Jen, and Leanne into a tight embrace. My life had become just as I always fantasized. ≋

Author's Note

I conduct private sessions by telephone, host teleseminars, and present in-person workshops across the U.S. and Canada. I would love to be of service to you! I can be reached through my e-mail or my website:

Website:
www.kimoneillpsychic.com

E-mail:
kimoneillpsychic@sbcglobal.net